A Compendious History Of New-England

To Which Is Added, A Short Abstract Of The History Of New-York, And New-Jersey : Designed For The Use Of Schools And Private Families

Jedidiah Morse, Elijah Parish

Alpha Editions

This edition published in 2021

ISBN : 9789354419652

Design and Setting By
Alpha Editions
www.alphaedis.com
Email - info@alphaedis.com

As per information held with us this book is in Public Domain.
This book is a reproduction of an important historical work. Alpha Editions uses the best technology to reproduce historical work in the same manner it was first published to preserve its original nature. Any marks or number seen are left intentionally to preserve its true form.

PREFACE.

Every person should possess some knowledge of the history of his own country. It seems necessary to the existence of true and enlightened patriotism. Youth is the fittest season to acquire this knowledge. It is the season of the most leisure; the memory is then less incumbered; this knowledge gratifies that curiosity, which is natural to the human mind, and which is peculiarly strong in the early period of life.

Among the first settlers of New-England were some of the best and wisest men of the age; men remarkable for their christian piety, patience, fortitude, and benevolent enterprize, deserving a rank among the worthies who have founded empires, enlightened nations, and given glory to the age and country in which they lived. Its history, in consequence, has been more entirely preserved, and better authenticated, from its first settlement, than that of any other portion of the globe, of equal magnitude and importance. No history is more replete with useful instruction and entertainment. It furnishes many important lessons to warriors, statesmen, and divines. It may be read and studied with much profit by our youth.

The abundant but scattered materials for the history of this favoured portion of the world, it has been our aim to reduce to a form, order, and size, adapted to the use of the higher classes in schools, and to families. We have endeavoured faithfully to bring into view the most operative causes, near and more remote, which led to the settlement of New-England, with the impelling motives of the immediate agents in this bold enterprize, and to trace the steps by which she has risen to her present distinguished rank in the political, literary and commercial world. To render the work interesting to youth, we have laboured to clothe our ideas in plain, familiar language, and to blend entertainment with instruction.

The sources whence we have derived our information have been very numerous, and the most authentic that our country affords. Among them many occasional sermons, miscellaneous publications, records and manuscripts, have been faithfully consulted, and their essence condensed into this little volume. In the use of these voluminous materials we have not been hurried. A considerable part of the work was compiled in 1802, for the Supplement of Dobson's edition of the Encyclopedia; and, by his permission, and the advice of some judicious friends, has been revised, enlarged, divided into chapters, and published in its present form, for more general benefit.

To extend the usefulness of this work, an abstract of the history of New York and New-Jersey has been added to this edition, with a view to its introduction into the schools of these respectable states; and that their pious and indigent youth, of promising talents, might enjoy the benefit of a portion of the avails of its sale, whatever this may be. One of the authors, who is sole proprietor of the work, having consecrated the net profits of all future editions of it to this purpose.

Conscious, that in compiling and publishing this little volume, we have been prompted by an upright regard to the best interests of our country, we commit it to the candour and patronage of the public. We hope the youth of the several states, a summary of whose history is here given, will read with pleasure and improvement what we have written for their particular use, with labour and delight; that while reading, they will admire, then love, then imitate the shining virtues of their pious forefathers, be emulous to preserve pure their wise institutions, and, like them, receive the applause and blessings of succeeding generations.

J. MORSE.
E. PARISH.

April, 1, 1820.

CONTENTS.

	Page.
INTRODUCTION	40

CHAP. I.

The flight of the Puritans to Holland; their sufferings during their residence there; their character; their determination to remove, and their reasons for removal   48

CHAP. II.

Measures adopted for removing; their voyage; their disappointment as to the place of their settlement, through the treachery of the Dutch; the form of government established; their landing at Cape Cod   55

CHAP. III.

Character of the first settlers; Discovery of New-England; Its boundaries, extent and settlement; Destructive wars and pestilence among the natives; nature of the Indian title to their lands   62

CHAP. IV.

Excursions for discovery; a child born; another voyage for discovery; attacked by Indians; discover the place which they afterwards named Plymouth; two men left; Capt. Standish elected commander in chief; dreadful winter; mortality; an Indian visits them; treaty with Massasoit   74

CHAP. V.

Increase of their number; sufferings; a massacre of Virginians; duel; Squanto dies; lands purchased; visit to Massasoit, who is sick; patent obtained; first cattle in New-England; death and character of Mr. Robinson   83

CHAP. VI.

A larger patent obtained; difficulties between the company in England and the planters; persecution of the Puritans; sports on the Lord's day established; Cromwell and others contemplate a removal to America; Massachusetts purchased; settled; charter obtained; its contents; first church formed at Salem; addition of 1500 to the colony; Indian conspiracy; scarcity; mortality; a number discouraged, return to England   93

CHAP. VII.

Church gathered in Charlestown; first court held there; Morton sentenced for stealing an Indian canoe; Boston, Watertown, and Roxbury settled; description of the former; scarcity and its good effects; arrival of Gov. Winthrop's family; account of Newbury; union of the two colonies   106

CHAP. VIII.

Complaint against the colonists; character of Rev. Mr. Higginson; Ipswich settled; further emigrations; representative government; code of laws enacted   115

CHAP. IX.

Character of the first settlers; New-Hampshire and Maine settled; Exeter planted   123

CHAP. X.

Settlement of Connecticut; character of Rev. Mr. Davenport   134

CHAP. XI.

History of Connecticut continued; character of Rev. Mr. Thomas Hooker   147

CHAP. XII.

Settlement of Rhode-Island; this colony refused admittance into the confederation; Narraganset Indians surrender their country to the king of England; Roman Catholics; charter surrendered 158

CHAP. XIII.

War with the Pequot Indians 166

CHAP. XIV.

Earthquake; Uncas visits Gov. Winthrop; Hampton settled; Harvard College founded; Indian plot at Kennebec; settlement of Rowley; character of Rev. Ezekiel Rogers 175

CHAP. XV.

Emigration ceased; settlement of Woburn; Consideration of the colonies; Eastham settled; character of Mr. Treat; Gov. Winthrop's speech; his character 184

CHAP. XVI.

Character of the natives who inhabited New-England 193

CHAP. XVII.

The society for propagating the gospel; the faithful labours of the New-England ministers to instruct the natives in the religion of Jesus Christ 198

CHAP. XVIII.

Quakers persecuted; apology for our forefathers; synod of 1662; character of Capt. Standish   205

CHAP. XIX.

Comet; Philip's war; life and character of Capt. Church   232

CHAP. XX.

Sufferings of the colonists; Synods of New-England   242

CHAP. XXI.

Loss of charter; state of New-England; Andros arrives; tenor of his administration; William and Mary proclaimed; Indian war; expedition against Canada and Nova-Scotia; New charter   254

CHAP. XXII.

Witchcraft   261

CHAP. XXIII.

French war; Complaint against Gov. Phips; his character; Indian and French ravages; Yale college; Indian war; Peace; death of Queen Ann; George I. crowned; Small-pox; Earthquake; Burnet governor; his death   270

CHAP. XXIV.

Public ferment in Massachusetts; Dreadful mortality; line established between Massachusetts and New-Hampshire; Shirley governor; Louisbourg taken; French invasion; Congress at Albany; Nova-Scotia taken; Braddock's defeat   275

CHAP. XXV.

Stamp act; Dartmouth college founded; Lexington and Bunker-hill battles; Expedition to Canada; Boston evacuated; Ticonderoga taken; descent on Rhode-Island; Tryon's expedition to Connecticut; American academy incorporated; New-London burnt; Insurrection in Massachusetts; Federal Constitution; Colleges in Vermont and Maine   286

CHAP. XXVI.

Population; Character; Amusements; Learning; Religion   292

CHAP. XXVII.

HISTORY OF NEW-YORK.

Discovery by the Dutch; Patent; Submission to the English; Government resumed by the Dutch, who erect a fort on Connecticut river; Their extravagant claims; Surrender of the country to the English; Its seizure by the Dutch, who soon surrendered it permanently to the English; Indians   297

CHAP. XXVIII.

Gov. Dongan recalled; Jacob Leister traitorously assumes the government; The French instigate the Indians to make war on the colonies; Dreadful massacre of the inhabitants of Schenectady; Leister and his son condemned to die, as guilty of treason; Commencement of dissentions between Episcopalians and Presbyterians; Indians cede a large tract of land to the English; Abortive plans for attacking Canada; Five sachems visit England, and are introduced to Queen Ann; 5000 Palatines from Germany, brought over by Gov. Hunter; Troubles with the merchants respecting the Indian trade; Project for a settlement of Highlanders, fails; Cession of lands to New-York by Massachusetts   308

CHAP. XXIX.

HISTORY OF NEW-JERSEY.

The Dutch settled East-Jersey, and the Swedes and Finns West-Jersey; Grant of this territory by Charles II. to the duke of York, and by him to others; Lands purchased of the Indians; The Dutch and Swedes inhabit the country together; Indian murders, causes and effects of them; Character and customs of the Indians; The Dutch conquered the country, but soon relinquished it; New Patent Division into *East* and *West* Jersey; Sold to Fenwick, who makes the first English settlement in Jersey; New partition of the country; Grant of West Jersey, and sale of East Jersey; Difficulties in managing the government; Surrendered to the crown 1702; Remained a royal government, till it became in 1776, an independent state; The patriotism and sufferings of its inhabitants during the war; College and Theological seminary at Princeton.

INTRODUCTION.

TO record the progress of human affairs, as directed by the providence of God; to exhibit the connexion of events, showing how an immense series is produced, as cause and effect; to display the character of man and of God, is the interesting office of a historian. The student in history, therefore, may learn the spontaneous results of human passions; the nature of the Divine government in this small province of the universe;—he may perceive the wisdom and the righteousness of God, in raising individuals to power and fame, and bringing them down to captivity, dependence and ruin; in his elevating cities and empires to greatness and glory, to science and religion—and in his overturning cities and empires, and subjecting them to the dominion of ignorance and vice;—he may discover the power of God to be peculiarly manifest in producing, from events trivial and common, those consequences, which are immensely important, and vastly distant in time and place. History, therefore, has always been considered an efficacious method of instructing mankind. Good men in every age have employed it for this invaluable purpose. It displays the felicities of goodness, and the miseries of vice; unfolds events, which have fulfilled prophecies that are past, and produces confidence in those, which remain to be fulfilled. Examples of individuals, great and good; of communities distinguished for wisdom and integrity, powerfully excite the student to imitate their virtues.

INTRODUCTION.

The settlement of New-England by a colony of Christians, may be remotely ascribed to the Reformation of Luther in Germany; or, to speak more exactly, to the rational and evangelical instructions of Wickliffe in England. While others were wrapt in papal darkness, he saw the true light. He was one of those uncommon men, one of an age, who appear in the world, as benefactors and instructors of the human race. He taught that the gospel of Christ was a perfect rule of life and manners; that St. Peter was not above the other apostles, nor the pontiff of Rome superior to the bishops.

A hundred and thirty years before Luther, Wickliffe rose, the morning star of the reformation. He was the first translator of the New-Testament into English, and wrote nearly two hundred volumes. These, with his bones, were burnt by order of the council of Constance, forty one years after his death. He taught, for substance, the same doctrines which Luther afterwards taught with so much greater success; the same doctrines which have since been professed by the Puritans, and which now constitute the creed of the great body of the New-England churches.

These new doctrines of Wickliffe roused the resentment of the papal church. Though for more than a thousand years, christians had not armed themselves with any weapons of force to punish their erring brethren; though their only means of restraining those who wandered from the footsteps of the flock, had been prayers and tears, admonitions and excommunications; yet now, finding these insufficient, the council of Lateran, A.D. 1215, in imitation of the pagan emperors, and instigated by papal influence, gave orders that all heretics shou'd be delivered over to the civil magistrate to be burned. Then blazed the first fire of persecution, kindled by professing christians; a fire which has sometimes carried misery and ruin through a whole nation; a fire, whose embers are now hardly extinguished on the altars of the church.

But the conflagration did not reach England till about two hundred years after its commencement; till near the close of the fourteenth century. In the reign of Richard II. and of Henry IV. and Henry V. laws were enacted, that heretics "might be burned to death before the people." The consequences were terrible. If any of the laity refused any profits, or any token of respect, which were supposed to be due to the priests of Rome, they were immediately suspected and accused of *heresy*, imprisoned, and put to death. By a law of Henry V. not only the followers of Wickliffe, but *whoever* else they were, "who should read the scriptures in the mother tongue, should forfeit land, cattle and goods, from their heirs forever, and so be condemned for heretics to God, and most arrant traitors to the land." To this iniquitous law hundreds fell victims. In such a state of things, Henry VIII. ascended the throne of England. This proud young monarch, during the first part of his reign, was a warm supporter of the papal power, and put to torture and to death multitudes of the bold confessors of the truth.

The effects o the Reformation by Luther, were now felt in England. The young king, possessing enough of scholastic learning to make him vain, and of zeal against the truth, to make him mad, engaged in a controversy with Luther, and published a book against him, which, "though it carried the king's name in the title," was actually written by another hand. "But whoever had the labor of the book, the king had the thanks, and the reward."* The Pope conferred on him for this act, the title of " *Defender of the Faith,*" which he had the weakness to value as " the brightest jewel in his crown."† This event happened in the year 1521.

A few years after this, an occurrence took place, which proved nearly fatal to the cause of popery in England, and in a wonderful manner favored the advancement of the Reformation. The king, who had lived with his wife Katharine nearly twenty years, became weary of her; and being as unprincipled as he was licentious, he pretended great compunction of conscience, because he had lived with her so long; she having been his brother's widow. The truth was, he had fallen in love with Anne Boleyn. In the ardor of this passion, he consulted with the universities of Europe; he applied to the pope for a divorce; but the pope from political motives, not yielding to his desires, Henry adopted a short and violent course. He declared himself and his kingdom independent of Rome, and himself " sole and supreme head of the church of England."‡ Under such malignant auspices the Reformation had its rise in the English nation. Though nothing could be more unscriptural or absurd, than for a vicious layman to assume the uncontrouled authority of reforming heresies, of establishing doc-

* Fox's Martyrology.

† His Jester, whom he kept at court, seeing the king overjoyed, asked the reason, and being told that it was occasioned by his new title, he said, " My good Harry, let thee and me defend each other, and let the faith alone to defend itself."

‡ This sacred title, the proud monarch, afterward, got annexed to the crown, by an act of parliament: and, incredible as it may seem, it is retained to this time.   *Heylin.*

trines, discipline, and modes of worship for the church of Christ; yet these daring measures have been followed with immense benefits to the cause of Christianity. So marvellously does God cause "the wrath of man to praise him." The wicked passions of Henry, though he meant not so, occasioned a light, which still shines to cheer millions of Christians scattered over the face of the earth; but for a season, it gleamed through much darkness. Henry himself became a persecutor. His Roman Catholic subjects he persecuted for their obedience to the Roman pontiff. The followers of Wickliffe he persecuted, because they were wiser and better than himself. The conceited tyrant felt entirely competent to direct the faith and worship of all his subjects. He was, in fact, the pope of England. One of the many evils, which grew out of this unwarrantable and wicked conduct of the king, was the prevalence of a variety of conflicting opinions. Soon it was an article of complaint to the court, that a diversity of doctrines were delivered from the pulpits. This was considered an insupportable evil. As an effectual remedy the king ordered all preaching to be suspended throughout the kingdom, from the 12th of July, 1536, to the 29th of September, that *he* might have time to adjust a system of orthodoxy, to guide the clergy in teaching their flocks.

In the summer of this year, (1536) the first reformed convocation in England assembled, over which lord Cromwell presided as the king's vicegerent in all spiritual matters.* To this assembly, by order of the king, he declared, "That it was his majesty's pleasure, that the rites and ceremonies of the Church should be reformed by the RULES OR

* Fuller's Church History.

scripture, and that nothing should be maintained, which did not rest on that authority; for it was absurd, since the Scriptures were acknowledged to contain the laws of religion, that recourse should be had to glosses or the decrees of popes, rather than to them."* Happy for the Church, for England and the world, had the king and the reformers adhered to the rules here prescribed. But the king did not stop here. He ordered his clergy to teach the people to believe not only the whole bible, but also the apostles, the Nicene and Athanasian creeds; that baptism was necessary to salvation; that contrition, faith and reformation were necessary to eternal life; that confession to a priest was necessary, if one can be obtained; and that his absolution is the same, as if it were spoken by God himself; that the bread and wine of the sacrament are truly of the same body which was born of the virgin; that justification implies a renovation of nature, &c. The worship of images and prayers to the saints were required; purgatory he left doubtful. In this manner truth and error were miserably blended. Thus was the dawn of the reformation overcast with clouds of darkness. All the people were required by law, to swear that the king was supreme head of the church of England; a number of papists were executed for refusing the oath. Among these were John Fisher, bishop of Rochester, and Sir T. Moore, then late lord chancellor of England. For a time this struck the people with panic, but did not long prevent insurrections in different places. In Lincolnshire, twenty thousand people rose, headed by a priest, and directed by a monk.

In 1538, a brighter light beamed on the church. The bible was printed in English; liberty was given to the people

* Burnet's Hist. of the Reformation.

to read it, one copy was ordered to be placed in every church; the clergy were required to preach the necessity of faith and repentance, and against trusting in pilgrimages, or the good works of other men; images were taken down, and praying to them was pronounced idolatry. These measures were consoling to enlightened Christians; but transubtantiation, the seven sacraments, purgatory, the celibacy of the clergy, prayers for the dead, auricular confession, were all retained; yet here was the utmost point of advance towards reformation, during the life of Henry. His subsequent measures proved him to be a miserable guide of the church. The next year, the law, called *the bloody statute*, was enacted. Its absurd title was " an act for abolishing diversity of opinions," &c. We may pertinently ask, why did he not first make a law, that all men should possess the same capacity, have the same education, the same temper, and be placed in the same circumstances? The absurdity and wickedness of this law was soon manifest from its effects; five hundred persons were thrown into prison. The year following, the temper of the king was strikingly displayed; Protestants and Papists were burning at the same time. Among the victims were three Lutheran clergymen. The Papists suffered for denying the king's supremacy, and adhering to the church of Rome.

In 1543, another law was made, which indicated the marvellous sagacity of the rulers! It was enacted, that all matters of christian faith, rules and ceremonies, shall be published by the king's advice, and shall be in every point *believed* and obeyed. It was also enacted, that all books of the Old and New Testament, being Tyndal's translation, comprising any articles of faith, contrary to the doctrines set forth by the king, shall be abolished. " No person shall

INTRODUCTION.

We have no conclusive evidence, that any other than *extempore* prayers were used in the church, till the latter part of the fourth century. Then written prayers are first mentioned; but it was left for every bishop to draw up a form of prayer for his own church. In the fifth century, they began to consult about an agreement of prayers; but no uniformity was established. In the darkest times of popery a great variety of forms were permitted in the Romish church. Every religious order had its peculiar rites. But the Episcopal church, as if they were resolved to outdo the Papists in absurdity and spiritual domination, resolved that her members should adopt *a complete uniformity*. On this dreadful rock was dashed the prosperity of the nation. They resolved to compel all men to agree in an exact uniformity of doctrines, (a thing impossible from the nature of the human mind) and of ceremonies of worship; and habits or dress of their clergy. All these things they considered equally *essential* in their religion.

About 1550, the sad consequences of retaining the popish garments became more evident. A dispute arose, however trivial it may appear to us, which produced consequences of incalculable importance to remote generations, and distant quarters of the world. All Germany was in a flame on the same subject. At this crisis Dr. Hooper, " a pious learned man"* arrived in England from Zurich; his mind filled with the zeal of those times against caps and gowns for the clergy. He devoted himself to preaching; was in the pulpit every day of the week; and so popular were his sermons, that the churches were crowded wherever he preached. His fame soon reached the court, and he and

* Bp. Burnet.

Dr. Poynet were appointed to preach the Lent sermons. To reconcile the people to the reformation, he was sent on a mission through the counties of Kent and Essex. Soon he was appointed bishop of Glocester, but he declined the office for two reasons: "the form of the oath was *impious*, and the habits to be worn, Aaronical." The king altered the oath with his own hand. The habits were not so easily changed. The prelates would not allow him to decline the bishopric, nor would they dispense with the habits. He entreated to be excused; urging that such a dress had no countenance from scripture or antiquity; that it was the invention of antichrist; that it had been abused to superstition and idolatry, and to use it was to harmonize with antichrist. All these reasons were disregarded. The bishops were resolved that he should be subdued and at all events, be made a bishop; that he should be consecrated, according to the customs of the episcopal church, and wear the common habits. He was, therefore, by order of council, silenced, and confined to his house. To be thus persecuted by his brethren of the same faith, about the color and shape of his clothes, was more than he could well understand. After a tedious imprisonment, during which his life is said to have been threatened,* a compromise, finally, took place. Hooper, after consulting both the universities, and the divines of Geneva and Switzerland, consented to be dressed in his habits, at his consecration, and when he preached before the king, or in his cathedral, or in any public place; but in all other places he had a dispensation. Accordingly, he preached before the king, "his upper garment of a scarlet color, reaching to his feet; under that, one of white lin-

* Peirce's Vindication, vol. i. p. 50.

en, which covered his shoulders; on his head was a square cap."

So imperfect was the reformation effected by young Edward, during his short reign; yet a majority of those engaged with him were undoubtedly great and good men. Advances toward primitive simplicity were, perhaps, as rapid as the state of the nation, and of the times permitted. They themselves considered the work incomplete. In one of their service books, they say, "they had gone as far as they could in reforming the church, considering the times in which they lived, and hope that those who come after them, will, as they may, do *more.*" But those who " came after them," instead of doing *more*, carried the church back toward Popery. The death of Edward, in July 1553, in the 16th year of his age, and seventh of his reign, for a long season terminated the work of reformation. He was succeeded by his sister Mary.

Here, before we proceed in our history, it is proper distinctly to remark, that in articles of faith, the first reformers followed St. Augustine, whose doctrines for substance have since been adopted and defended by Calvin, as the doctrines of scripture. Predestination, original sin, justification by faith, effectual grace, and the necessity of good works, with the doctrine of the Trinity, and the divinity of Christ, were leading articles of their faith, and considered as fundamental in the Christian scheme of religion. They also held, that bishops, and priests, and pastors were the same. The great practical error of the early reformers, was their abandonment of the first principle, on which they justified their own revolt from the church of Rome; viz. the right of private judgment, and the sufficiency of the scriptures as a rule of faith. Losing sight of this, they absurdly employed the civil power, to enforce their creeds and rites of worship. By such a course they labored to suppress a proper freedom of inquiry, to check the progress of improvement, and to a certain extent they did in fact transform themselves into that very corrupt church, from which they had separated.

To prevent the return of Popery, Edward, by the advice of his council, sat aside the succession of his sisters, and by *will* settled the crown on Lady Jane Grey, who was next in blood after those princesses. But Mary, by stratagem and falsehood, defeated the design of her brother. At first, she promised the Protestants that she would make no alteration in religion. This procured her an army. Next, she told her council that she was resolved not to *compel* others, except by the *preaching* of the *word*.* Finally, on a tumult being excited, while a Roman Catholic was preaching against the reformation, the queen forbid all preaching through the kingdom, unless by special license; but declared, "she would not compel her subjects to adopt her religion, *till public order should be taken by common consent*."† Here the mask falls. As soon as she can obtain a law, persecution shall begin. The blackening storm was seen rising; the Protestant pulpits were shut; Cranmer and Latimer were sent to the Tower, Hooper to the Fleet, and more persons fled from the kingdom.

The queen was crowned Oct. 1, 1553; and on the 31st, a bill was sent to the commons, repealing the law of Edward in favor of the reformation, and severe punishments were decreed against all who resisted Popery. The carvers of images and crosses had now a brisk and profitable business.

---

* Burnet's History of the Reformation. † Ibid.

The most eminent preachers of London were in prison; and of sixteen thousand clergymen, it was supposed twelve thousand were silenced. In Nov. 1554, the statutes of former reigns for burning heretics were revived; and in Feb. John Rogers was burned, as was Mr. Saunders soon after; his last words were, " Welcome the cross of Christ, welcome everlasting life." Doctor Taylor suffered next. In July, Rev. J. Bradford, who had been a celebrated preacher, became a victim; the persecution spread over the country. In June and July one woman and eight men suffered; in August and September twenty-five more. The most affecting sacrifice was yet to come. On the 16th of October, bishops Ridley and Latimer were burned at the same stake. Ridley was a long time in torment, before the fire seized on his body; his last words were, " Be of good cheer brother; God will assuage the fury of the fire, or enable us to bear it." Latimer replied, " Be of good comfort; we shall this day light such a candle in England, as I trust by God's grace shall never be put out." The martyrdom of archbishop Cranmer followed. In him is seen the vanity of human glory; lately he shone a star of splendor, a luminary of the church, the second man in the empire. Now behold him a fast bound prisoner, a gazing stock of the multitude, clothed in rags, and led to execution. In a moment of terror, to save his life, he had *subscribed* to the doctrines of Popery. His repentance was deep and pungent, as his sin had been grievous. Bound to the stake, the fire burning, he stretched out his right hand to the flame, never moving it but once to wipe his face, till it dropped from his arm, often crying out, " that unworthy hand." His last words were, " Lord Jesus, receive my spirit." Not content with burning heretics singly, Bonner sent them in companies to the flames. In less than six years, the period of Mary's reign, two hundred and seventy seven persons suffered death, or according to other accounts, two hundred and eighty eight, and even four hundred.* These Papists, not content to make war upon the living, assailed the dead. They caused the bones of Fagius and Bucer to be dug up. and then cited them to appear before their ghostly tribunal, to give an account of their faith; but these good men, totally disregarding the summons, were, for this non-appearance, burned under the gallows.

In this day of terror, many hundred people fled into Flanders, France, Germany, Geneva, and Switzerland. These exiles were most numerous at Frankfort, where a contention arose, which gave one party the name of *Puritans;* whose history is traced in the following pages. This name is so interesting to all the children of New-England, that we may well spend a moment in developing its origin.

The good magistrates of Frankfort offered the English exiles the use of their church, during those hours of the sabbath, when it was not occupied by their own citizens, on the two following conditions; they must subscribe the French confession of faith, and not quarrel about ceremonies. The strangers accepted the offer, and agreed not to answer aloud after the minister, and not to use the litany or surplice. They adopted, for substance, that mode of worship, which is still practised in our congregational churches. They invited Messrs. Knox, Haddon, and Lever, to be their ministers. Soon after, they received letters from their friends, residing at Strasburgh, exhorting them to conform to the mode of worship, adopted by king Edward. Wishing

---

* Some say 800

to show all due respect to their brethren, they wrote to the celebrated Calvin for his advice. He replied, that in the book of Edward were many tolerable weaknesses; but he could not see why men should be so fond of Popish dregs. By this the members of the congregation at Frankfort were confirmed in their own practice. Not long after, Dr. Cox, who had been tutor to king Edward, with a number of his friends, coming to Frankfort, interrupted the public service, by answering aloud after the minister. As if this outrage on decorum had not been sufficient, the next sabbath, one of the company, without the consent of the congregation, ascended the pulpit and read the whole litany. This produced a dispute, a division, and at last a separation. By art and management, by a violent and overbearing conduct, Cox finally obtained the ascendancy; and the old congregation left the city. A majority of these went to Geneva, chose Messrs. Knox and Goodman their pastors, adopted the Genevan discipline, and were afterwards called PURITANS.

In England, the reformers, by order of Mary, were sacrificed without mercy. At Oxford, the persecutors burned all the English bibles and books of heresy, which they could find. But the hand of God was against queen Mary and her government. Her measures were unsuccessful; her husband abandoned her; her health declined, and she died of a broken heart, in the forty-third year of her age, and sixth of her reign.

Mary, with all her malignant efforts, did not extinguish the light of the reformation in England. Many, who loved the gospel more than their lives, endured and survived the storm. One of the largest of the congregations of this sort of people, consisting of about 200. was in London, and held their meetings with the utmost secrecy, and often in the dead of night, and experienced many remarkable deliverances. Clark, in his Martyrology, relates the following: "On one of these nocturnal occasions, being assembled in a house on the bank of the Thames, they were discovered by their enemies, and the house so effectually guarded, that they were sure none could escape, and waited for the morning to secure their prey. But among them was a worthy mariner, who, through a back door, which opened to the river, escaped; swam to a boat, which he brought, received the good people into it, made oars of his shoes, and during the night conveyed them all away in safety."

The accession of Elizabeth gave new life to the reformers. They expected she would favor their cause, though she was known to be fond of magnificence in her devotions, and thought that her brother had gone too far in stripping religion of her ceremonies. The exiles hastened home from the continent. Freedom of opinion and speech was enjoyed without fear of arrest, of prison, or of death.* Soon the jarring sounds of controversy were heard from the pulpits. To suppress this evil, the queen immediately prohibited all preaching. The Papists were soon vanquished; but to satisfy the different sections of the reformers, required all the wisdom of the sagacious Elizabeth. While some were engaged for the service and discipline of Geneva, others were as zealous for the service book of Edward, and for receding

* When the exiles came forward in public, a gentleman, it is said, made suit to the queen, in behalf of *Matthew*, *Mark*, *Luke* and *John*, who had long been imprisoned in a Latin translation, that they also might be restored to liberty, and walk abroad as formerly, in the English tongue. Her majesty promptly replied, "that he should first know the minds of the prisoners, who perhaps desired no such liberty as he requested." *Heylin's Hist. of the Reformation.*

no further from the Romish church than was necessary to secure the purity of their doctrines, and their freedom from foreign power. But an act was passed requiring *uniformity* in the common prayer, and service, and administration of sacraments; an act, which for near a century produced incalculable mischief in the church of England. Both parties agreed but two well in admitting a uniformity in ceremonies and habits to be necessary; and in using the sword and fire to enforce their own system, whenever they could obtain the power. So a partial reformation was established by a law of the realm. Crosses and images were banished from the churches. To avenge the blood of the martyrs, shed in the late reign, the populace collected crucifixes, surplices, altar-cloths, and books, and made bonfires of them in Smithfield, and other places. These proceedings displeased the queen. Keeping an altar, a crucifix, an organ, with other instruments, and lighted candles in her own chapel, her service rivalled the splendor of Papal worship. In her chapel, the English language was used. This was the chief point of difference. The disputes of those times did not respect the doctrines of the gospel, and had the Popish habits of the ministers, and the ceremonies of worship, been left to the discretion of the churches, those unhallowed fires of dissention might easily have been extinguished.

If any are disposed to question the wisdom of the Puritans in their unyielding zeal against the Popish garments of the clergy, let them recollect as their apology, and perhaps as their complete justification, that those garments were supposed, by a great part of the people, to give the right of office, and even a miraculous power, to those who wore them. To continue their use was to countenance such impious superstition, and to connive at idolatry.

It was found impossible to supply the vacant pulpits with men of character and learning; their antipathy to rites and robes, imposed by authority, was violent. Learning and piety were lost to the churches; mechanics, and men the most illiterate, assumed the office of ministers. These were disregarded and despised by the people, and a cloud of odium covered the reformation. If the parson could read the service, and sometimes a homily, this was thought sufficient. Few sermons were preached in the kingdom. Knox, having returned from Geneva, where he and Coverdale had completed the translation of the bible, extended the reformation into Scotland.

In 1560, archbishop Parker visited his diocese, and found the greater part of his clergy ignorant mechanics, or Popish priests; in some counties not a sermon was preached in the circuit of twenty miles. The prospects of the church were dismal; she had little hope from the universities. Their instructors were chiefly Papists, and had trained the youth in those principles. The reformation proceeded heavily. The lips of those ministers who had the power to awaken and instruct the nation were silent. The two great luminaries of the kingdom were obscured by a dark eclipse, the queen was hostile to the marriage of the clergy; she often lamented that she had proceeded so far; and very reluctantly parted with her images, her crucifixes, and her candles.

In 1564, many instances of non-conformity were reported to the queen. Her majesty was highly displeased. It appeared that some of the clergy performed divine service " wearing a square cap, some a round cap, some a button cap, some a hat, some in scholar's clothes, and some in others." However unimportant or ludicrous such a controversy may appear in the present day, the merits of these habits were then solemnly debated by the gravest doctors and bishops of England, and by the most learned divines of Europe. Their disputes were useless. The strong arm of authority decided the question. The bishops published their "advertisements" to the clergy, prescribing an *exact* uniformity, as to the fashion of their dress, "gowns, caps, cuffs, capes, sleeves, and tippets." By this measure another portion of the most serious and useful ministers, who had continued to preach, were expelled from their pulpits, and shut up in prison. They refused to *conform*. Some of them became physicians, some became chaplains in private families; some fled to Scotland; others to the continent; some resorted to secular business; and many, with large families, were reduced to want and beggary. The churches were shut; the public mind was inflamed; six hundred people repaired to a church in London to receive the sacrament; the doors were closed; no minister would officiate. The cries of the people reached the throne; but the throne was inexorable, and the archbishop had rather see his flock perish for the waters of salvation, than dispense with the clerical robes of the Papal church.

Despairing of relief from the government, the suspended ministers appealed to the world, and published an able defence of their conduct. Other publications followed. These were answered by the bishops. The Puritans replied; the public mind was agitated and inflamed; multitudes of the common people refused to attend worship where the minister wore *the habits*. The government was roused. The Star Chamber decreed, that no person should publish any book against the queen and ordinances, or their *meaning*. Booksellers were compelled to enter into bonds to observe this law. This measure hastened the controversy to a signal *crisis*.

The suspended ministers finding themselves in a pressing dilemma, having lost all hope of relief, had a solemn consultation, and agreed, "that since they could not have the word of God preached, nor the sacraments administered without *idolatrous geare, it was their duty to break off from the public church, and to assemble in private houses and elsewhere.*" This agreement took place about the year 1566, and was the event that constituted the memorable era of SEPARATION from the church of England, and the establishment of the denomination of DISSENTERS.

Here we see people of the same country, believing the same religious doctrines, separating, chiefly on account of a few ceremonies, and the use of certain garments. Other less interesting points of difference might have been settled, if the queen and the bishops would have allowed the people to worship God in a manner more agreeable to their consciences. But this fire of contention, which at first might have been easily extinguished, was suffered to burn deeper and wider, like a volcano, till finally, in a fatal explosion, it destroyed the king, the government, and the constitution.

In June, 1567, the sheriff of London discovered and broke up an assembly of about one hundred Puritans, most of whom were arrested, and several sent to bridewell, where they were confined more than a year. In all suspected places, spies were employed to prevent these religious assemblies. In 1572, about one hundred clergymen were deprived of their support, for not subscribing to the articles of the church. Doctor Clark was expelled from the university of Cambridge, which by this time was considered "a nest of Puritans," for preaching that "Satan introduced into the church the different orders of the clergy."

Though the pulpits of the Puritans were daily silenced, and they were not allowed to print a page, still their cause gained ground; the spirit of their principles spread continually through the mass of society. Their zeal was inextinguishable. They employed printing presses, which secretly travelled through the country. Their pamphlets were scattered in every direction. The sober part of the community were addressed with powerful arguments; humor, sarcasm, and intolerable satire, were scattered every where by invisible hands. To no purpose did Parker, for a long time, employ his agents to discover their presses. Deplorable was the state of morals and religion. Oppression and invective had sharpened the spirit of the parties. In some places Popery was openly professed; the bishops were loaded with riches; the people were neglected, and the court was corrupt, and reputed even to be the residence of licentiousness and atheism.

While the bishops were driving the Puritans from their pulpits, many of the nobility received them into their families, as their chaplains, and tutors of their children. Thus sheltered from their oppressors, they preached to the family, and catechised the children. This doubtless had a powerful effect on the rising generation. Still the spirit of persecution did not rest.

In June, 1583, two ministers of the Brownists were executed. This year the troubles of the Puritans were increased. Archbishop Grindal, who was rather favorably disposed towards them, was succeeded by Whitgift, a cruel persecutor. He ordered that all preaching, catechising, and praying should cease in every house, when any person was present beside the family. In 1584, no less than thirty eight clergymen were suspended in the county of Essex.

More effectually to arrest the Puritan pens, the Star Chamber forbade having any printing presses in any private place, or any where in the kingdom, except in London, and the two universities. These must be licensed by the archbishop of Canterbury, or bishop of London. Nor might any book be printed, till it had been perused by them or their chaplains. The Lord's day being greatly profaned by plays and sports, the Rev. Mr. Smith, preaching before the university of Cambridge, urged the unlawfulness of such practices. For this he was summoned before the vice chancellor; yet so reasonable was the course of duty, that without any law, the observance of the sabbath became more common, and afterwards was considered as the badge of a Puritan. So oppressive was the Episcopal party, that the dissenters were not permitted to keep a common school.

In 1586, the Puritan ministers again petitioned parliament. They state, that after the most laborious and exact survey, they find that one third of the ministers have been expelled from their pulpits; that there are in England only two thousand ministers to supply ten thousand churches; that many people, in order to hear a sermon, must travel twelve or twenty miles. But the spirit of mercy had forsaken the government.

Another terrific law was made by the parliament, which opened February 19, 1591. It was enacted " that if any person, above the age of sixteen, shall for one month refuse to attend at some Episcopal church, and after conviction, shall not in three months make a humble confession, he shall go into *perpetual* banishment, if he do not depart in the time appointed, or if he return without the queen's license, he shall suffer death, without benefit of clergy." The moderate Puritans evaded this dreadful law by going to church when the services were near closing. But on the Brownists, who had conscientiously separated from the church, of whom there were twenty thousand in Norfolk, Essex, and about London, this law burst like a fatal thunderbolt. Though they conducted their meetings with all practicable secresy, and changed the place of their worship from time to time to prevent discovery, it was not long before the officers of government fell upon one congregation, and arrested fifty-six of them, who were all sent to prison, where many of them perished, and others, after several years of confinement, were executed or banished. At their examination, they confessed, that for years they had met in the fields, in summer, at 5 o'clock A. M. on the Lord's day, and in the winter at private houses.

Till about this time, the controversy had chiefly respected habits, discipline, and ceremonies; but doctrines now began to be disputed. The Puritans and the universities denied the descent of Christ into hell, advocated the sanctity of the sabbath, and the opinions of Calvin, his Institutions being read in their schools; while the Episcopal party took the opposite side, and espoused the system of Arminius. The cause of the Puritans advanced; the bishops lost the respect due to ministers of religion. If any among the clergy or laity were distinguished for their pure morals, or ardent piety, they were immediately supposed to be Puritans. For some time, however, before the death of the queen, the zeal of controversy had gradually subsided, and the aspect of public affairs was more favorable to the rights and interests of the Puritans. Those of their opposers, who had been the most intimate friends of the queen, whom she had most favored, and through whose influence she had been led to do many things against the Puritans, when her case became desperate, and she could no longer serve them, deserted her, and scarce afforded her any of their company. She died March 1603, and was succeeded by James I. who came to the throne by hereditary right, as well as by the appointment of queen Elizabeth.

The Puritans had high hopes of relief from the new king, who had been educated in their religion. But unfortunately for himself and the nation, James had not abilities to soften the violence of party asperity, nor conscience enough to support the friends of a thorough reformation; but immediately became a dupe to the flattery of the bishops, and a tool of their ambition. The men who forsook Elizabeth, and seduced the king to act against his own principles and interests, became his confidants. Though he had given the most solemn pledges of favor to the Presbyterians, " thanking God that he was king of the purest church in the world;" yet in nine months he renounced his former professions, and became the champion of Episcopacy. The church of Rome he called *his mother church*, declaring, " I will have one doctrine, one discipline, one religion in substance and *ceremony*." " I will make them *conform*, or I will hurry them out of the land, or else worse."

The execution was as fatal as the threatening was absurd and wicked. Whitgift was succeeded by Bancroft, as archbishop of Canterbury, a man of rough temper, and an open foe to civil and religious liberty. By enforcing the observance of festivals, and the use of surplices, and caps and hoods; and by requiring the clergy, *from the heart* to subscribe certain articles, he very soon silenced more than three hundred Puritan ministers. Some were excommunicated, some imprisoned, and others driven into exile. The greater part of those who left the country were Brownists, whose leaders were Johnson, Ainsworth, Smith, and the well known John Robinson; who has since been considered the father of that portion of the Puritans, who were the founders of the New-England colonies; of whom a more particular account will be given in the subsequent history.

Abbot, a sound Protestant, and thorough Calvinist, succeeded Bancroft, who died in 1610, in the archbishopric of Canterbury. Still, in 1612, several persons were burned for heresy at Smithfield and Litchfield; but so evident was the commiseration of the people, that it was thought more prudent to let the prisoners languish out their days in Newgate.

On the death of James, in March, 1625, he was succeeded by his son Charles I. who inherited his father's love of power, and hatred of puritanism. The good archbishop Abbot, having lost his influence, and Laud being bishop of London, and prime minister, the work of persecution proceeded with new vigor. Ministers were daily suspended, nd their families ruined; no shelter from the terrific storm could be discovered in the realm of England. The sufferers were roused. What could they do? A colony formed of the exiles in Holland, had already settled at Plymouth, in New-England; and these sufferers now projected the planting of a second colony on Massachusetts bay, which was effected in 1629.

The history of these colonists, and of those who afterwards followed them to this retreat from oppression, and of their posterity down to the present time is given in the following pages.

We close this Introduction with a few of the many testimonials in favor of the character of the Puritans at this period.

Though few men ever suffered more reproach and calumny than the Puritans, yet candid and sensible men, not of their number, and opposed to their principles, have done them more justice. Bishop Burnet, in his history of his time, says, "The Puritans gained credit as the bishops lost it. They put on the appearance of great sanctity and gravity, and took more pains in their parishes, than those who adhered to their bishops, often preaching against the vices of the court. Their labors and their sufferings raised their reputation, and rendered them very popular." Hume, who has ridiculed their principles, and spoken contemptuously of them in other respects, says,* "So absolute was the authority of the crown, that the precious spark of *liberty* had been kindled, and was preserved by the *Puritans alone ;* and it was to *this sect* that the English owe *the whole freedom of their constitution.*" Higher praise, and this too from an enemy to their religion, could hardly be bestowed on the Puritans. More of their true character and worth will be brought into view in the following chapters.

* Hist. of Eng. vol. v. p. 134.

HISTORY

OF

NEW-ENGLAND.

CHAP. I.

The flight of the Puritans to Holland; their sufferings during their residence there; their character; their determination to remove, and their reasons for removal.

In 1602, there was an extensive revival of religion in the counties of Nottinghamshire, Lancashire and Yorkshire in England, and the converts were numerous. They saw the vanity of their former superstitions; sought more evangelical instruction; and a *purer* church. A separation from the established church, as already noticed, was the consequence. They resolved, " whatever it should cost them," to enjoy liberty of conscience. On account of their distance from each other, they formed themselves into two churches. Of one, Mr. JOHN SMITH, a man of " able gifts and a good preacher," became pastor; but these, adopting some errors in the Low Countries, became neglected, and their history is unknown. Of the other, the history of which will constitute a considerable part of the following pages, the Rev. RICHARD CLIFTON, a man " of grave deportment and a successful preacher," had the pastoral care. Many were hopefully converted under his ministrations. Mr. JOHN ROBINSON was a member of this church, and afterwards their pastor. Mr. WILLIAM BREWSTER was an elder and preacher.

After they separated from the establishment, on account of its retaining so much of Popery,* and were organized

* As the Papists are often mentioned in this work, the following epitome of their principles may be useful to the reader.

The Papists, of the age of which we are speaking, believed the Pope to be supreme head of the church, under Christ, and that his jurisdiction extended over all christians. They believed infallibility to be an attribute of their church, though they were not agreed whether it resided in the Pope, in a general council, or in both united. They believed that Jesus Christ instituted seven sacraments, baptism, confirmation, the eucharist, penance, extreme unction, orders, and matrimony. They believed in the doctrine of human merit, that men not only deserved the grace of God; but life and glory hereafter. The right of indulgences, they supposed left with the church by Jesus Christ. By this, they did not mean liberty to commit sin, nor pardon for sins to come; but released from temporal punishment, after pardon had been obtained by repentance and confession. They also believed in works of supererogation, or that a man may and did often perform more than duty or the command of God required; that in this way an immense stock of merit was procured, which the church might dispense of in indulgences to those who needed. The celibacy of the clergy, and the use of pictures and images in religious worship were articles of their creed; but they denied that these were worshipped. As the Protestant read a chapter or section to refresh his mind with certain truths or facts, so the Catholic, with a glance, *instantly* affected his heart. The council of Trent enjoined intercession to the saints reigning with Jesus Christ. These saints, they did not profess to worship; but addressed as mediators with God, as Moses interceded for Israel, and as saints now ask a daily remembrance in each other's prayers. They honored the relics of the saints, and pronounced a curse on all, who say, that mass ought to be celebrated only in the vulgar tongue. The traditions of the church, they supposed, supplied the defects of scripture, and had the same authority. They believed in a purgatory, where the souls of gracious persons were confined, who find relief in the prayers and alms of the faithful. In the mass, they maintained that propitiatory sacrifice is offered for the living and the dead: and that in the eucharist was really present the body and blood, the soul and divinity of the Lord Jesus Christ.

churches, having covenanted " to walk in all the ways of God made known, *or to be made known to them*, according to their best endeavors," the spirit of persecution rose like a flood, with new fury. Beside the trial of cruel mockings, they were watched by officers, and were often imprisoned, or obliged to fly from their houses and means of subsistence.

In this deplorable situation, with " joint consent," they resolved to go into the Low Countries, " where they heard was freedom of religion for all men." Hard was their lot, to leave their dwellings, their lands, and relatives, to go they knew not whither, to obtain a living they knew not how. Having been employed only in agriculture, they were ignorant of the trades and business of the country, which they had selected as the place of their exile. Though persecuted, they were not dismayed; though distressed, their courage did not forsake them. Still another affliction, more unreasonable, if possible, than any former one, stared them in the face. They could not stay in peace, nor were they allowed to depart. The strong arm of *law* barred every harbor and vessel against them. They could effect their escape only by secret means, or by bribing the mariners, and then were they often betrayed, their property seized, and themselves punished. The following facts will show their distressing and forlorn situation.

A large company, intending to embark at Boston, in Lincolnshire, hired a ship, agreed with the master to take them on board at a certain day, at an appointed place. They were punctual; he kept not the day, but finally came and received them on board in the night; then, having agreed beforehand with the searchers and other officers, he delivered the passengers and goods to them, who put them in boats, rifled and searched them " to their shirts," treating the women with indelicacy and rudeness, carried them back

to the town, where they were spectacles of scorn to the
multitude, who came to gaze. They were carried before
the magistrates, and imprisoned for a month ; the greater
part were then sent to the place whence they came: but
the principal characters were kept in confinement, or bound
over to the next assizes.

Distressed, but still persevering, the next spring a number of these, with others agreed with a Dutch captain to
carry them them to Holland. He was to take them from a
large common between Grimsby and Hull, a place remote
from any town. The women, children, and goods, were
sent to the place in a small bark; the men travelled by
land ; but the bark arriving a day before the ship, and the
sea being rough, and the women very sick, the seamen put
into a small creek. The next morning the ship came, but
the bark was aground. That no time might be lost, the
captain sent his boat to receive some of the men, who were
on shore. As the boat was returning for more, the captain
saw a great company of horse and foot, coming armed from
the country ; at which he weighed anchor, hoisted sail, and
having a fair wind was soon out of sight. The men on
board were thus separated from their wives and children,
without a change of garments, or money in their pockets.
They wept and entreated, but tears and entreaties were
vain. Soon after, they were tossed in a storm, and driven
on the coast of Norway. They saw neither sun, moon, nor
stars, for seven days. The mariners despaired of relief,
and once they supposed the ship actually going down ; with
shrieks and cries, they exclaimed, *we sink, we sink*, the water overflowing them to their mouths ; yet the Puritan
passengers, in this scene of horror and desperation, without
any great distraction, cried, " Yet, Lord, thou canst save ;
Lord, thou canst save," with other similar expressions. The
ship soon recovered herself, and the fury of the storm abated.

But to return to the people on shore. The men escaped, excepting those, who voluntarily staid to assist the women and children. Here was a moving scene of distress; husbands and fathers carried to a foreign country; children crying with fear, and shivering with cold. Charity and humanity would have cheered the weeping throng; but these heavenly spirits were not here. Persecution raised her voice, terrible as death; she hurried them from one place to another, from one officer to another, till they were tired of their victory. To imprison so many innocent women and children would have excited public indignation; homes they had none, for they had disposed of them; they were glad to be rid of them on any terms. From these sufferings their cause received advantage. Their meekness and christian deportment made a favorable and deep impression on the hearts of many spectators, which produced considerable accessions to their number. But by courage and perseverance they all finally crossed over to Holland, and united with their friends, according to the desire of their hearts, in grateful praises to God.

In Holland they saw the bustle of business, the splendor of cities, and the independence of amazing wealth; poverty, however, arrested them with the strength of an armed man. Messrs. ROBINSON and BREWSTER were the last who arrived, having, like valiant generals, remained to see the feeblest safe on board; they arranged their church affairs in regular order, and continued about a year at Amsterdam. Mr. ROBINSON and some others, seeing the evils in which the other English church under Mr. Smith was involved, thought it prudent to remove to Leyden. Though they here expected less employment and profit, than in the capital, they were cheerful in this sacrifice of worldly good, in hope of being more free from temptations, and enjoying more uninterruptedly the blessings of the gospel.

Religion was always the first object in all their calculations and arrangements. Engaging in such trades and employments, as they could execute, and which gave them comfortable support, they had great comfort in each other's society, great satisfaction in the ordinances of the gospel, under the able ministry and prudent government of Messrs. ROBINSON and BREWSTER. They grew in gifts and graces: " They lived in peace, and love, and holiness;" numbers came to them from England: they had a great congregation, and at one time three hundred communicants. If at any time sparks of contention were kindled, they were immediately quenched; or if any one proved obstinate, he was excommunicated; but instances of this kind rarely happened. Perhaps this church approached as near the pattern of apostolic churches, as any since the first ages of christianity.

Their integrity and piety procured them esteem and confidence in a land of strangers. Though they were poor, when they wished to borrow money, the Dutch would readily take their word, because they always found them honest and punctual. They saw them very industrious in their callings, and therefore preferred them as customers; they found them upright and faithful, and therefore gave the preference to their work. Just before these fathers of New-England left the city, the magistrates, from the seat of justice, gave this honorable testimony of their worth. In addressing the Walloons, who were the *French* church, " These English," say they, " have lived among us now these twelve years, and yet we never had *one* suit or action come against them; but your strifes and quarrels are *continual.*"*

* Morton.

The interest of religion being constantly impressed on their minds, pursuing it with unabating ardor, it was natural for them to think of changing their residence, as new and favorable prospects opened before them. Great minds pursue great objects; as their means increase, their views expand. Having enjoyed the comforts of evangelical instruction from the courtesy of strangers, they were unwilling to possess so precious a jewel by so precarious a tenure. Their removal, therefore, was not the effect of a fickle disposition, but the result of undaunted perseverence for the attainment of an end, which absorbed all other considerations.

Other more imperious reasons seemed to enforce the measure. They found that but few, comparatively, came to them from their native country, and that fewer still remained with them. They loved their cause, approved their magnanimity, but after making the trial themselves, they could not endure the excessive labor, the hard fare, and other inconveniences to which all were obliged to submit. Many preferred prisons in England, to liberty in Holland, accompanied with such sufferings. It was supposed, that if a place of more comfortable living could be found, great numbers would flock to them. Mr. Robinson used to say that, "Many in England, who then wrote and preached against them, would conduct as they did, if they had liberty and could *live comfortably*." Many found that they were growing old without any property for their support. Not only themselves and servants, but their children also, were obliged to labor beyond their strength, their vigor of life consuming before it was mature. Others they saw overcome by the temptations of the place, or enlisting as soldiers or sailors. These were distressing events to affectionate, religious parents.

They were also animated with the hope of carrying the gospel of salvation to Pagan countries, and of saving many souls ready to perish. The business was the subject of much conversation. Some urged and encouraged their companions to the undertaking. Others proposed very serious and weighty objections. Their want of property for such an enterprise, the dangers of the voyage, the cruelty of savages, and improbability of finding subsistence in a world of forests, were mentioned with deep conviction of their reality. To these things it was replied, that all great achievements were attended with great difficulties, and required corresponding courage and zeal. It was acknowledged that the obstacles were great, but not insuperable; the dangers formidable, but not desperate. Some of the difficulties, though probable, they conceived were not certain; others they hoped to conquer, or bear with fortitude. It was also urged, that the twelve year's truce was expired; that war between the Dutch and Spaniards would greatly endanger them; that the beating of drums and the alarm and parade of war, which had already begun, showed them what to expect: that the conquering Spaniard might prove as cruel as the savage; and the famine and pestilence of war be as dreadful, as the woods of America; that they were exiles, their condition miserable, their dangers imminent, and something must be done. The ministers of New-England, in a letter to Mr. Ducy, assign as the reasons, (and probably they are the true ones after all,) which finally influenced them to leave their country, and settle a wilderness, were, " that the ancient faith and true worship might be found inseparable companions in their practice, and that their posterity might be undefiled in religion." " It was therefore fully concluded by the major part to put the design of removal into execution, and prosecute it by the best means in their power."

CHAP. II.

Measures adopted for removing ; their voyage ; their disappointment as to the place of their settlement, through the treachery of the Dutch ; the form of government established ; their landing at Cape Cod.

Having resolved on a removal, the first measure they adopted was a meeting for prayer, to seek direction and assistance from God. A general conference was then holden to consult on the subject, and determine to what particular place they should remove. Some, and those not the least respectable, preferred Guiana, in South America, on account of the warmth of the climate, the fertility of the soil, and the ease with which they might be supported. To these arguments were objected, the unhealthiness of all hot countries, and the hostility of the Spaniards. The objection against Virginia was, that they should be exposed to the persecution of the English government, without the privilege of its protection ; finally, it was concluded to live in a distinct body by themselves, under the general government of Virginia, and " by their friends to sue his majesty for liberty and freedom of religion." This they were encouraged to hope they should obtain by the agency of some persons of rank and quality, who were their friends.

Two persons were then chosen and sent to England, to make application to the Virginia company, whom they found ready to grant them a patent with as ample privileges, as they had themselves, and to afford them all the assistance in their power. The principal persons of the company believed that the king would grant their request. as to freedom of religion. This was found impossible. Though the leading members of the Virginia company, with their friends, and one of the chief secretaries of state, urged the king, and others made application to the archbishop, all was vain. The king intimated that he would not disturb them in their religion, while they conducted peaceably. This hope of his connivance was all they could obtain. The Virginia company, presuming that they would not be troubled, urged them to proceed. The agents returned to Holland; some were discouraged, but they finally concluded to proceed, " resting on God's providence, as they had done in other things."

Upon this resolution, Messrs. ROBERT CUSHMAN and JOHN CARVER were sent to conclude the business with the Virginia company, to obtain as good a patent as they could, and agree with such merchants and friends, as were disposed to encourage the voyage. Written instructions were given them, beyond which they were not to proceed without further advice. New difficulties occurring, these agents returned to Holland to confer with their brethren.

After a long and troublesome negociation, which began in 1617, the patent was obtained in 1619; yet God so ordered their affairs, that this patent, which had cost them so much expense, labor, and anxiety, was never of the least advantage to them, as they did not settle in a part of the country within the Virginia patent. So precarious are the most sanguine hopes of man.

Having received the patent and proposals from the merchants and friends on whom they depended for assistance, they began to " prepare themselves with all speed." A ship of sixty tons was hired in Holland, and another of one hundred and eighty in England. All things being in readiness for their departure from Leyden, they kept a day of solemn humiliation and prayer. Their pastor preached from Ezra viii. 21. " Then I proclaimed a fast at the river

Ahava, that we might afflict ourselves before our God, to seek of him a right way for us and for our little ones, and for all our substance."

The time of their departure being come, they were accompanied by most of their brethren several miles to Delft Haven, where the ship waited to receive them. They now left the pleasant city of Leyden, which had been their hiding place for twelve years. They found the ship and all things ready. Friends from Leyden, who could not embark with them, followed and arrived before their departure; friends from Amsterdam came to take their leave of them. The night was spent with little sleep, but " with friendly entertainment, and christian discourse, and real expressions of purest love."

The next day the wind was fair; they went on board, their friends with them. Distressing was the sight of that sad and mournful parting. The sighs and sobs and prayers, which burst from every lip, were sufficient to melt the coldest heart; tears gushed from every eye; the kindest speeches were stifled by unutterable tenderness of soul. The Dutch strangers, who were present, could not refrain from weeping. Unfeigned love glowed in every heart; but the tide, which waits for no man, called them away; the moment was overwhelming. Their pastor fell on his knees, and they all with him, with cheeks bedewed with tears, commended themselves with most fervent prayer to God; then with mutual embraces and many tears, they parted. To many this was a final parting on earth. A prosperous gale soon bore them to the English shore. At Southampton they found the larger ship, and the rest of their company ready to sail for America.

After their parting, Mr. Robinson wrote a letter to Mr. John Carver,* and another to the company, both full of

* This interesting letter is preserved in Hazard's Hist. Col. vol. i. p. 96

affection, and of confidence in their wisdom and goodness, and of wise and most salutary advice.

Mr. Robinson's letter to the company was read before they left Southampton, and very gratefully received; afterward it produced the most happy effects. A governor and two or three assistants being chosen for each ship, they sailed from the old for the new world, Aug. 5, 1620. New calamities befel them; one of their vessels sprung a leak, and they were obliged to return, and make repairs; again they sailed, and again were they beaten back, and obliged to leave their small vessel. Being all crowded into one ship, they put to sea again, Sept. 6; but a dreadful storm opposed their passage, and they seriously contemplated relinquishing the voyage, and returning home.

These repeated disasters gave them full opportunity deliberately to " count the cost" of their designs, to estimate and feel their dangers and distresses, to compare them with the value of those religious privileges, which were the object of all these daring enterprises, of all these overwhelming sufferings. Never did martyrs, dying for their religion and their Saviour, have a more favorable time for cool reflection, to form a deliberate judgment, and to examine the rock on which they built their best hopes.

In their native country their sufferings had been great and of long duration, giving them full time to reflect and recant, had they felt that to be their duty. In Holland for twelve or thirteen years, they had endured trials and labors, which had exhausted their strength, and produced a premature old age. Still, however, they persevered, pursuing their design with unappalled resolution. Every effort to gain the American coast, was a new demonstration of the reality, the infinite value, and the invincible energy of the *Christian Religion*, when it reigns in the hearts of good men. Was there ever an object presented to mankind, which could more powerfully persuade them to believe the gospel, than this company of *holy puritans*, crossing the stormy ocean in search of a place to worship God in peace and purity of conscience? Must not that religion be from heaven, which could sooth, support, comfort, and animate people in circumstances so painful and hazardous? Nor were these daring efforts prompted by the passion of the moment; they had been repeated and continued for eighteen years. They were not like meteors, which blaze, dazzle, and expire; but the sun, shining in his strength to enlighten the world.

After being tossed more than two months on the boisterous deep, they descried, Nov. 9th, the bleak and barren shores of Cape Cod. Two days after, they anchored in Cape Cod harbor. But this bleak and barren region was not the place which they had in view for their settlement.

Their intention was to have settled at the mouth of Hudson's river; but the Dutch, intending to plant there a colony of their own, privately hired the master of the ship to contrive delays in England, and then to conduct them to these northern coasts, and there, under the pretence of shoals and winter, to discourage them from venturing to the place of destination. Although Cape Cod harbor, in which they first anchored, was good, the surrounding country was sandy and barren. These were discouraging circumstances; but the season being far advanced, they prudently determined to make the best of their present situation. As they were not within the limits of the patent, and consequently not under the jurisdiction of the Virginia company, and having some factious persons among them, in the capacity of servants, who, possessing a portion of the modern spirit of *liberty and equality*, had intimated, that when on shore, they should be under no government, and that one man would then be as good as another, the more judicious thought it necessary to establish a separate government for themselves.

Accordingly, before they landed, having devoutly given thanks to God for their safe arrival, they formed themselves into a body politic, under the following *covenant* or *contract*, which they all subscribed, and made the basis of their government. "In the name of God, amen. We whose names are under written, the loyal subjects of our dread sovereign lord, king James, by the grace of God, of Great Britain, France and Ireland, king, defender of the faith, &c. Having undertaken for the glory of God, and the advancement of the christian faith, and honor of our king and country, a voyage, to plant the first colony in the northern part of Virginia; do by these presents, solemnly and mutually, in the presence of God, and of one another, covenant and combine ourselves together into a civil body politic, for our better ordering and preservation and furtherance of the ends aforesaid; and by virtue hereof to enact, constitute and frame such just and equal laws, ordinances, acts, constitutions, and offices, from time to time, as shall be thought most meet and convenient for the general good of the colony; unto which we promise all due submission and obedience: In witness whereof, we have here under subscribed our names at Cape Cod, the 11th of November; in the year of the reign of our sovereign lord, king James of England, France and Ireland, the eighteenth, and of Scotland, the fifty-fourth: Anno Domini, 1620."

This instrument was signed by twenty-four heads of families, with the number in their respective families annexed, and seventeen single men, making in the whole one hundred and one souls.

Afterwards by a unanimous vote, they chose JOHN CARVER their governor for one year.

Having thus established and organized their government, in its form truly republican, their next object was to fix on a convenient place for settlement. In doing this, they were obliged to encounter numerous difficulties, and to suffer incredible hardships. Many of them were sick in consequence of the fatigues of a long voyage. Their provisions were bad, the season uncommonly cold, and they unacquainted with the coast.

Immediately after their landing, they fell on their knees, " with hearty praises to God, who had been their *assurance*, when far off on the sea." They were truly in a new world. Whales sported in the water; oaks, pines, sassafras, juniper, and other sweet wood, shaded their harbor, and plenty of fowl flew around them. Few particulars of their voyage have been preserved. " The people were close stowed, continually wet, the vessel leaky, one person died, and one child was born, named *Oceanus*."

CHAP. III.

Character of the first settlers. Discovery of New-England. Its boundaries, extent, and settlement. Destructive wars and pestilence among the natives. Nature of the Indian title to their lands.

Before we proceed in the details of our history, some further preliminary remarks and information seem necessary.

If any country deserves the notice of history, *New-England* is that country. Other nations, in reverting to their origin, have been constrained to look for it in deep obscurity, in mere traditionary legends, without the aid of written records; or "to trace a lawless ancestry into the caverns of ravishers and robbers."* But the first settlers of New-England were men of influence, "illustrious by their intrepid valor, no less than by their Christian graces;" men eminently distinguished in the age in which they lived, for their learning, their wisdom, and their piety. "Theirs was the fortitude of patience, and the heroism of martyrdom." No country on earth, it is believed, was ever favored in its first settlement, with such a body of men as were the fathers of New-England. The records, which they have left us of our early history, are ample, complete and authentic. Nothing important is left to conjecture. They looked in long prospect before them, and laid deep and broad foundations for the improvement and happiness of their posterity.

The part of our country where our fathers first landed, and in which they settled, was discovered as early as 1597; but no attempt was made for a permanent settlement till more than a century afterwards. A long night of obscurity covered this part of the American coast. The people of England were living at ease in the land of their nativity; the church was not prepared to fly for rest into this "wilderness."

New England, now the northeastern grand division of the United States of America, lies in the form of a quarter of a circle around the great bay, or part of the Atlantic ocean, which sets up to the northwest between Cape Cod and Cape Sable. It contains the six states of Vermont, New-Hampshire, Maine, Massachusetts, Rhode-Island and Connecticut; and is situated between 41° and 48° N. lat. and 64° 54' and 73° 39' W. longitude from Lon-

* J. Q. Adams, Esq.

don. Its extreme length, from the northeast corner of Maine, to the southwest corner of Connecticut, is about 626 miles; its breadth is very unequal, from 50 to 200 miles. It contains about 72,000 square miles; and is bounded N. by Lower Canada, E. by the British province of New-Brunswick and the Atlantic ocean, S. by the same ocean and Long Island sound, and W. by the state of New-York. The soil, in this portion of our country, is not the most fertile, the climate is forbidding, yet the wealth of its inhabitants is greater, and the population more numerous, than in any other portion of the United States. There is much truth in the remark of a European writer; " Were not the cold climate of New-England supplied with *good laws* and *discipline*, the barrenness of that country would never have brought people to it, nor have advanced it in consideration and formidableness above the other English plantations, exceeding it much in fertility and other inviting qualities."

In 1605, Capt. Weymouth, in search of a passage to India, discovered the Penobscot, or the Kennebec, river, and carried thence five of the natives to England. Three of these, viz. *Manida, Sketwarroes,* and *Tasquantum,* were placed in the family of Ferdinando Gorges. They were docile and intelligent. Their account of the country gave a new impulse to the spirit of enterprise. Sir John Popham, lord chief justice of King's Bench, with other noblemen and knights, styled the Plymouth Company, obtained a patent of North Virginia, of which the country afterwards called New-England was a part.

This company in 1606 sent out Henry Chalong and Captain Prynne in two ships, for further discoveries in the country, whence the Indians had been brought, two of whom were on board with Chalong; but he was taken by the Spaniards, and carried to Spain. Prynne surveyed the coast, its rivers and harbors, and carried home such an account, that a colony of one hundred adventurers sailed from Plymouth in two ships, May, 31, 1607. After falling in with the island of Monhigan, they landed at the mouth of the Kennebec, then called the Sagadahoc, Aug. 11. The spot selected for a residence was on Parker's island, where they raised a fortification, and called it Fort St. George. They brought two natives with them, who procured them a cordial welcome from different tribes. The emperor Bashaba at Penobscot, to whom the sachems west, as far as Naumkeag, acknowledged subjection, sent his son to visit the president of the English colony, and to open a trade for furs. In December the ships sailed for England, leaving forty-five persons; but their hard fare, the severity of a Kennebec winter, the burning of their store, and the death of their president Popham, so discouraged them, that with the next vessel they all returned to England. So commenced and ended the first colony on this coast within a year.

The Norridgewog tribe have this tradition, that this company engaged a number of Indians, who had come to trade with them, to draw a cannon by a long rope, that the moment they were arranged in a straight line, the white people discharged the piece, which killed and wounded a number. Such was the indignation of the natives in consequence of this barbarous treachery, that they compelled the company to embark to save their own lives.

From this time, till 1620, no settlement was made on these shores. Sir John Popham and some others, however, carried on the fisheries, which produced considerable profit.

In April, 1614, Capt. John Smith, with two ships, commenced a voyage of discovery to the northern coasts of America. He first made the island of Monhigan, then computed to be in lat. 43° 30', where he built seven boats, in one of which, with eight men, he ranged the coast from Penobscot to Cape Cod, entered and surveyed Massachusetts Bay, and made his observations on other parts of the coast. He discovered the Isles of Shoals, and called them Smith's Isles. The whole country he found peopled by various tribes of Indians. After his return to England, he wrought these surveys and observations into a map, which he presented to Charles, prince of Wales, (afterwards king Charles I.) who gave his own name to the river, which divides Boston from Charlestown, and to the whole country that of NEW-ENGLAND.

When he sailed for England, he left Captain Hunt behind to complete his cargo of fish for a Spanish market. Hunt, destitute of justice and humanity, decoyed twenty-four Indians on board, carried them to Spain, and sold them for slaves. This outrage on the laws of hospitality was long resented by the inhabitants of the country.

About this period the emperor of Penobscot, with his family, was destroyed by the Tarrateens, a tribe east of the Penobscot, upon which a contest for the sovereignty rose among the sachems, and a bloody civil war raged through the empire. Immediately a terrible pestilence followed. By these two calamities, nineteen twentieths of the natives on the shores of Massachusetts, it was estimated, were destroyed. This disease was probably the yellow fever, the bodies of the people being " exceeding yellow, both before and after they died."* Another circumstance is mentioned, which coincides with this opinion ; foreigners were not susceptible of the contagion. Richard Vines and crew, on a voyage of discovery, travelled into the country, and lodged in their wigwams, but were not affected, though the natives were dying in such numbers, that the living could not bury

* Gookin.

them. It is known, that *sometimes* strangers do not take the yellow fever, where it is most malignant. Had it been the small pox, as some have supposed, these Europeans would certainly have taken it, or have recognized the visible marks of the disease. On the spot where is now the town of Plymouth, though before very populous, "every human being died of the pestilence."* Uncultivated fields, numerous graves, and human bones unburied, confirmed this account.

An extraordinary occurrence, relative to this pestilence, has been mentioned. " A French ship had been wrecked on Cape Cod; the men were saved with their provisions and goods. The natives kept their eyes on them till they found an opportunity to kill all but three or four, and divide their goods. The captives were sent from one tribe to another as slaves. One of them learned so much of their language as to tell them, that " God was angry with them for their cruelty, and would destroy them, and give their country to another people," They answered "that they were too many for God to kill." He replied that " if they were ever so numerous, God had many ways to kill them, of which they were ignorant." Afterwards, when this extraordinary pestilence came among them, they remembered the man's words, and when the Plymouth settlers arrived at Cape Cod, the few survivors imagined, that the other part of his prediction would soon be accomplished."†

The events we have now mentioned, respecting the depopulation of this country, by wars and pestilence, considered in reference to the settlement of our fathers in the desolated places, are certainly very remarkable. The dangers to which they were exposed from these untutored tribes, were greatly lessened; and the lands which they occupied being depopulated and deserted, the rights of no man

* Belknap. † Ib.

were infringed. The Pilgrims of Plymouth obtained their right of possession to the territory on which they settled by titles as fair and unequivocal as those by which any human property can be held."* Happy, had this been the case in the subsequent progress of settlements in this country.

An important question has arisen, since the settlement of this country, in regard to the nature of the title of the Indians to the lands which they occupied, and still occupy. It is asked, whether a nation may lawfully take possession of a part of a vast country, in which there are found none but erratic nations, incapable, by reason of the smallness of their numbers, to people and cultivate the whole? The answer given by a writer of authority† is, that the possession of the Indians cannot be taken for a true and legal possession; the earth belongs to the human race in general, and was designed to furnish it with subsistence: but if each nation had resolved from the beginning, to appropriate to itself a vast country, that the people might live only by hunting, fishing, and wild fruits, our globe would not be sufficient to maintain a tenth part of its present inhabitants. People have not then deviated from the views of nature in confining the Indians within narrow limits. However, we cannot help praising the moderation of the English puritans who first settled in New-England; who, notwithstanding their being furnished with a charter from their sovereign, purchased of the Indians the land they resolved to cultivate. This laudable example was followed by William Penn, in the settlement of Pennsylvania.

Another law writer, of eminence in our country, states his opinion on this question as follows: "The European settlers of the country claimed to have a right to appropriate

* J. Q. Adams, Esq. Anniversary Oration at Plymouth, 1802.

† Vattel's Law of Nations.

it to themselves, and the mildest and least exceptionable form in which they exercised that right, was to treat the aboriginal inhabitants, as entitled to a limited or qualified, property,—a right to occupy and enjoy, under certain modifications, but with no power to convey, nor indeed to do any other acts of ownership. The right of soil, or the absolute property, and the jurisdiction over it, were in the meantime deemed to belong to the Sovereign or State, under whose authority the discovery and settlement were made, and to the grantees of such sovereign or state."*

So large a tract of country inhabited by Indian tribes is now embraced within the limits of the United States, that the question concerning the nature of the Indian title has become extremely important, and should be deliberately settled on sound and equitable principles.

CHAP. IV.

Excursions for discovery ; a child born ; another voyage for discovery ; attacked by Indians ; discover the place which they afterwards named Plymouth ; two men left ; Capt. Standish elected commander in chief; dreadful winter ; mortality ; an Indian visits them ; treaty with Massasoit.

THE day they landed, they sent an armed party to make discoveries, who returned at night, having found nothing but water, wood, and sand hills. The next day was the sabbath, and they all rested. Monday the men went on

* Hon. John Sergeant, Esq.

shore to refresh themselves, the women to wash, attended by a guard, and the carpenter began to repair the shallop for coasting.

Wednesday, Capt. Miles Standish took a party of sixteen men, well armed, and went to make further discoveries. About a mile from the sea they saw five Indians, who fled. They pursued them about ten miles, but night coming on, they placed sentinels, kindled a fire, and rested quietly. In the morning they continued the pursuit to Pamet river, without discovering inhabitants or habitations; they returned to a pond of fresh water in Truro, and lodged there that night.

In the course of the day, in one place, they found several heaps of sand, one of which was covered with old mats, and an earthen pot at one end; on digging, they found a bow and arrows; presuming it was a grave, they replaced every thing. In another place they found an old iron kettle, and near it another pile of sand, in which was buried three or four bushels of Indian corn. They hesitated, but finally took the kettle and a part of the corn, resolving, if ever they found the owners, to return the kettle, and pay them for the corn. They afterwards discovered the owners, and liberally paid them. The corn was in a basket handsomely made. Afterward they found a place fortified with palisadoes. They were also amused with a trap to catch deer, in which one of them was caught without harm. The next day they returned, and were joyfully received by their companions.

The corn, which they found, was the first fruit of the land to them, and incalculably important. Snow covering the ground immediately after, it was impossible to find any more, and without seed they could have had no harvest the next year. As soon as the shallop was ready, a party was sent in her to examine the shore; but they found no suitable place for settlement. They brought away the rest of the corn which they had before discovered, and found some graves, and two wigwams, but saw no Indians.

About this time Mr. White had a son born, who was named *Peregrine*. He was the first English child born in New-England. He died July, 1704. aged 84.

Wednesday, December 6th, they set out upon a fourth expedition for discovery. The ground had been several days covered with snow, and the weather was extremely cold; the water freezing on their clothes, made them stiff as coats of mail; two persons were already sick. The first day they saw ten or twelve Indians, who fled; a number made a fire and slept in the woods the first night, whence they saw the smoke of the fires kindled by the Indians. The next day, after passing some corn fields, they discovered a curious burying yard, encompassed with palisadoes, driven close together, while some of the individual graves within were fenced in the same manner; at night they returned to the shallop. About midnight they were alarmed by the sentinel, and fired two guns, but saw no enemy. At five in the morning, after they had prayed together, there was again a cry of *Indians! Indians!* when a shower of arrows was poured upon them, attended with savage yells, terrible to the English. But the report of guns was equally novel and terrific to the Indians, who soon fled. Their arrows, which were taken up, and sent to Europe as curiosities, were pointed with brass, and deer's horn, and eagle's claws. Thence, after coasting further in vain, they directed their course for a harbor, which their pilot had mentioned. After great dangers in a storm, they landed on Clark's island, and rested all night; the next day, being Saturday, they concluded to remain over the Sabbath, which they passed in a religious manner.*

* Morton

The 17th of December, they discovered the place where Plymouth now stands, of which they gave the following account, after examining the harbor and vicinity several days. The first day they marched into the land, " they found cornfields and little running brooks, a place very good for situation. Returning to the ship, the good news comforted their hearts. The bay is encompassed with good land, and in it are two fine islands, on which are nothing but woods, oaks, pines, walnut, beech, sassafras, vines, and other trees which we know not." " The bay is a most hopeful place, with innumerable fowls and fish." The 18th they continued to explore the country, well pleased.* " The 20th, of Dec. after landing and viewing the places again, as well as they could, they came to a conclusion, by most voices, to settle on the main land, on the high ground, which had been planted with corn three or four years before, where is a sweet brook, and many delicate springs of good water." This night twenty of their number remained on shore. A violent storm, which continued the two following days, detained them on shore, and prevented all intercourse with those on board the vessel.†

Saturday the 23d,‡ they began to cut timber, and provide materials for building. This business found them employment, when the weather would permit, till about the 19th of February. The single persons united with the families, which were in all nineteen. Each family built their own cottage ; but all engaged in building a storehouse, twenty feet square, for common use. From the time of their arrival on the coast, till the day of their permanent landing, the weather was unusually stormy and severe. The men who were employed in exploring the harbors to find the best place for settlement, were exposed to extreme hardships

* Winslow. † Prince. ‡ Winslow.

from watchings and fastings, wet and cold. Here we find one cause of the mortal sickness, which afterwards prevailed. During the month of December, six of their number died, and many others sickened of grievous colds, of which they never recovered.

On the Lord's day, December 31st, they attended public worship for the first time on shore, and named the place PLYMOUTH; partly because the harbor had been so named by Capt. Smith, and partly from gratitude for the kind treatment they had received at Plymouth, the last port in England which they had left. The *rock* on which they first stepped has been divided, and one part of it placed in the centre of the town, where it is known by the name of "Forefather's Rock," and is visited with a degree of reverence by strangers.

The anniversary of their landing has been celebrated on the 22d of December, by their immediate descendants at Plymouth, as a religious festival. A discourse is delivered adapted to the occasion; after public worship, more forcibly to impress their minds with the circumstances of their meritorious forefathers, clams, fish, ground nuts, and victims from the forest, constitute a part of their grateful repast. For a number of years the same anniversary was celebrated in Boston by the descendants of the Plymouth pilgrims, and others. Here too the festal board displayed the style of other times; treasures, which had been hidden in the sand, and game from the woods, mingled with other provisions of the table. It is a festival, rational and happy in its tendency. It reminds the guests of the virtues and sufferings of their fathers; by a comparison of circumstances, it excites transports of gratitude, elevates the affections, and mends the heart.

On the 12th of January, John Goodman and Peter Brown walking into the woods " to gather thatch, lost themselves."

After wandering all the afternoon, they were obliged, though "slenderly" clothed, to make the ground their bed; it snowed, and the cold was severe. Their distress in the night was increased by hearing, as they supposed, three *lions* roaring; one of which they thought was very near them. In their terror they resolved to climb a tree, though an intolerably cold lodging place. They stood ready to ascend when the lions should come, and continued walking round the tree all night, which probably saved their lives. In the afternoon, from a hill, they saw the islands in Plymouth harbor, and in the evening reached their friends, faint with hunger and cold. Goodman's feet were so frozen that they were obliged to cut off his shoes.

Many of the first settlers, it seems, imagined they heard the roaring of lions. Neither the wolf nor the lion was at this time generally known in England; hence it is not strange they should mistake the howlings of a wolf for the roaring of a lion. Wood says, " I will not say that I ever saw lions myself, but some affirm they have seen a lion at Cape Ann. Some, likewise, being lost in the woods, have heard such terrible roarings as have made them much aghast, which must be either lions or devils, there being no other creatures which used to *roar*."

In February, they arranged their military concerns. Miles Standish was chosen Captain, and received "authority to command in military affairs." The third of March they rejoiced to find that the winter was past, "the birds sang in the woods most pleasantly," it thundered, and there was a steady rain. For this climate, the winter, providentially, had been remarkably mild. Still it had been a dismal winter to them. Never did human beings suffer more, nor display greater fortitude and christian magnanimity.

The whole company that landed consisted of but *one hundred and one* souls; their situation was distressing, and their prospects discouraging. Their nearest neighbors, except the natives, were the Dutch at Albany and Bergen, a French settlement at Port Royal, and the English in Virginia; the nearest of these was two hundred miles from them, and utterly incapable of affording them any relief in time of famine or danger. Wherever they turned their eyes, distress was before them. Persecuted for their religion in their native land; grieved for the profanation of the holy sabbath, and other licentiousness in Holland; fatigued by their long and boisterous voyage; disappointed through the treachery of their commander, of their expected country; forced on a dangerous and inhospitable shore in the advance of a cold winter; surrounded with hostile barbarians, without any hope of human succour in case of an attack; denied the aid or favor of the court of England; without a patent, without a public promise of a peaceable enjoyment of their religious liberties, worn out with toil and sufferings, and without convenient shelter from the rigor of the weather:—Such was the situation, and such the prospects of these pious, solitary christians. To increase their distresses, a general and very mortal sickness prevailed among them, which swept off *forty-six* of their number before the opening of the next spring. Some part of the time two and three died in a day. At times there were not five who had health to nurse the sick.

To support them under these trials, they had need of all the aid and comforts, which christianity affords; and these were sufficient. The free and unmolested enjoyment of their religion reconciled them to their humble and lonely situation. They bore their hardships with uncommon patience, and persevered in their pilgrimage of almost unparalleled trials, with such resignation and calmness, as gave proof of great piety, and unconquerable virtue.

No sooner had this little colony completed their landing at Plymouth, than they began to lay out the town into streets, and lots, and to erect buildings for their accommodation. They first built a storehouse with a thatched roof, in which they deposited, under a guard, their whole stock of ammunition and provisions. On the 14th of January, the thatched roof of the storehouse accidentally caught fire, and was consumed; but by the timely exertions of the people, the lower part of the building with its contents, which were indispensable to their support, was preserved.

On the 3d of November, 1620, King James, being informed that an extensive country in America had lately been depopulated by sickness, and that no part of it was then inhabited by the subjects of any christian prince, and being desirous to advance the christian religion, and extend the boundaries of his own dominions, signed a patent, incorporating the duke of Lenox, the marquisses of Buckingham and Hamilton, the earls of Arundel and Warwick, Sir Francis Gorges, with thirty-four others and their successors, styling them, " The council established at Plymouth, in the county of Devon, for the planting, ruling, ordering, and governing, of New England in America."*

To this council he granted all that part of America, which lies between the 40th and 48th degrees of north latitude. They were invested with powers of jurisdiction over the country, and authorized to exclude all others from trading within their boundaries, and from fishing in the neighboring seas. This charter was the great *civil basis* of all the subsequent grants and patents to the settlers of New-England.

" This charter, from the omission of several powers necessary to the future situation of the colony, shows how inad-

---

* This patent, which was early surrendered, was published for the first time in Hazard's Hist. Coll.

equate the ideas of the parties were to the important consequences, which were about to follow from such an act. The governor, with the assistants and freemen of the company, it is true, were empowered to make all laws, not repugnant to those of England: but the power of imposing fines, imprisonment, or other lawful correction, is expressly given in the manner of other corporations of the realm; and the general circumstances of the settlement, and the practice of the times, can leave us no doubt that this body politic was viewed rather as a trading company, residing within the kingdom, than what it very soon became, a foreign government, exercising all the essentials of sovereignty over its subjects."*

In 1623, Dec. 30, the council of New-England " granted and confirmed unto Robert Gorges, his heirs and assigns forever, all that part of the main land in New-England, commonly called or known by the name of Messahuset, lying on the N. E. of the bay called Massachusetts together with all the coasts and shores along the sea for ten English miles, in a straight line towards the N. E. and 30 English miles into the main land through all the breadth aforesaid, with all the islands within three miles of the main, excepting such as have been granted to others."†

On the 16th of March, 1621, the inhabitants at Plymouth were alarmed at seeing a sturdy Indian walk into their settlement, and, passing by the houses, go directly where the people were collected. He saluted them in broken English, and bid them welcome. He was affable, told them his dwelling was five days travel thence, that he was a sagamore or prince. He understood the geography of the country, gave an account of the different tribes, their sagamores and number of men. He had been acquainted with

* Minot.   † Hazard.

the English, who had taken fish at Monhigan, and knew the names of their captains. He was naked, excepting a leather belt about his waist, with a fringe a span wide. He had a bow and two arrows, was tall and straight, his hair long behind, and short before. They kindly entertained him and gave him a horseman's coat. He tarried all night, and informed them that the place where they were, was Patuxet, and that about four years before, all the inhabitants had died; that not a man, woman or child survived. On his departure, he received a knife, a bracelet and ring, and promised in a few days to pay them another visit. He came according to promise, and brought five others with him. They sang and danced, and were very friendly and familiar.

The 22d of March, their first visitant, *Samoset*, came again and brought Squanto, or Tisquantum, who had been carried away by Capt. Hunt and sold in Spain, whence he went to London, and thence came to America. By this event he escaped the universal mortality of his tribe at Patuxet. Three others accompanied them, and gave information that Massasoit was near. He soon appeared on the top of a hill with 60 men. Mr. Edward Winslow was sent to treat with him, carrying to the king two knives and a copper chain, with a jewel in it; to Quadepina, his brother, a knife, a jewel for his ear, " a pot of strong water," some biscuit and butter. After presenting them these trinkets, and saluting them with love and peace, they were desired to visit the governor. The king, with twenty attendants, proceeded to the governor, leaving their bows and arrows, Mr. Winslow remaining with the rest as a hostage; the English keeping six or seven of them. Capt Standish and Mr. Williamson, with half a dozen soldiers, met the king at the brook, and conducted him and his train to the governor, who met them at a house appointed, with drum and trumpet sounding, and other military parade. A green rug, and three or four cushions, were spread for the company. The governor kissed the king's hand, and the king his, and both sat down. "Strong water" was then given to the king, "who drank a great draught, that made him sweat all the while after." Victuals was then set before them. After which they entered into a formal and very friendly treaty, in which they agreed to avoid injuries on both sides, to punish offenders, to restore stolen goods, to assist each other in all justifiable wars, to promote peace among their neighbors, &c. Massasoit, and his successors for fifty years, inviolably observed this treaty. The English are much indebted to this powerful chieftain for his friendship, and his memory will ever be respected in New-England. Massasoit returned, but Squanto continued at Plymouth, and was extremely useful as their interpreter and pilot to different parts of the coast. He taught them how to cultivate Indian corn, and where to take fish.

The Narragansets, disliking the conduct of Massasoit, declared war against him, which occasioned much confusion and fighting among the Indians. The Plymouth colony interposed in favor of Massasoit, their good ally, and terminated the dispute to the terror of their enemies. Even Canonicus himself, the terrific sachem of the Narragansets, sued for peace.

In April of this year, Governor Carver, while engaged in labor with the rest of the settlers, was seized with a pain in his head, which shortly after deprived him of his senses, and, in a few days, of his life, to the great grief of these afflicted people. He was buried with all the honors in their power to bestow.

Of this gentleman the following character is given by his biographer. "He was a man of great prudence, integrity, and firmness of mind. He had a good estate in England, which he left in the emigration to Holland and

America. He was one of the foremost in action, and bore a large share of sufferings in the service of the colony, who confided in him as their friend and father. Piety, humility, and benevolence were eminent traits in his character; and it is particularly remarked, that in the time of general sickness, which befel the colony, and with which he was affected, after he had himself recovered, he was assiduous in attending the sick, and performing the most humiliating services for them without any distinction of persons or characters."*

He was succeeded by William Bradford, then in the thirty-third year of his age, a man of "wisdom, piety, fortitude, and goodness of heart," and on these accounts much respected and beloved by the people. Isaac Allerton was chosen his assistant in the administration of government. One of the first official acts of Gov. Bradford was to send an embassy to Massasoit. His objects were to explore the country, to carry presents, and confirm the league with that chief; to survey his situation and strength, to establish a friendly intercourse, and to procure seed corn for the next season.

Edward Winslow and Stephen Hopkins, with Squanto for their guide, composed this embassy. This sachem lived about 40 miles southwest of Plymouth, (now Warren) in Rhode-Island. As they passed through the country, they observed the marks of the ravages, which the pestilence had made a few years before. They were received with friendship, and accomplished the business of their mission to the satisfaction of the governor.

The prudent and upright conduct of the Plymouth colony toward the Indians secured their friendship and alliance. Through the influence of Massasoit, nine of the petty

* Belknap.

sachems in his neighbourhood, who were jealous of the new colonists, and disposed to give them trouble, came to Plymouth, and voluntarily subscribed an instrument of submission to the king of England. Hobbamac, another of these subordinate chiefs, came and took up his residence at Plymouth, where he continued a faithful guide and interpreter till his death. The Indians of the island of Capawock, which had now obtained the name of Martha's or Martin's Vineyard, also sent messengers of peace. These transactions are so many proofs of the peaceful and benevolent disposition of the Plymouth settlers. Their successive continuing peace, also, shows what probably might have been done, had their descendants maintained the same peaceful temper. All the subsequent wars might have been avoided.

In September, 1621, governor Bradford sent ten men, with Squanto, in a shallop, to explore the bay, now called Massachusetts. They found that the islands in this bay had been cleared of wood, that they had been planted, but were now almost without inhabitants. The few who remained received them very hospitably, expressing great fears of the Tarateens, a people at the eastward, who often came and robbed them of their corn, and killed some of their people. The superior fertility of the islands in the bay, made them wish they had settled there. Having very happily recovered their health, they began to repair their cottages before winter. In October, they gathered in their harvest. Their English grain was poor, but their corn was very good, and they had plenty of fish and fowl, and were very happy.

CHAP. V.

Increase of their number; sufferings; a massacre of Virginians; duel; Squanto dies; lands purchased; visit to Massasoit; who is sick; patent obtained; first cattle in New-England; death and character of Mr. Robinson.

In November, a ship with thirty-five passengers arrived from England. Unfortunately for the little colony, the ship was short of provision, and the colonists, out of their scanty pittance, were obliged to victual her home. In consequence, before the next spring they were reduced to great straits, and obliged for some time to subsist on fish and spring water, being for two or three months destitute of bread. To heighten their distresses, the Narraganset chief, Canonicus, threatened the peace of the colony by a message sent in "the emblematical style of the ancient Scythians, viz. a bundle of arrows bound with the skin of a serpent." The governor returned the skin filled with powder and ball, which had the desired effect. Afraid of its contents, the chief returned it unopened, and remained quiet.

About this time a part of the colony of Virginia was surprised, and massacred by the Indians. From this circumstance, and the hostile disposition of the Narragansets, the colonists, feeble as they were from famine, found it expedient to fortify their town. Accordingly, they surrounded it with a stockade and four flankers, divided their company into four squadrons, and alternately kept guard day and night. Their guns were mounted on a kind of citadel erected on the top of the town hill, with a flat roof; the lower story of which served them for a place of worship.

The practice of *duelling*, which has never prevailed in New-England, was introduced by two servants, who quarreled, and fought with *sword* and *dagger*. Both were wounded, neither of them mortally. For this disgraceful conduct they were formally tried before the whole company, and sentenced to have "their heads and feet tied together, and so to remain twenty-four hours, without meat or drink." In consequence of their penitence, a part of their punishment was remitted.

The summer of 1622 being dry, and the harvest scanty, the colonists were obliged to seek a supply from the Indians. Governor Bradford, with the faithful Squanto for his guide and interpreter, made an excursion for this purpose; during which, Squanto fell sick and died. On his death bed he requested the governor to pray for him, that he might "go to the Englishman's God in heaven." This Indian deserves to have his name recorded with honor in the history of New-England. Forgetting the perfidy of those, who, by base artifice, had made him a prisoner, and a slave, he became a hearty friend of the English, and so continued till his death, rendering them in various ways most essential services. Though faithful to the English, he had his share of art, cunning, and dishonesty. He would often send word privately to the Indians that the English were coming to kill them, but asssuring them at the same time, that he had influence to persuade them to peace. By these means he not only obtained large presents, but raised himself to such importance in view of his countrymen, that they sought to him as a protector, and he became more respected than their sachems. He also, to give consequence to the English and himself, informed the natives that the English kept the plague buried in a cellar, which was their magazine of powder, which they could send forth to the destruction of any people, while they remained at home themselves. Governor Bradford was treated with great respect by the several tribes which he visited, and the trade was conducted on both sides with justice and confidence. He purchased in the whole twenty-eight hogsheads of corn, for which he paid in goods received from England.*

In the spring of 1623, Massasoit fell sick, and sent intelligence of it to the governor, who immediately sent Mr. Winslow, and Mr. *John Hamden*, (the same man who afterwards distinguished himself by his opposition to the arbitrary and unjust demands of Charles I.) to pay him a visit. They carried with them presents, and some cordials for his relief. Their visit and presents were very consolatory to the venerable chief, and their medicines were the means of his recovery.

In return for their kindness, he informed them of a dangerous conspiracy among the neighbouring Indians, the object of which was, the total extirpation of the English. By means of this timely discovery, and the consequent spirited exertions of the governor, whose wise plans were executed by the brave Capt. Standish, the colony was once more saved from destruction. Afterwards, in 1639, at the termination of the Pequod war, Massasoit, who then changed his name to Woosamequen, brought his son to Mooanam to Plymouth, and desired that the league, which he had formerly made might be renewed, and made inviolable. The sachem and his son voluntarily promised, "for themselves and their successors, that they would not needlessly, nor unjustly raise any quarrels, nor do any wrong to other natives to provoke them to a war against the colony; and that they would not give, sell or convey any of their lands, territories, or possessions to any person, without the privity or consent of the government of Plymouth, other than to such as the said government should send or appoint. The whole court did then ratify and confirm the aforesaid league, and promise to

* Belknap.

the said Woosamequen, (or Massasoit) his son and successors, that they would defend them against all such as should unjustly rise up against them, to wrong or oppress them."*

The "contract" entered into by the colonists at Cape Cod, on their arrival, was intended only as a temporary substitute for legal authority from their sovereign. Accordingly, as soon as they were informed of the establishment of the "council at Plymouth, for planting New-England," before mentioned, they applied for and obtained a patent. It was taken out in the name of John Pierce, in trust for the colony. "When he saw that they were well seated, and that there was a prospect of success to their undertaking, he went, without their knowledge, but in their name, and solicited the council for another patent of greater extent; intending to keep it to himself, and allow them no more than he pleased, holding them as his tenants, to sue and be sued at his courts. In pursuance of this design, having obtained a patent, he bought a ship, which he named the Paragon; loaded her with goods, took on board upwards of sixty passengers, and sailed from London for the colony of New Plymouth. In the Downs he was overtaken by a tempest, which so damaged the ship that he was obliged to put her into dock. Here she lay several weeks, and her repairs cost him one hundred pounds. In December, 1622, he sailed a second time, having on board one hundred and nine persons; but a series of tempestuous weather, which continued fourteen days, disabled his ship, and forced him back to Portsmouth. These repeated disappointments were so discouraging, that he was easily prevailed upon by the adventurers to assign his patent to them for five hundred pounds. The passengers came over in other ships."

* Morton.

This spring, (1623,) there was an alarming drought. For six weeks after planting, there was scarcely a drop of rain. The corn changed its color, and was just withering to die. Instead of labouring in common, which they had before practised, each now laboured by himself on his own plot. By this they hoped to compel the idle to diligence, and to excite all to greater exertions. But the drought threatened to blast all. In this crisis of trouble, the wreck of a vessel was driven on the coast, which they supposed was the one which had sailed several months before to bring them relief. A deep concern was fixed on every countenance. Individuals examined their hearts before God. The magistrates appointed a day of fasting and prayer. In the morning the heavens were clear; the earth powder and dust. The religious exercises continued eight or nine hours. Before they separated, the sun was obscured, the clouds gathered, and the next morning began soft and gentle showers, which continued, with some intervals of delightful weather, for fourteen days. The corn revived and grew luxuriantly, and the hearts of the people were filled with hope and praise. The Indians in town inquired the cause of the public solemnity, and were deeply impressed with the consequences; saying that their "conjurations" for rain were followed with storms and tempests, which often did more harm than good.

In July and August arrived two ships with supplies, and a number of new settlers. In September, one of the ships returned, in which Mr. Winslow went passenger, as an agent for the colony. The other went south, on a voyage of discovery.

In the year 1624, the charter of the Plymouth council was attacked by the British parliament, and some strong resolutions were passed in the house of commons, which so far deprived the council of their resources, that, it seems, they no longer thought it practicable to settle a plantation, though they appointed a governor general for New-England. In consequence, the patentees prudently concluded to divide the country among themselves. Accordingly, in the presence of king James, they drew lots for the shares that each one was to possess, as his exclusive property; the royal confirmation was to be obtained to each particular portion. This was not, however, immediately given, and they continued a few years longer to act as a body politic, and to make grants of different portions of the country to various societies.

In March, 1624, Mr. Winslow, who had been sent to England for the purpose, arrived with a supply of clothing, and brought with him a *bull*, and *three heifers*, which were the first neat cattle imported into New-England. None of the domestic animals were found in America.

At the close of this year, the Plymouth colony consisted of one hundred and eighty persons, who lived in thirty-two dwelling houses. Their stock consisted of the cattle brought over by Mr. Winslow, a few goats and a plenty of swine and poultry. Their town, half a mile in compass, was impaled. On an elevated mount in the town, they had erected a fort, and a handsome watch tower.

The year following, March, 1625, that venerable and good man, the Rev. John Robinson, whose memory is precious in New-England, died at Leyden, in the 50th year of his age, greatly lamented, both in Holland, and by that part of his congregation, who had settled at Plymouth. In a few years after, part of his people, who had remained with him in Holland, removed, and joined their brethren at Plymouth.

Among these were his widow and children. His son Isaac lived to the age of ninety, and left male posterity in the county of Barnstable. Mr. Robinson, though never in the country, deserves to be numbered among the founders of New-England. He possessed a strong mind, cultivated with a good education. His doctrines were Calvinism; he admitted the articles of the church of England, and the confession of faith, professed by the French reformed churches. He held that every church of Christ is to consist only of such as appear to believe in, and to obey him; that infants are to receive baptism only when, at least, one of the parents is a member of the church, which is also declared in the French confession of faith.* As a disputant, he was celebrated. At the time of his living in Leyden the dispute was warm between the Calvinists and Arminians. Polyander, a professor of divinity in the university, with the ministers of the city, invited Mr. Robinson to hold a public disputation with Episcopius, the Arminian professor of divinity in the university. At first Mr. Robinson modestly declined the discussion; but, being importuned, he thought it his duty, and "in view of a numerous assembly, he defended the truth, foiled his learned opposer, and put him to an apparent nonplus." Evidences of his goodness meet us in every incident of his life. Several months before the removal of his people to New-England, to confirm the wavering, and remove the scruples of those who doubted, he set apart a day for solemn prayer, and preached from 1 Sam. xxiii. 3, 4. "And David's men said unto him, behold, we be afraid here in Judah, how much more then if we come to Keilah against the armies of the Philistines? Then David inquired of the Lord yet again. And the Lord answered him, and said, arise, go down to Keilah; for I will deliver the Philistines into thine hand."

In July following, another day of prayer was observed, when he preached from Ezra viii. 21. In this sermon are the following passages worthy of notice. "Brethren," said he, "we are now quickly to part from one another, and whether I may live to see your face on earth any more, the

* Hazard, Belknap.

God of heaven only knows; but whether the Lord hath appointed that or not, I charge you before God and his blessed angels, that you follow me no further, than you have seen me follow the Lord Jesus Christ. If God reveal any thing to you by any other instruments of his, be as ready to receive it, as ever you were to receive any truth by my ministry; for I am verily persuaded, I am very confident, that the Lord has yet more truth to break forth from his holy word. For my part, I cannot sufficiently bewail the condition of the reformed churches, who are come to a period in religion, and will at present go no further than the instruments of their reformation. The Lutherans cannot be drawn to go beyond what Luther saw. Whatever part of his will our good God has revealed to Calvin, they will rather die than embrace. And the Calvinists, you see, *stick fast* where they were left by that great man of God, who yet saw not all things. This is a misery much to be lamented, for though they were burning and shining lights in their times, yet they penetrated not into the whole counsel of God; were they now living, they would be as willing to embrace further light, as that which they first received. I beseech you, remember it is an article of your church covenant, "That you be ready to receive whatever truth shall be made known to you from the written word of God."

Such was the mutual love and respect between this worthy man and his flock, that it was hard to judge whether he delighted more in having such a people, or they in having such a pastor. Beside his singular abilities in divine things, he was discreet in civil affairs, and assisted his people in their temporal as well as spiritual concerns. None were so odious to him as the selfish, "those who were close and cleaving to themselves, and retired from the common good." Those who were stiff and rigid in small affairs; those, who inveighed against the faults of others, but were careless of their own conduct, were odious in his view. His people esteemed and revered him while living, but more after his death; when they felt the want of his counsel and assistance. Not only his own flock, but the people of Leyden held him in high esteem. They gave him the use of one of their churches, in the chancel of which he was buried. The whole city and university regarded him as a great and good man: his death they sincerely lamented, and honored his funeral with their presence.

CHAP. VI.

A larger patent obtained; difficulties between the company in England and the planters; persecution of the Puritans; sports on the Lord's day established; Cromwell and others contemplate a removal to America; Massachusetts purchased; settled; charter obtained; its contents; first church formed at Salem; addition of 1500 to the colony; Indian conspiracy; scarcity; mortality; a number discouraged, return to England.

In 1629, when the plantation consisted of about 300 souls, a patent of a larger extent, than the one which Pierce had obtained and relinquished, was solicited by Isaac Allerton, and taken out in the name of "William Bradford, his heirs, associates, and assigns."* This patent confirmed their title, as far as the crown of England could confirm it, to a tract of land, bounded on the east and south by the Atlantic ocean, and by lines drawn west from the rivulet of Connohasset, and north from the river of Narraganset, which lines meet in a point, comprehending all the country

* Hazard.

then called Pokanokit. To this tract they supposed they had a prior title from the depopulation of a great part of it by a pestilence, from the gift of Massasoit, his voluntary subjection to the crown of England, and the protection they gave him. In a declaration published by them in 1636, they asserted their "lawful right in respect of vacancy, donation, and purchase of the natives,"* which, together with their patent from the crown, through the council of New-England, formed "the warrantable foundation of their government, of making laws, and disposing of lands." In the same patent was granted a large tract bordering on the river Kennebec, where they had carried on a traffic with the natives for furs, as they did also at Connecticut river, which was not equally beneficial, because the Dutch were their rivals.† The fur trade was found to be much more advantageous than the fishery.

The company in England, with which they were connected, did not supply them in plenty. Losses were sustained by sea; the returns did not answer their expectations; they were discouraged, threw many reflections on the planters, and finally refused them any further supplies;‡ but still demanded the debt, and would not permit them to connect themselves in trade with any other persons. The planters complained to the council of New-England, but obtained no redress. And after the expiration of seven years, (1628) for which the contract was made, eight of the principal persons in the colony, with four of their friends in London, became bound for the balance; and from that time took the whole trade into their own hands. These were obliged to take up money at an exorbitant interest, and to go deeply into trade at Kennebec, Penobscot, and Connecticut; by which means, and their own great industry and economy, they

---

* Hazard. † Hutchinson and Prince.
‡ Bradford's Letter's, Historical Collection.

were enabled to discharge the debt, and pay for the transportation of thirty-five families of their friends from Leyden, who arrived in 1629.*

The persecution of the Puritans in England, under archbishop Laud, now raged with unrelenting severity; and while it caused the destruction of thousands in England, proved to be a principle of life and vigor to the infant colonies in New-England. Among other expedients for vexing the Puritans, who were now composed both of the dissenters from the established church, and the opposers of despotic monarchy, " a system of sports and recreations on the Lord's day, which had been originated in the last reign, was revived and established by the king. This measure was directly calculated to obviate the objections of the Roman Catholics to the suppression of feasts and revels, to conciliate their favour; and to wound the feelings of the Puritans, and embarrass their clergy; as they were remarkable for a strict attention to the fourth commandment, still so decently observed by their descendants. The magistrates had found these sports, which consisted of dancing, leaping, vaulting, and various other games, to be introductory of profanation, and attempted to suppress them; but so great was the zeal of the court to root out Puritanism, that the representations of the magistrates were overruled, and the order, establishing the book of sports, was directed to be read in every parish. This was a net to entangle the clergy, and many lost their livings, for conscientiously refusing to read the order. In short, it became evident, in the star chamber language of the earl of Dorset, that to be guilty of drunkenness, uncleanness, or any less fault, might be pardonable; but that the sin of Puritanism and non-conformity was without forgiveness."†

* Belknap.   † Minot.

Though the current of popular opinion, at that time, was directly opposite to superstition; though it was with difficulty, that many rites and ceremonies rendered venerable by long custom, and sanctified by the practice of the first reformers, could be retained in public worship; yet so violent and rash was archbishop Laud, that he chose this time to introduce new rites and ceremonies. This gave the English church a strong resemblance to the church of Rome, which the English in general, and the Puritans in particular, viewed with detestation and horror. They supposed the design was to throw them back into the darkness and delusions of Popery. The court of Rome expected the same result, and repeatedly offered Laud a cardinal's hat.* Is it strange, that the indignation of the public should be roused; that their measures of redress should be bold, persevering, and successful?

In this situation of affairs, several men of eminence, who were the friends and protectors of the Puritans, entertained a design of settling in New-England, should they fail in establishing liberty and the reformation of religion in their own country. They solicited and obtained grants in New-England, and were at great pains in settling them. Among these patentees, were the lords Brook, Say, and Seal, the Pelhams, the Hampdens, and the Pyms; names which afterwards appeared with great eclat. Sir Matthew Boynton, Sir William Constable, Sir Arthur Haslerig, and Oliver Cromwell, were actually on the point of embarking for New-England; when archbishop Laud, unwilling that so many objects of his hatred should be removed beyond his reach, applied for, and obtained, an order from the court to put a stop to these emigrations. While some had fled to foreign countries, others were not so fortunate as to obtain

* Hume.

this dreadful privilege, but were detained as hostages for the good conduct of their brethren abroad."* However, he was not able to prevail so far as to hinder New-England from receiving vast additions of the clergy, who were silenced and deprived of their livings, and of the laity, who adhered to their opinions. As in all countries where persecution rages, so here, the wisest, and most useful members of the community, were compelled to leave their country. "Multitudes of pious and peaceable Protestants were driven by the severities of their persecutors, to leave their native country, and seek a refuge for their lives and liberties, with freedom for the worship of God, in a wilderness, in the ends of the earth."† By such people New-England was first settled. A body of men more remarkable for their piety and morality, and more respectable for their wisdom, never commenced the settlement of any country.

The Independents, or Congregationalists, as they have since been called, ever distinguished themselves as the patrons of religious liberty. This is allowed, not only by Neal and other writers friendly to their cause, but by those, who, in other respects, speak of them with derision. Thus Mr. Hume is constrained to confess, that, "Of all Christian sects, this was the first, which during its prosperity, as well as its adversity, always adopted the principle of toleration." His account of the Presbyterians is very different. "But nothing was attended with more universal scandal, than the propensity of many in parliament towards a toleration of the Protestant sectaries. The Presbyterians exclaimed, that this indulgence made the church of Christ resemble Noah's ark—and rendered it a receptacle for all unclean beasts. They menaced all their opponents with the same persecu-

* Minot. † Dr. Owen.

tion, under which they themselves had groaned, when held in subjection by the hierarchy.

As early as 1626, a few people from Plymouth, conducted by Mr. Roger Conant, commenced a settlement on Naumkeag river. Discouraged by the difficulties they had to encounter, they had determined to quit America and return to England; but, encouraged by the Rev. Mr. White, of Dorchester in England, who, with other influential persons, assured them they should receive a patent, supplies, and friends, they relinquished their design, and concluded to wait the event. Accordingly, on the 19th of March 1627, Sir Henry Roswell, and several other gentlemen, in the vicinity of Dorchester, purchased of the council of Plymouth, all that part of New-England, included within a line drawn from the Atlantic ocean, three miles south of Charles river, and three miles north of the Merrimac, to the South Sea. But as the council gave them no powers of government, they afterwards obtained a charter of incorporation from Charles I. constituting them a body politic, by the name of the "Governor and Company of Massachusetts Bay in New-England," with powers as extensive as any other corporation in England.

Under this charter, Matthew Cradock was elected the first governor, and Thomas Goff, deputy governor; Capt. John Endicott, who the year before had gone over with one hundred persons to Salem to prepare the way for the settlement of a permanent colony, was appointed, by the Plymouth company, governor for the plantation.*

In May, 1629, about three hundred and fifty persons, with the Rev. Messrs. Skelton, Higginson, and Bright, embarked for New-England, and arrived at Naumkeag, now Salem, on the 29th of June, having with them 115 head of cattle,

* Hutchinson

among which were 4 goats, and some conies, &c. One hundred persons the same year, "dissatisfied with the situation of Salem"* removed and laid the foundation of Charlestown. Messrs. Skelton and Higginson remained at Salem, where they formed, and were ordained over, the first church in that town; Mr. Bright removed with the others to Charlestown. Religion being the great object of these colonists, they immediately proceeded to form themselves into churches. Those of Salem, with the approbation of their governor, consulted with their brethren at Plymouth, who informed them how they had proceeded, as they believed, according to the word of God.

At the time appointed for organising their church, messengers from the church at Plymouth attended to witness the proceedings. The day was devoted to prayer and fasting, and thirty persons, who had desired to be of the communion, consented publicly to a confession of faith, which they had previously examined; after which they signed a solemn covenant. Mr. Skelton was then chosen pastor, and Mr. Higginson teacher, and Mr. Houghton their ruling elder. These were consecrated to their several offices by imposition of hands, by some of the brethren appointed by the church. Several other persons were then admitted to the church; some by expressing their consent to the confession of faith and covenant; some by writing an account of their faith and hope, and some by making a verbal declaration of their religious experience before the whole church. None were admitted without satisfactory testimonies of their sober life and conversation. The only necessary term of communion was to give, in some way, satisfaction to the church concerning their faith and manners. The *mode* of giving this evidence was left entirely to the direction of the church-

* Hist. of New-England, vol. iv. p. 139–40.

officers. Here, and at Plymouth, children of the church were considered members. Before admission to the Lord's supper, they were examined by the officers of the church, and if they were found "tolerably acquainted with the principles of religion, and were free from scandal, and willing to own the covenant, publicly, they were received. Accordingly Mr. Higginson's son, 15 years of age, was privately examined by Mr. Skelton, and admitted into the church."* Here we see nearly half a dozen different *modes* of admitting members, to the communion of this church. It is not strange that other churches have used several other methods. It is yet to be ascertained, which is the best manner of admitting members to the communion of our churches.

The colony was formed on the plan of the East-India company; for, though the object of the *settlers* was *religion*, the *company* had no motive but *profit*. Those, who came over, expected liberty of *conscience*; the company, who sent them, waited for *furs* and other articles of *commerce*. Accordingly the governor, deputy governor and assistants were all residents in England. The nominal governor here was merely their agent. Mr. Endicott was the first.

But the situation of the persecuted Puritans in England becoming more and more intolerable, interested respectable and wealthy people in their behalf, and converted them to their principles. Several persons of note had formed a resolution to emigrate to Massachusetts, *provided* they should be permitted *to carry the charter with them*. They were aware of the inconvenience of being governed, in a new and distant country, different in most respects from England, by men, over whom they had no controul; they wished to govern themselves. They insisted therefore that the charter should be transmitted with them, and that the corporate

* Neal, Mather.

powers, which it conferred, should in future be executed in New-England. Though the legality of the proposed measure was questioned, yet the importance of engaging men of wealth and influence in the enterprise, by which greater profits were expected, induced governor Cradock, who entered fully into their views, to call a general court, August 29th, 1629, to whom he submitted the question; when it was unanimously resolved "That the patent shall be transferred, and the government of the corporation removed from London to Massachusetts Bay." The members of the corporation, who remained in England, were, by agreement, to retain a share in the trading stock, and its profits, for seven years; but it does not appear that any dividend was ever made, or that any trade was carried on for the company.

On the 20th of October, 1629, the company proceeded to a new choice of officers, to elect such persons only, as had determined to go over with the charter. John Winthrop was chosen governor, John Humphrey deputy governor, Sir Richard Saltonstall and seventeen others, assistants. The deputy governor and several of the assistants never came to America. Their places were supplied by a new choice. Thomas Dudley was chosen deputy governor in place of Mr. Humphreys.

In the spring of 1630, these officers, with about fifteen hundred emigrants, embarked at various ports in England, in eleven vessels, fitted at the expense of more than £21,000 sterling, having their charter on board. This was the first charter that ever arrived in New-England, and the only one under which Massachusetts ever acted, till king William granted them another after the revolution. After a tedious voyage, they arrived at Salem in June, and at Charlestown the beginning of July. In consequence, the 8th day of this month was celebrated in all the plantations in New-England, as a day of public thanksgiving to God, "for all his goodness, and wonderful works to them."*

But there were several circumstances, which operated to damp their joys on this occasion. An extensive and formidable conspiracy of the Indians, as far as Narraganset, for the purpose of extirpating the English colonists had been discovered, to the inhabitants of Charlestown, by John Sagamore. The alarm and terror, which this event occasioned, had scarcely subsided. Of three hundred persons, who were previously at Salem and Charlestown, eighty had died the preceding winter. There was not corn enough to supply their necessities for a fortnight; and their other provisions, in consequence of their long voyage, were reduced to a scanty pittance. They were obliged to let their servants, who had cost them from fifteen to twenty pounds each, go free, and provide for themselves. Under all these disadvantages, they had but a few months to prepare shelter and food for a long and cold winter.

To increase their calamities, a mortal sickness soon commenced its ravages among them, and before December, two hundred of their number died. Among these was lady Arabella, who "came from a paradise of plenty and pleasure, in the family of a noble Earl, into a wilderness of wants;" also Mr. Johnson, her husband, highly esteemed for his piety and wisdom, and one of the assistants, and Mr. Rossiter, another of the assistants. To console them under their severe distresses, Mr. Wilson preached to them on the subject of Jacob's behaviour, who was not disheartened by the death of his nearest friends on the way, when God called him to remove. This worthy minister was liberal, almost to an extreme, in administering to the

* Prince.

relief of the necessitous: he was at all times a father to the poor; the wretched Indians often tasted his bounty.

Discouraged by such calamities, and gloomy prospects, about an hundred persons, who had lately arrived, of "weaker minds," and not of the best characters, returned to England in the vessels which brought them over. The return of these was considered as no loss to the plantation. Among the people lately arrived, some from the west of England, but more from the vicinity of London, were persons of all trades and occupations, necessary for planting a new country. As the buildings were not sufficient for such a number of people, the artificers among them erected tents and booths for their temporary accommodation.

CHAP. VII.

Church gathered in Charlestown; first court held there; Morton sentenced for stealing an Indian canoe; Boston, Watertown, and Roxbury settled; description of the former; scarcity and its good effects; arrival of governor Winthrop's family; account of Newbury; union of the two colonies.

As the great object of these christian pilgrims, in leaving their native country, was to " enjoy the ordinances of the gospel, and worship the Lord Jesus Christ according to his own instructions," governor Winthrop, lieut. governor Dudley, Mr. Johnson, and the Rev. Mr. Wilson, on the 30th of July, 1630, entered into a formal and solemn covenant with each other, and thus formed the church in Charlestown. On the 27th of August following, Mr. Wilson was ordained pastor of the church at Charlestown. This was the first ordination that took place in Massachusetts.*

On the 23d of August, 1630, the first court of assistants, was held at Charlestown, on board the Arabella, consisting of gov. Winthrop, deputy governor Dudley, and Sir Richard Saltonstall, Messrs. Ludlow, Rossiter, Newell, T. Sharp, Pynchon, and Bradstreet, assistants. This court was formed for the determination of great affairs, civil and criminal. Justices of the peace, invested with the same authority, as like magistrates in England, and other officers were appointed for the preservation of the public peace. The first question that came before them was, " How the ministers should be maintained?" On the proposal of Messrs. Wilson and Phillips, the court ordered that houses should be built for them at the public charge, and the governor, and Sir Richard Saltonstall, were appointed to carry the order into effect. Thomas Morton, of Mount Wollaston, who had stolen a boat from the Indians, was ordered to be brought before them for trial.

On the 7th of September, a second court was held at Charlestown, before which Morton was tried, condemned, and sentenced to be set in the *bilbows*, and afterwards to be sent prisoner to England by the ship called the *Gift*, now returning; that all his goods shall be seized to defray the charges of his transportation, payment of his debts, and to give satisfaction to the Indians for the canoe he had unjustly taken from them; and that his house be burned in sight of the Indians. All persons were forbidden to plant within the limits of their patent, without leave from the court; those persons who had set down at *Agawam* were ordered to remove. Trimountain, they named *Boston*, Mattapan, *Dorchester*, and the town on Charles river, *Watertown*.

* Prince.

Before the following winter, Sir Richard Saltonstall, with Mr. Phillips and others, removed and formed a plantation at *Watertown;* the greater part of the church in Charlestown, with Mr. Wilson, removed and settled in Boston. Another company, with Mr. Pynchon at their head, settled at Roxbury.*

At Charlestown they had been very sickly, which they ascribed to the water; the only spring, they had discovered, was overflowed at high water; and, being informed by one Blaxton, who had been over to Boston and slept there, that he found good water in that place, Mr. Johnson and others crossed Charles' river, and began a settlement in November. Governor Winthrop soon followed them. Here they erected for themselves huts, and spent the winter.

On the 6th of December, the governor and assistants met, and agreed to fortify Boston neck; but the design was soon relinquished, and they concluded to build, the next spring, a fortified town on the spot near where Harvard University has since been established, then called Newtown. In the spring following, the governor accordingly began to erect a house; and the deputy governor finished his, and removed his family. But the neighbouring Indians manifesting a friendly disposition, the plan of a fortified town was relinquished. The governor determined to settle at Boston.†

This place was called *Shawmut* by the natives, but now *Trimountain* by the English on account of its three hills. Afterward, from respect to Mr. Cotton, who came from Boston, in Lincolnshire, this peninsula was named Boston. The doubt and hesitancy exhibited by the first inhabitants respecting this spot, as a place for their principal settlement, proved that they had little apprehensions of its physical advantages or future importance. For some time Dorchester

* Prince. † Hutchinson.

was a larger town, and Cambridge its powerful rival. So indifferent was its figure, that sarcastically it was called *Lost Town*.

On the 24th of May, 1631, a fortification was begun on Fort Hill. The next day the people of Charlestown went over and assisted: the day following the people of Dorchester went; Roxbury also lent their aid. But previous to this, in March, the court had ordered a market to be established in Boston, to be kept every Thursday, which was lecture day. On the fourth of this month, Samuel Cole had set up the first house of entertainment, and John Cogan the first merchant's shop. On the 16th of March was the first fire in Boston; two dwelling houses were consumed. The fire caught about noon in the chimney of Mr. Sharp's house, "the splinters of which it was made not being clayed." Catching "the thatch" on the roof, the wind drove the fire to Mr. Colburn's house, which was destroyed, though most of the goods were saved. This so alarmed the people, that, for the prevention of the like evil, it was ordered that in Newtown (now Cambridge) "no man should build his chimney of wood, nor cover his house with thatch." In August the congregation of Boston and Charlestown began to build the first meeting-house in Boston.* It was erected in Cornhill.

The following account of Boston was written by a learned Englishman, who had visited Massachusetts, in 1633. "Boston," saith he, "is two miles northeast of Roxborough. The situation is pleasant, being a peninsula, the bay of Roxborough on the south, Charles river on the north, marshes on the back side, not forty rods over, so that a little fence will secure their cattle from the wolves. The greatest wants are wood and meadow land, which never

* Winthrop.

were in this place; their timber, and firewood, and hay, are brought from the islands. They are not troubled with musquetoes, wolves, or rattlesnakes. Those who live here on their cattle, have farms in the country, the place being more suitable for those who trade.

"This neck of land is not above four miles in compass, in form almost square, has on the south side a great broad hill, on which is a fort, which commands the still bay. On the north side is another hill, equal in bigness, on which is a windmill: to the north west is a high mountain, with three little rising hills on the top of it, wherefore it is called Tramount. Although this town is not the greatest, nor richest, it is the most noted and frequented, being the centre of the plantations, where the monthly courts are kept. The town has very good land, *affording rich cornfields*, and fruitful gardens, sweet and pleasant springs. The inhabitants keep their swine and cattle at Muddy river, in the summer, while their corn is on the ground, but bring them to town in the winter."*

In 1638, Boston was rather a village than a town, there not being above twenty or thirty houses.† Though this town has suffered greatly by the smallpox, by war, and by many terrible fires, it is the largest town in New-England. In 1676, a fire destroyed forty-five dwelling houses; three years after, eighty dwelling houses, seventy stores, and several vesels, were destroyed by fire. In 1711, a fire broke out in the centre of the town, and consumed all the houses on each side of Cornhill, from School street to Market square; but the most terrible conflagration was in 1760, when one hundred and seventy-four dwelling houses were swept away, with one hundred and seventy-five warehouses, shops, and other buildings. The loss was estimated at

* Wood. † Josselyn.

£100,000 sterling. In 1787, and 1794, the fires consumed about two hundred buildings. Beside the fires mentioned, there have been many others, which destroyed a great number of buildings, and property of immense value. The siege in 1775 was calamitous to Boston; it was supposed as many buildings were destroyed there, as were burned in Charlestown.

As the first winter approached, provisions became extremely scarce; the people were compelled to subsist on clams, muscles, groundnuts, and acorns, and even these, while the snow covered the ground, were procured with great difficulty. These trials discouraged many; and when it was announced that "the governor had the last batch of bread in the oven," they almost despaired of receiving seasonable relief. They were also full of fears lest a ship, which had been despatched to Ireland for provisions, had either been cast away, or taken by pirates. But God, in his good providence, sent them timely relief. In their trouble, they had appointed a day to seek the Lord by fasting and prayer. Before the day came, the ship, with provisions arrived, and they changed the day of fasting into a thanksgiving.*

After a winter of great sufferings, the court convened in the spring of 1631, and ordained, "that the governor and assistants should in future be chosen by the freemen alone; that none should be admitted to the freedom of the company, but such as were chosen members, who had certificates from their ministers, that they were of orthodox principles; and that none but freemen should vote at elections, or act as magistrates or jurymen." This law continued in force, till the writ of *quo warranto* in 1684, annihilated the government.†

In November this year, governor Winthrop's wife and family arrived at Boston. When they came on shore, they

* Rev. Mr. Abbot's M.S. notes. † Chalmers.

were honoured with a discharge of artillery; the militia assembled and "entertained them with a guard and divers vollies;" the judges of the court and most of the people near the town went to salute them. For several days plenty of provisions was sent to them, "cows, fat hogs, kids, venison, poultry, geese, and partridges." Never had there been such rejoicing in New-England. The eleventh of November was a day of religious thanksgiving.

The distresses endured the preceding season induced the colonists to pay great attention to the raising of provisions for their future support. To encourage a spirit so laudable and necessary, the court enacted "that Indian corn should be deemed a legal tender in discharge of debts." A great part of the cattle, which had been imported from England, had died; and a milch cow was now valued at twenty five or thirty pounds sterling.

The Plymouth settlers had erected a trading house at Penobscot about the year 1627; of this the French from Accadie had taken possession. This gave rise to complaints on both sides, of encroachments on their respective rights, which led on finally to war between the parent countries.

In 1633, arrived a number of people in the ship Hector, who settled at Quafcacunquen. In May, 1634, arrived Mr. Thomas Parker and Mr. James Noyes. Mr. Parker and about a hundred, who came over with them, sat down at Ipswich, where he continued about a year, while Mr. Noyes preached at Medford. In May, 1635, some of the principal people of Ipswich petitioned the general court for liberty to remove to Quafcacunquen, which was granted, and the place incorporated by the name of Newbury.* This was the tenth church gathered in the colony. Mr. Noyes was chosen teacher, and Mr. Parker pastor of the church.

* Town Records, Magnalia, Winthrop's Journal.

The beautiful river, on whose banks they first settled, was, in honour to their Rev. pastor, named Parker river: tradition says, because he was the first, who ascended it in his boat. This he might easily effect from Ipswich, where he had lived the year before; it being only about eight miles of smooth water through Plum Island Sound. A writer in 1652, gives the following account of Newbury.

"This town is twelve miles from Ipswich; it has meadows and upland, which hath caused some gentlemen, who brought over good estates, to set upon husbandry, among whom that religious and sincere hearted servant of Christ, Mr. Richard Dummer, sometime a magistrate in this little commonwealth, hath holpen on this town. Their houses are built very scattering, which hath caused some contending about removal of their place for sabbath assemblies. Their cattle are about four hundred, with store of cornland in tillage; it consists of about seventy families the souls in church fellowship are about one hundred. The teaching elders of this congregation have carried it very lovingly towards their people, permitting them to assist in admitting persons into church society, and in church censures, so long as they act regularly, but in case of their mal-administration, they assume the power wholly to themselves; their godly life and conversation hath hitherto been very amiable, and their pains and care over their flock not inferiour to many others."

Another account of Quafcacunquen, or Newbury, in 1633,[*] the year of its settlement, is in these words. "Merrimac lies eight miles from Ipswich, is the best place; the river is navigable twenty leagues; all along the river's side are fresh marshes, in some places three miles broad. In this river are sturgeon, salmon, and bass, and divers other

[*] Wood.

kinds of fish. The country scarce affordeth that which this place cannot yield."

These quotations are not made on account of their geographical accuracy, for they are both defective; but as curiosities.

The first person born in Newbury was Mary Brown, afterwards, Godfrey. She lived to be eighty-two years of age, had a good report as a maid, a wife, and widow, and left a numerous posterity. The first male child was Joshua Woodman, who died 1703, aged sixty-seven.*

Few churches of New-England, have sent forth more branches than this in Newbury. Beside a meeting of friends and part of a congregational society, the other part lying in Rowley, there are eleven churches within the ancient limits of Newbury.

A curious specimen of style, and that fondness, which the man retains for "the play place of his tender years," is left us by a native of this town.

"As long as Plum island shall faithfully keep the commanded post, notwithstanding all the hectoring words and hard blows of the proud and boisterous ocean; as long as any salmon or sturgeon shall swim in the streams of Merrimac, or any perch or pickerel in Crane Pond; as long as the sea fowl shall know the time of their coming, and not neglect seasonably to visit the places of their acquaintance; as long as any cattle shall be fed with the grass growing in the meadows, which do humbly bow down themselves before Turkey Hill; as long as any sheep shall walk upon Old Town hills, and thence pleasantly look down upon the river Parker, and the fruitful marshes lying beneath; as long as any free and harmless doves shall find a white oak or other tree within the township to perch, or feed, or build a

* Gravestone in Byfield.

careless nest upon, and shall voluntarily present themselves to perform the office of gleaners after barley harvest; as long as nature shall not grow old and dote, but shall constantly remember to give the rows of Indian corn their education by pairs; so long shall christians be born here, and being made meet shall hence be translated to be made partakers of the inheritance of the saints in light."* So pleasing were his anticipations, and so readily did he find in his native town, all the images of duration to satisfy his taste.

The ministers of this ancient church have been respectable for their talents and purity of character. Their first pastor, the Rev. Thomas Parker, was the only son of the Rev. Robert Parker, who with some other ministers was driven out of England, in the reign of queen Elizabeth, for Puritanism. Mr. Thomas Parker was born in 1595. He had been admitted into Magdalen college, in Oxford, before his father's exile; after which he removed to Ireland, where he pursued his studies under the famous Dr. Usher. Thence he went after his father to Holland, where he enenjoyed the assistance of Dr. Ames. His labours were indefatigable, and his progress answerable. Before the age of twenty-two, he received the degree of Master of Arts. In his diploma it is said "Illum non sine *magna admiratione* audiverimus." He soon returned to Newbury, in England, to pursue his theological studies, where he also for a time preached and kept a school. He thence with a number of christians from Wiltshire, came over to New-England in the year 1634. The next year, with a number of those, who left England with him, and others, he settled at Newbury, where for a long course of years, by the holiness and humility of his life, he gave his people a lively commentary of

* Description of the New Heaven, by S. Sewall, Fellow of Harvard College, printed 1727.

his doctrine. He was a hard student, and by his incessant application, became blind several years before his death. Under this extreme loss, he supported an easy and patient temper, and would, in a pleasant manner, say, "Well, they will be restored shortly in the resurrection." He died April, 1677, in the eighty-second year of his age, and fifty-second of his ministry. He was a man of charity, and for some peculiarity of opinions, experienced some difficulties with his neighbours. He was considered one of the first scholars and divines of the age.

Mr. Parker's confidence in the success of New-England settlements, may be inferred from the text he selected for a sermon preached at Ipswich, just before he and his people left England. It was Exodus i. 7, "And the children of Israel were fruitful, &c. and the land was filled with them."

Mr. Parker and also his colleague considered the sabbath as beginning the evening preceding, yet both kept sabbath evening, as their people did. Being asked why he adopted a practice different from his opinion, Mr. Parker replied, "Because I dare not depart from the footsteps of the flock, for my own private opinion." When he kept a small school he refused any reward, saying, "He lived for the church's sake, therefore he was not willing to receive any scholars, but those, who were designed for the ministry. His whole life was employed in prayer, study, preaching, and teaching school.

Mr. James Noyes was born in 1608, at Chouldertown, of godly parents; his father being minister of the town. Mr. Noyes was called from college, in Oxford, to assist Mr. Parker in his school at Newbury, in England. In his youth he was admired for his piety; after receiving a call at Watertown, he chose to settle with his beloved Parker, and the people, who came over with him, who invited him to Newbury. He was much beloved by his people, and his memory is respected there to the present day. A catechism, which he composed for the children of his flock, has lately been reprinted by them. He was their teacher for more than twenty years; and after a long and tedious sickness, which he bore with patience and even with cheerfulness, he died Oct. 22, 1656, in the 48th year of his age. He married Sarah Brown, before he left England, by whom he left six sons and two daughters, who all lived to have families. Though Mr. Noyes fled from the church of England, he was not so high a republican in religious affairs, as his brethren in general. "He no way approved the governing *vote* of the fraternity, but took their consent in a silential way." He held a profession of faith, and repentance, and subjection to ordinances, to be the *rule* of admission to church fellowship, but admitted to baptism the children of those, who had been baptised, without requiring the parents to own any covenant, or being in church fellowship. Mr. Parker and Noyes kept a private fast together once a month, while Mr. Noyes lived, as they often had done in England, and while on their passage to this country. Mr. Parker continued the practice after the death of Mr. Noyes. They were the most cordial and intimate friends; in England they instructed in the same school; they came over in the same ship; they were ministers in the same church; and as Mr. Parker never married, they lived in the same house; nothing but death could separate them.

Mr. John Woodbridge succeeded Mr. Noyes as a teacher of the church with Mr. Parker, his uncle, his mother being Mr. Parker's sister. Mr. Woodbridge was born in 1613, the son of a pious clergyman of Wiltshire." John was "trained up in the way he should go," and when prepared, sent to Oxford to receive an education. But not choosing to take the oath of conformity, he left college, and pursued his studies in a more private way. The ceremonies of the church being rigorously enforced, young Woodbridge, in 1634, came over to New-England with Mr. Parker. With the rest he took up lands in Newbury, and continued his studies, till, by reason of his father's death, he was called to England; having accomplished his business and married a daughter of governor Dudley, he returned to New-England, in the the infancy of Andover, where he was ordained, Sept. 16, 1644. Here he continued with reputation, till by the invitation of friends, in 1647, he once more crossed the Atlantic to the pleasant isle of his nativity. There he continued, useful and happy, till the Bartholomew act, in 1663, banished him once more to America. Soon after his arrival on these shores, the church in Newbury invited him to be an assistant of his aged uncle, and to them he devoted his labours. But after some time, a difficulty concerning church discipline rose between him and his people, and he was dismissed. Soon after, he was remarkably blessed "in his private estate," which supplied the loss of his salary. His reputation was good, and he was appointed a justice of the peace, and magistrate of the colony. He had twelve children; eleven of whom lived to be men and women. He had the comfort of seeing three sons, and two sons-in-law, employed in the gospel ministry, and four grandsons candidates for the same work. He was a man of an excellent spirit, and gave good evidence "that he had been sanctified from his infancy." He was of a remarkably patient, pleasant temper, noted for his readiness to forgive injuries, rarely or never disturbed by worldly disappointments. A messenger once brought him word of great loss of property; his reply was, "what a mercy it is that this is the first time that I ever met with such a disaster." On a sabbath day in March, 1695, after a distressing disease, he died, aged 82 years. To him succeeded the Rev. John Richardson, who was ordained teacher of the first church in Newbury, with

Mr. Parker, Oct. 20, 1675. He died April 27, 1696, in the 50th year of his age, and 21st of his ministry. The Rev. Mr. Tappan was his successor. He, and Dr. Tucker, who followed him, both enjoyed a good old age.

The Massachusetts colony being threatened by the surrounding Indians, prudence dictated that union should be established between the two infant colonies. To bring about a measure so necessary to their safety, the governor, with the Rev. Mr. Wilson and others, proceeded to Plymouth, forty miles through the wilderness on foot. They were kindly and respectfully received by governor Bradford, and the principal gentlemen at Plymouth. The result of this embassy was a lasting friendship between the colonies.

CHAP. VIII.

Complaint against the colonists; character of Rev. Mr. Higginson; Ipswich settled; further emigrations; representative government; code of laws enacted.

THE colonists, in their zeal to preserve the unity and purity of the faith, had expelled from among them some, whose principles and conduct they disapproved. These persons complained to the king of the wrongs they suffered. Their complaint was referred to the privy council for colonies, January, 1632; but most of the charges being denied, and "to avoid discouragement to the adventurers, and in hopes that the colony, which then had a promising appearance, would prove beneficial to the kingdom," the complaint was dismissed.*

* Chalmers.

On the 15th of March, 1630, died the Rev. Francis Higginson, first pastor of Salem church. He was educated at Emanuel college, Cambridge, in England, and had been pastor of a church in Leicester. His preaching was evangelical, his great object being to produce that change of heart, without which no man can see the kingdom of God. The effect was such as might be expected; a remarkable revival of religion was the reward of his labours, and many were effectually turned from sin to holiness; but like many other good men, for his non-conformity, he was deprived of his pulpit. At this time burst forth the weight of his influence; the arm of ecclesiastical power could not obscure the lustre of his talents. Such was the pathos and enchanting persuasiveness of his eloquence, that the people could not be denied the pleasure of his instructions. "He was unto them, as a very lovely song of one that hath a pleasant voice." The people obtained liberty for him to preach a lecture on one part of the sabbath, and on the other to aid an aged clergyman, who needed his assistance. The people supported him by a free contribution; while it was safe, all the conforming ministers in the town invited him into their pulpits. He preached to another congregation a mile out of town. Thus did the field of his labours enlarge. But as it often happens in similar cases, while one part of the community was delighted and encouraged in their public and private religion, another part, feeling themselves rebuked and condemned, became more violent opposers and more cruel persecutors.

Mr. Higginson openly avowed his opinion, that ignorant and immoral people ought not to be admitted to the table of the Lord Accordingly, after preaching a sermon from this text, "Give not that which is holy to dogs," and being about to administer the sacrament, he saw a known swearer and drunkard before him, to whom he publicly said, he was not willing to give the Lord's supper to him, unless he professed his repentance to the satisfaction of the brethren, and desired him to withdraw. The man went out in a rage against Mr. Higginson, and with horror in his conscience; he was immediately taken sick, and in a few days expired, crying out, "*I am damned.*" Another profane person being offended with his wife, for attending Mr. Higginson's preaching, vowed revenge upon *him.* Accordingly, he resolved on a journey to London, to complain to the high commission court against him. All things being made ready for his journey, as he was mounting his horse, an insupportable pain of body seized him; his conscience was terrified: he was agitated with horrour; being led into his house, he died in a few hours.

A number of respectable and wealthy merchants having obtained a charter of Charles the first, and being incorporated by the name of the governor and company of Massachusetts Bay, in New-England, determined, in 1629, to send over some ships to begin a plantation. Hearing Mr. Higginson's situation, they sent two messengers to invite him to join their company, engaging to support him on the passage.

These messengers, understanding that Mr. Higginson was in daily expectation of officers to carry him to London, determined to have some sport. Accordingly, they went boldly to his door, and with loud knocks, cried where is Mr. Higginson, we must speak with Mr. Higginson. His affrighted wife ran to his chamber, entreating him to conceal himself. He replied, "No, I will go down and speak with them, and the will of the Lord be done." As they entered his hall with an assumed boldness, and roughness of address, they presented him some papers, saying, Sir, we come from London; our business is to carry you to London, as you may see by these papers. "I thought so," exclaimed Mrs.

Higginson; indeed all the people in the room, as well as she, were confirmed in their opinion, that "these blades were pursuants." Mr. Higginson soon found himself invited to Massachusetts by the governor, and company; he welcomed his guests, had a free conversation, and after taking proper time to ascertain his duty, resolved to cross the Atlantic. His farewell sermon was from Luke xxi. 20, 21. "When ye see Jerusalem encompassed with armies, &c. then flee to the mountains." Before a vast assembly he declared his persuasion that England would be chastised by war, and that Leicester would have more than a common share of sufferings. Soon after Leicester, being strongly fortified, received the wealth of the adjacent country. It was then beseiged, taken by storm, given up to plunder and violence, and eleven hundred of the inhabitants were slain in the streets. He soon took his journey with his family to London, in order to embark for New-England, when the streets, as he passed along, were filled with people, bidding him farewell, with prayers and cries for his welfare.

They sailed from the Isle of Wight, May, 1629, and when they came to the land's end, Mr. Higginson, calling up his children and other passengers to take their last sight of England, said, "Farewell England, farewell the church of God in England, and all the christian friends there," concluding with a fervent prayer for the king, church and state of England. The 24th of June, they arrived in Salem harbour. Mr. Skelton, who had been his companion in the voyage, united with him in forming a church, who immediately chose these two their spiritual teachers. Happy were the people in their instructions, and the ample privileges they enjoyed; but this, as well as the other colonies, was doomed to suffer a dreadful mortality, the first winter after their arrival; almost one hundred persons died at Salem,* and two hundred at Boston, Charlestown, and the vicinity.

While others were dying around him the first winter, Mr. Higginson fell into a hectic. The last sermon he preached was from Matth. xi. 7, "What went ye out into the wilderness to see." From which he reminded the people of their design to promote true religion in coming into this country. Mr. Higginson "was grave in his deportment, and pure in his morals. In person he was slender, not tall: not easily changed from his purposes, but not rash in declaring them." His posterity are still among the most respectable people of the commonwealth.

In March, 1633, J. Winthrop, a son of the governor, with twelve men, began a plantation at Agawam, which afterwards was called Ipswich. The next year a church was gathered, being the ninth in the colony. In April, the people being destitute of a minister, the governor travelled on foot from Boston to Ipswich, spent the sabbath with them, and "exercised by way of prophecy."† In 1634, the Rev. Nathaniel Ward came over from England, and became their minister for about eleven years."‡

The spirit of persecution still raged in England. Many of the persecuted, less enterprising than their brethren, who had already gone to America, had been waiting with solicitude to know their situation and prospects. Satisfied on these points from the accounts they had received, great numbers embarked this year, 1633, for New-England. So numerous, and of such character were these emigrants, that the king in council thought fit to "stay the ships until further orders."

These orders, however, in consequence of an able vindication of the conduct of the governor and colonists of New-

---

* Mather. † Winthrop's Journal. ‡ Mather.

England, by such of the company as were present, did not put a stop to emigrations. In some of the summer months of this year there arrived twelve or fourteen ships filled with passengers. Among the distinguished characters who came over about this time, were Mr. Haynes, Sir Henry Vane, and the Rev. Messrs. Cotton, Hooker and Stone. The first was afterwards many years governor of Connecticut. The second was the next year elected governor of Massachusetts. The three last named were among the most eminent divines of that day, and their coming to New-England drew after them multitudes of the persecuted Puritans. Mr. Cotton is said to have been more useful and influential in settling the civil as well as ecclesiastical polity of New-England; than any other person.

Until this period the legislative powers had been exercised by the governor, deputy governor, and assistants, and the whole body of freemen in person, though the latter had been permitted to have but little share in the government; but the colony had now become so numerous that it was inconvenient, and indeed impracticable, to legislate in one assembly; nor was it safe, surrounded as they were, with hostile Indians, for the freemen to leave their families for so long a time unprotected; necessity, therefore, obliged them to establish a *representative form of government*, which they did by general consent, though no express provision was made for it in the charter. Accordingly, the freemen elected twenty-four deputies, who appeared in general court, April, 1634, as their representatives. Their first business was to assert the rights of the people by passing the following resolutions; viz. "That none but the general court had power to make and establish laws, or to elect and appoint officers as governor, deputy governor, assistants, treasurer, secretary, captains, lieutenants, ensigns, or any of like moment, or to remove such upon misdemeanor, or to set out the duties or powers of these officers. That none but the general court hath power to raise monies and taxes, and to dispose of lands, viz. to give and confirm proprieties."

After these resolutions, they proceeded to the election of magistrates. They further determined, "That there shall be four general courts held yearly, to be summoned by the governor for the time being, and not to be dissolved, but by consent of the major part of the court. That it shall be lawful for the freemen of each plantation to choose two or three, before every general court, to deal in all affairs of the commonwealth, wherein the freemen have to do, the matter of election of magistrates and other officers only excepted, wherein every freeman is to give his own voice." And to show their resentment, they imposed a fine upon the court of assistants for going contrary to an order of the general court.* The legislative body, thus organized, continued without alteration, (except that the number of general courts annually, was reduced, in 1644, from four to two) till the loss of the charter in 1684. This is supposed to have been the second house of representatives that ever assembled in America. A house of burgesses met for the first time in Virginia, May, 1620.

Having thus established their form of government, a code of laws was the next business in course. The leading characters among the colonists, were of opinion that the subjects of any prince or state had a natural right to emigrate to any other state or country, when deprived of liberty of conscience, and that upon such a removal their allegiance ceased. They considered their subjection to the crown of England as voluntary, and founded on mutual compact, and this compact was their charter. They maintained their

* Hutchinson.

right to make their own laws, and to elect their own magistrates, but acknowledged that their laws must not be repugnant to those of England; and that by their compact they had no right to seek protection from any foreign prince. With these sentiments, and without any partiality for the laws of their mother country, it is not surprising that they did not adopt the laws of England, as the foundation of their code. The peculiarity of their situation indeed rendered necessary, corresponding laws and regulations. And as their leading object in coming to this country, was to enjoy liberty of conscience, and to support and transmit pure to their posterity, the religion of the bible; and, finding in this book the leading principles of good government, and a system of laws for the general regulation of human conduct, they adopted it as their "principal code of law, and declared, as an article in their bill of rights, that no man should suffer, but by an express law, or *by the word of God.*"

"Their capital offences were idolatry, witchcraft, blasphemy, murder, bestiality, sodomy, adultery, manstealing, bearing false witness, conspiracy, rebellion, cursing, or smiting a parent, *unless when neglected in education*, or provoked by extreme and cruel correction, rebellious and stubborn conduct in a son, disobeying the voice and chastisement of his parents, and living in notorious crimes, rape, and arson. Other offences were made capital upon a second or third conviction, and the degree of the offence was in some instances increased by the circumstance of its being committed on the sabbath.

"In the inferiour classes of crimes, were many peculiar to the situation of the colony, especially with regard to sumptuary regulations, and the enforcing of industry. In these there are strong proofs of the disposition which prevailed of shewing respect to particular descriptions of families by distinctions in their favour.

"The rigour of justice extended itself to the protection of property, and to the moral habits of the people; a remarkable instance of this is shown in the power given to creditors, over the persons of their debtors. The law admitted of a freeman's being sold for service to discharge his debts, though it would not allow of the sacrifice of his time, by his being kept in prison, unless some estate was concealed." A most reasonable law.

"The governor and assistants were the first judicial court; to this, inferiour jurisdictions were added; and the house of representatives coming into existence, the judicial authority was shared by them, as in the words of their law, the second branch of the civil power of this commonwealth. The subordinate jurisdictions were, the individual magistrates, the commissioners of towns, and the county courts. These seem, in some sense, to have acted as the deputies of the general court, since, in difficult points, they were allowed to state the case without the names of the parties, to that court, and receive its declaration of the law.

"As in their government, hereditary claims were rejected, their public officers being all periodically chosen from the body of the freemen, and without regard to distinct orders, so in the descent and distribution of real or personal estates of intestates, the exclusive claim of any one heir was not admitted, but equal division was made among all, reserving only to the eldest son a double portion. This in a numerous family, which is common in a young country, effectually prevented the undue accumulation of property. These two regulations may be said to be the great pillars on which republican liberty in Massachusetts is supported. There was an inestimable advantage gained to the cause of freedom by a law, in 1641, which declares the lands of the inhabitants free from all fines and licences upon alienation, heriots, wardships, and the whole train of feudal exactions, which have so grievously oppressed mankind in other parts of the world. More recently the double claim of the eldest son has been abolished, and all the children now have equal portions. They tendered hospitality and succour to all Christian strangers, flying from the tyranny of their persecutors, or from famine, wars, or the like compulsory cause.

But while they have thus scrupulously regulated the morals of the inhabitants within the colony, and offered it as an asylum to the oppressed among mankind, they neglected not to prevent the contagion of dissimilar habits, and heretical principles from without. A law was made, in the year 1637, that none should be received as inhabitants within the jurisdiction, but such as should be allowed by some of the magistrates. It was fully understood, that differing from the religious tenets generally received in the country, was as great a disqualification, as any political opinions. In a defence of this order it is advanced, that the apostolic rule of rejecting such as brought not the true doctrine with them, was as applicable to the commonwealth as the church, and that even the profane were less to be dreaded, than the able advocates of erroneous opinions.*

CHAP. IX.

Character of first settlers; New-Hampshire and Maine settled; Exeter planted.

THE first settlers of New-England were certainly a remarkable people; of a character peculiarly adapted to those important designs they were to execute. They were destined to plant and subdue a wilderness, filled with savage

* Minot.

enemies; to lay the foundation of a great empire, under the jealous eye of their parent country. Accordingly, they were enterprising, brave, patient of labour and sufferings, with a zeal for religion bordering on enthusiasm. They had also among them their full proportion of the learned and best informed men of that age. A body of men more remarkable for their piety, more exemplary in their morals, more respectable for their wisdom, never before, nor since, commenced the settlement of any country. What have been considered as blemishes in their character seemed necessary in their situation. "Less rigour would have disqualified them for discharging the heavy duties they had to perform, and, perhaps, more liberality would have introduced sectaries, which would have weakened the community by divisions, and profligates who would have corrupted it by their vices."*
"Religious, to some degree of enthusiasm it may be admitted they were, but this can be no peculiar derogation from their character, because it was at that time almost the universal character, not only of England, but of Christendom; had this, however, been otherwise, their enthusiasm, considering the principles on which it was founded, and the ends to which it was directed, far from being a reproach, was greatly to their honour. For I believe it will be found universally true, *that no great enterprise for the honour or happiness of mankind was ever achieved without a large mixture of that noble infirmity*. Whatever imperfections may be justly ascribed to them, which, however, are as few as any mortals have discovered, their judgment in forming their policy was founded on wise and benevolent principles; it was founded on revelation and reason; it was consistent with the best, greatest and wisest legislators of antiquity."

* Minot.

Inextinguishable zeal for liberty was a prominent feature of their character. Not the mad democracy of modern growth, but a rational and safe enjoyment of civil and religious privileges, was the great object of their pursuit. For several years the government was administered by the governor, deputy governor, and judges of the court of assistants. In 1630, it was voted by the freemen of the commonwealth, that they would choose the assistants themselves, that the assistants should choose the governors from their own body, who, with the assistants, should have the power of making laws, and of appointing officers to execute them. This surely was not democracy.* But a regard for religion was their master passion, which directed all the rest; this is evident, not only from their constant professions, but from their customs, their institutions, their laws, and various other circumstances by which the character of a community is known.

A learned writer observes, "that laws are the best index of the spirit of a government; that had commerce been the object of those, who settled New-England, their laws would have been commercial; but their object was religion; the first laws of New-England were wholly adapted to promote religion."

A law of Massachusetts, 1646, declares, that "if any one shall contemptuously treat the gospel preached, or the faithful preacher, in any congregation, or like Korah cast reproach upon the doctrine or minister, he shall for the first offence be reproved by the magistrate at some lecture, and bound to his good behaviour. For a second offence, he should pay 5£ to the public treasury, or stand two hours openly on a block or stool four feet high, on a lecture day, with this sentence in capitals on his breast: *An open and*

---
* Hazard.

obstinate contemner of God's holy ordinances." The same year it was enacted that whoever neglected to attend public worship on the sabbath, and on those fast and thanksgiving days, appointed by authority, "without just and necessary cause," should be fined 5s. for every such neglect.* All persons not worth 200£ wearing gold or silver lace, or button or blue lace above 2s. per yard, or silk hoods or scarfs, may be presented by the grand jury, and shall pay 10s. for every offence. Every person who dresses above his rank may be assessed at 200£. Nor may we with justice pass over their generous and cordial attachment to "the mother country." An English writer, who early visited New England, declares, "no people are more loyal, none more fond of the distinguished name of Englishmen." If there can be any doubt of this fact, an address, made by the founders of Massachusetts colony, to the church of England, when they left their native country, must give perfect satisfaction. "We esteem it our honour," say they "to call the church of England our dear mother, and cannot part from our native country, where she especially resideth, without much sadness of heart, and many tears, ever acknowledging that such hope and part as we have in the common salvation, we have received in her bosom, and from her breasts; we have it not, therefore, loathing the milk, which has nourished us, but blessing God for our parentage and education; as members of the same body, we shall always rejoice in her good, and grieve for her sorrow, desiring her welfare and the enlargement of her bounds. Commend to the prayers of your congregations the necessities of your neighbours, the church springing out of your own bowels. We conceive much hope, that your prayers will be a prosperous gale in our sails. We also entreat of you, that are minis-

* Hazard.

ters of God; we crave it of our private brethren at no time to forget us in your private solicitations at the throne of grace."—Did ever children leave a parent's house in a more affectionate manner?

In the years 1621 and 1622, captain John Mason, and Sir Ferdinando Gorges obtained grants of the Plymouth council of which they were members, of all the country between Naumkeag, (now Salem) and Sagadahock river; and back to the lakes of Canada. The tract between Naumkeag and Merrimac, which was granted to Mason, he called *Mariana*. The rest, granted jointly to both, they named *Laconia*.

The next year, 1623, they planted a colony, and established a fishery on Piscataqua river. About the same time a variety of other little settlements were formed, on the coast between the Merrimac and Sagadahock rivers. But none of them flourished, being "rather temporary establishments for traffic, than seed plots of future plantations."

In 1629, the southeastern part of the present state of New-Hamsphire was purchased of the Indians, and a deed obtained of them by John Wheelright and others from Massachusetts. The same year Capt. Mason procured a new patent from the council of Plymouth for a still larger tract, including this Indian purchase. This tract was now named NEW-HAMPSHIRE.

For several years after this, the adventurers paid very little attention to agriculture. They imported their bread corn from England and Virginia. Their views were chiefly turned to the discovery of the lakes, and of mines, to the cultivation of grapes, to the peltry trade, and the fisheries. The peltry trade was of some value, and the fisheries supported the inhabitants; but neither lakes nor mines were found, and their vines perished. Discouraged by ill success, the adventurers in England sold their shares to Mason and Gorges, who became the sole proprietors. They, in 1634, renewed their exertions to increase the colony, and appointed Francis Williams, a wise and popular man, its governor.

An attempt was made by Mason and Gorges about this time, to divide New-England into twelve lordships, under the direction of a general governor. This scheme was countenanced at court, but was never adopted, and produced no material injury to the rights of the settlers.

The religious views and sentiments of Mason and Gorges, did not accord with those of the planters in Massachusetts; the object of the latter was to establish a christian community enjoying liberty of conscience; while that of the former was to plant colonies, which should yield them wealth and power. The enterprise of Mason and Gorges was, however, at this period, exemplary and useful, as it served to excite a spirit of emulation in other adventurers, and their memory deserves respect. Capt. Mason died in the winter of 1635-6. Governor Winthrop in his journal makes the following remark on his death, which shews the temper of those times. "He was the chief mover in all attempts against us, the Massachusetts colony, and was to have sent the general governor; and for this end was providing ships. But the Lord, *in mercy*, took him away, and all the business fell on sleep."

In April, 1639, Gorges obtained from Charles I. a confirmation of his patent, and "his limits were now extended to one hundred miles from the rivers southwestward into the desert." This tract was called MAINE. By this patent Gorges was invested with all the royal rights of a Count Palatinate, with greater powers than had ever been granted by a sovereign to a subject. Encouraged by these attentions, and invested with authority, the following year he established civil government within the province, appointed

Josselyn and others his counsellors, and transmitted to them (March 1640) ordinances to regulate them in the administration of justice. But he possessed not the talents requisite to the government of a colony; the constitution he had formed for Maine, was merely executive, without any legislative powers, nor did it provide any assembly in which the people might be represented. Encouragement was not given to emigrants to purchase and cultivate his lands. Agriculture was neglected. Lands were granted, not as freeholds, but by leases, subject to quit rents, and no provision was made for the regular support of the clergy. With such a government and such regulations, it could not be expected that the colony would flourish; on the contrary "the province languished for years in hopeless imbecility. Its languors ceased, and a principle of life was infused, only when he ceased to be its proprietary and lawgiver." The town of York, however, was incorporated by him, with city privileges, in 1641; but this circumstance seems to have added neither to its wealth nor importance.

The Rev. John Wheelwright, brother of the famous Ann Hutchinson, finding opposition too powerful, quitted Massachusetts, and with a number of his followers, planted the town of Exeter. Sensible of the necessity of government and laws, of which they were destitute, thirty-five persons in October, 1639, "combined themselves in the name of Christ, to erect such a government as should be agreeable to the will of God." They considered themselves as subjects of England, acknowledged the laws of the realm, and promised obedience to such laws as should be made by their own representatives, and chose a Mr. Underhill for their governor. Their situation, however, was neither happy nor prosperous.

Not long after, a small but more respectable number of persons from England, settled at Dover, and in October,

1640, these people, and those who had planted themselves at Portsmouth, under Williams, formed themselves into a body politic.

Four distinct governments, including one at Kittery, north of the river, were now formed on the branches of the Piscataqua. These combinations being only voluntary agreements, liable to be broken or subdivided on the first popular discontent, there could be no confidence in their continuance. The distractions in England, at this time, had cut off all hope of the royal attention, and the people of the several settlements were too much divided in their opinions to form any general plan of government, which could afford a prospect of permanent utility. The more considerate persons among them, therefore, thought it best to treat with Massachusetts, about taking them under their protection. That government was glad of an opportunity, to realize the construction, which they had put upon the clause, of their charter, in which their northern limits are defined; for a line drawn from east to west at the distance of "three miles to the northward of Merrimac river, and of any and every part thereof," which would take in the greater part of New-Hampshire, and Maine, so that Mason and Gorges' patents must have been vacated. They had already intimated their intention to run this east and west line, and presuming on the justice of their claim, they readily entered into a negociation with the principal settlers of Piscataqua respecting their incorporation with them. The affair was more than a year in agitation, and was at length concluded by an instrument subscribed in the presence of the general court, by George Wyllys, Robert Saltonstall, William Whiting, Edward Holiock, and Thomas Makepeace, in behalf of themselves and the other partners of the two patents; by which instrument they resigned the jurisdiction of the whole to Massachusetts, on condition that the inhabitants should enjoy the same liberties with their own people, and have a court of justice erected among them. The property of the whole patent of Portsmouth, and of one third part of that of Dover, and of all their improved lands, was reserved to the lords and gentlemen proprietors, and to their heirs forever.*

Thus New-Hampshire ceased to be a separate province. Each of the associations beforementioned dissolved their respective compacts, which had been productive of much contention and anarchy, and peaceably submitted to Massachusetts.

CHAP. X.

Settlement of Connecticut; character of Reverend Mr. Davenport.

THE present territory of Connecticut, at the first arrival of the English, was possessed by the Pequot, the Mohegan, Podunk, and many other smaller tribes of Indians.

The Pequots were numerous and warlike. Their country extended along the seacoast from Paucatuck to Connecticut river. About the year 1630, this powerful tribe extended their conquests over a considerable part of Connecticut, over all Long Island and part of Narraganset. SASSACUS, was the grand monarch. The seat of his dominion was at New-London; the ancient Indian name of which, was Pequot.

The Mohegans were a numerous tribe, and their territory extensive. Their ancient claim comprehended most of New-London county, almost the whole county of Windham, and a part of the counties of Tolland and Hartford. UNCUS,

* Belknap.

distinguished for his friendship to the English, was the sachem of this tribe.

The Podunks inhabited East Hartford, and the circumjacent country. The first sachem of this tribe, of whom the English had any knowledge, was Tatanimoo. He was able to bring into the field more than 200 bowmen.

The first grant of Connecticut was made by the Plymouth council, to the earl of Warwick, in 1630, and confirmed by his majesty in council the same year. This grant comprehended "all that part of New England which lies west from Narraganset river, 120 miles on the seacoast." The year following, the earl assigned this grant to lord Say and Seal, lord Brook, and nine others, who held it in trust for the Puritan emigrants from England.

In the year 1631, Wahquimacut, a sachem of a tribe on Connecticut river, visited the governors of Massachusetts and Plymouth, and earnestly besought them to make a settlement upon that river. Wahquimacut was induced to make this request from a hope that the English might protect him and his nation against the Pequots, who, from their number and power, threatened to exterminate the river tribes. To persuade the English to comply with his request, he represented to them the fertility of the country, and its advantages for trade, and promised to give them eighty beaver skins, and an annual supply of corn. Mr. Winthrop, the governor of Massachusetts, was not inclined to accept the offer. Mr. Winslow, the governor of Plymouth, thought it worthy of consideration, and, that he might judge of the sachem's representations, visited the river the latter part of this year.

The next year a more particular examination of the river and adjoining territories was made by the people of Plymouth, with design to fix the proper site for a trading house. Having done this, they endeavoured to engage governor

Winthrop and his council to unite with them in this new settlement; but not having succeeded in this attempt, they resolved to undertake it by themselves. Accordingly, in Oct. 1633, William Holmes of Plymouth, with a small company of men, sailed up the Connecticut, and erected a trading house a short distance below the mouth of the little river in Windsor. This was the first house that was erected in Connecticut. The English, thus established, treated the Indians with justice and kindness; and the Indians in return testified, in every possible manner, their affection and good will. The fierce and high spirited Pequots were the only people, who refused this interchange of good offices, and who thus early manifested a deep animosity toward the English.

The same year, a little before the arrival of the English, a company of Dutch traders came to Hartford, and built a house which they called the *Hirse of Good Hope*, and erected a small fort, in which they planted two cannon. The remains of this settlement are still visible on the bank of the river. They erected another fort among the Indians at Totoket, now Branford. These were the only settlements of the Dutch in Connecticut in those times. The Dutch, and after them the province of New-York, for a long time, claimed as far east as the western bank of Connecticut river.

In 1634, lord Say and Seal, &c. sent over a small number of men, who built a fort at Saybrook, and held a treaty with the Pequot Indians, who, in a formal manner, gave to the English their right to Connecticut river and the adjacent country.

The same year the inhabitants of Dorchester, Watertown, and Newtown, applied to the general court of Massachusetts for permission to remove to Connecticut. After warm and long debates, this permission was refused. Nevertheless, the body of the people of Dorchester, and the towns of Newtown, Cambridge, and Watertown, concluded to remove.

In the summer of 1635 many of them performed the dangerous and laborious journey across the wilderness to Connecticut river. At the time of their removal, the Dutch had extended their claim to the river, and made a settlement a few miles below Windsor. About one hundred men, women and children took their departure from the three towns mentioned, to travel through an unexplored wilderness. They were fourteen days performing the tedious journey. The forests, through which they passed, for the first time resounded with the praises of God. They prayed, and sang psalms and hymns, as they marched along; the Indians following them in silent admiration.

They arrived at this river, the object of their ardent expectation, near the mouth of Scantic river in East Windsor. The Dorchester people, with Mr. Wareham for their minister, began the settlement of Windsor on the west side of the river; they suffered great hardships the first winter, and their cattle perished for want of food; to carry much provision or furniture through a pathless wilderness was impracticable. Their principal provisions and household furniture had been put on board several small vessels, which, by reason of delays, and the tempestuous season, were either cast away, or did not arrive. Several vessels were wrecked on the shore of New-England, by the violence of the storms. Every resource appeared to fail, and the people were under the dreadful apprehensions of perishing by famine. They supported themselves in this distressing period with that heroic firmness and magnanimity, for which the first settlers of New-England had been so eminently distinguished.*

* Trumbull.

The Indians near the river were numerous. Three sachemdoms were in the vicinity. The seat of one was near the mouth of Podunk river, lying in the southwest corner of East Windsor. A second at Middletown, twenty miles below; and the third at Farmington, about twelve miles west of Windsor.

Some of the first settlers of Windsor were gentlemen of opulence and education, as were those of Hartford and Weathersfield. The right of settling here they purchased of the old Plymouth company in England, and they paid the Indians for the soil. They had sent men the year before to make the purchase of the natives, whom they viewed as the only rightful proprietors.

In October following, a number of people from Watertown, settled Weathersfield. The 31st of the next March, Mr. Hooker, with most of his congregation, removed from Newtown, and settled Hartford. Mrs. Hooker was carried in a horse litter; they drove one hundred and sixty cattle and fed on their milk by the way. The inhabitants of these towns met and formed a constitution of government, and entered into a solemn agreement, dated January 14, 1638. Under this original constitution, formed by the people themselves, an independent government was established and administered till 1662. During this time many more towns were settled and christian churches organized. Application was then made to the king of England for a charter, that they might enjoy the protection and liberties of free born Englishmen. The petition was heard, and the charter granted, on condition the people paid to the king one fifth part of the gold and silver ore, which should be discovered.* This charter, which established *the substance of the constitution they had formed for themselves*, retained its force in periods of

* Governor Trumbull's Letter.

political fanaticism, and revolutionary frenzy; it saw the constitutions of neighbouring states rise and fall like billows of the deep; itself, like a rock in the surge, unmoved, and unhurt. Notwithstanding its strong democratic features, it was the pride of its subjects, and the boast of legislators. It remained in force till 1818, when a new constitution was adopted.

The first settlers of Connecticut encountered serious difficulties, though not so great as their brethren of Massachusetts and Plymouth, nor perhaps so great as they themselves had experienced on their arrival. There is no account of such fatal sickness among them as the other colonies had suffered. Still they had full opportunity to exercise their self denial and fortitude.

In November, two shallops, going with goods to Connecticut, were cast away in a northeast storm on Brown's island, near the Gurnet's Nose, and the men all drowned.

The same month a pinnace returning from Connecticut, way cast away in Manemit bay; the men, six in number, were saved, and wandered ten days in extremely cold weather, and a deep snow, before they reached Plymouth; without meeting even an Indian. Soon after ten men arrived in Massachusetts from Connecticut. They had been ten days on the journey, having lost one of their number, who fell through the ice and was drowned; and had they not found a friendly wigwam, all would have been starved.

The fifteenth of Nov. Connecticut river was frozen over. The people of Windsor, who removed their cattle, lost the greater part of them this winter; yet some, which came too late to be carried over the river, took good care of themselves, and looked well without hay. They lost £2000 worth of cattle, and were reduced themselves to great sufferings for want of food, being obliged to eat acorns, malt, and grains.*

* Winthrop.

The next fall, a bark sailing down the river, the people went on shore; the Indians killed one, made another prisoner, whose hands and feet they cut off, and tortured to death.

The following spring the Pequots, near Weathersfield, killed six men, while at work in the field; three women also were killed, and two maids taken captive; at the same time they killed a horse, and twenty cows.*

The first court held in Connecticut was at Weathersfield, April 26, 1636. The next year the colony carried war into the country of the Pequots.

Upon the forced surrender of the Plymouth company's patent to the crown, in 1635, the whole territory of New-England was regranted in large partitions, to a number of lords and proprietors. Among the rest, in 1635, were granted to the duke of Hamilton all the lands between Narraganset and Connecticut rivers, and back into the country indefinitely.

This covered a part of the Earl of Warwick's patent, and occasioned some disputes in the colony. There were several attempts to revive the Hamilton claim, but they were never prosecuted. The patent of lord Say and Seal prevailed.

In consequence of the Pequot war, 1637, the English obtained the country east of the Dutch settlements, by right of conquest. The pursuit of the Indians led to an acquaintence with the lands on the seacoast, from Saybrook to Fairfield. It was reported to be a very fine country. Messrs. Eaton and Hopkins, two very respectable London merchants, and Mr. Davenport, a man of distinguished piety and abilities, with their company, who arrived this year from London, made choice of this part of the country as the place of their settlement. Their friends in Massachusetts, sorry to part with so valuable a company, laboured to dissuade them

* Winthrop.

from their purpose. Influenced, however, by the promising prospects which the country afforded, they determined to proceed. Accordingly, in the fall, they sent four men, who wintered at Quinipioke, and in March, 1638, a body sufficient for three towns removed from Boston, under the direction of Mr Eaton, and settled at New Haven, and laid the foundation of a flourishing colony of which Quinipioke, now New Haven was the chief town. The first public worship in this new plantation was attended on Lord's day, April 18, 1638, under a large spreading oak. The Rev. Mr. Davenport preached from Matth. iii. 1, on the temptations of the wilderness. Connecticut and New Haven formed themselves into distinct commonwealths, and remained so till their union in 1665.

The first church was gathered in New Haven in 1639, and consisted of seven members. These were chosen by the settlers, after Mr. Davenport had preached from the words of Solomon, "Wisdom hath builded her house, she hath hewed out her *seven* pillars." These men were indeed the pillars of the church, to whom the rest were added as they became qualified. They were also the court to try all civil actions.

Mr. Davenport; a father to this infant colony, was an eminent christian, a learned divine, and a great man. He was born at Coventry, in 1597, of respectable parents, and sent to college at Oxford, before he was fourteen years old. Thence he was called to preach in London, at the age of nineteen, where his rare accomplishments, and his courage in visiting the sick in the time of a terrible plague, soon brought him into notice. By his great industry and midnight studies, he became an universal scholar, and his sermons were distinguished by the labour with which they were prepared. In his delivery he had a gravity, an energy, a pleasantness, and engaging eloquence, not common among his brethren. His enemies allowed him to be an excellent *preacher*.

Finding himself obnoxious, and in danger from the ruling party in London, he convened the principal people of his charge, desiring their opinion and advice, acknowledging their right to him as their pastor, and declaring that no danger should drive him from any service for their benefit, which they should require or expect. With a noble disinterestedness of soul, which did them honour, and demonstrated the tenderness of their affection, they relieved him from his scruples of conscience; they advised him to resign his office for his own safety. Instead of enjoying the quiet he now expected, he found himself more officiously watched than ever. He therefore, in 1633, retired to Holland, where he was immediately invited to be a colleague of Mr. Paget, pastor of a church in Amsterdam. But very soon his objections against their promiscuous mode of baptizing children excited formidable opposition, and he early found that he must baptize children where was no charitable evidence of their belonging to christian parents, or give up his relation to his people; he was too well informed to entertain any doubts; he was too honest to hesitate. In 1635, he retired from his pulpit in Amsterdam, and opened a catechetical exercise at his lodgings, every Lord's day, in the afternoon, an hour after the public services of the city were over. But the popularity of his talents soon collecting considerable numbers, jealousies were indulged, and opposition broke forth. He returned to England, telling his friends, that he "thought God had carried him to Holland on purpose to bear witness against that promiscuous baptism, which bordered on a profanation of the holy ordinance."

It was an observation of his, that when a reformation of the church had been effected in any age or country, it was seldom that any advance was made afterward beyond the improvements of the first reformers. He observed, that Noah's ark might as easily be removed from Ararat, as people persuaded to proceed beyond the first remove of their leaders. This coincides with a remark of the celebrated Robinson. "The Calvinists," says he, "stick just where that great man left them."

Very soon after, in 1637, Mr. Davenport, with several eminent christians and their families, came over to New-England. "Among these were Mr. Eaton and Mr. Hopkins, two merchants of London, men of fair estates, and of great esteem for religion and wisdom in outward affairs."* When they arrived, they found the colony of Massachusetts agitated with the wickedness and absurdities of antinomian and enthusiastic opinions, the influence of a "bold" woman having shaken the pillars of the government, and threatened the existence of the churches. She held public assemblies at her house, and expounded the scriptures to them.*

Mr. Davenport arrived just before the synod met at Cambridge to consider the errors of the day. His influence there was very happy; at the close he declared the result, and preached a sermon from Phil. iii. 15, in which he "shewed the occasion of differences among christians, and with much wisdom and sound argument, persuaded to unity."*

In March, Mr. Davenport, Mr. Predden, and a brother of Mr. Eaton, all ministers of the gospel, sailed for Quinipioke, and with them many families removed from Massachusetts to settle there, having conceived a high opinion of the soil, and expecting to escape the power of a general governor, whom they feared would soon be sent. The

* Gov. Winthrop.

people of Massachusetts parted very reluctantly with these valuable brethren. Charlestown made them large offers to induce them to settle there. Newbury generously offered them their whole town; the legislature offered them any place they should choose, which had not already been granted.*

At his new plantation, afterward called New Haven, Mr. Davenport endeavoured to establish a civil and religious order more strictly according to the word of God, than he had seen exhibited in any other part of the world. He was an original genius, and the plan he adopted was his own: if success be any evidence of merit, he certainly has high claims to the veneration and gratitude of nations. There the famous church of New Haven, says his biographer, and also the neighbouring towns, enjoyed his ministry, his discipline, his *government*, and his *universal direction* for many years.†

The holiness, the watchfulness, the usefulness of his ministry, are worthy of remembrance among all those, who would have before them an example of ministerial excellence. His attention and influence extended to all the churches. He was a man of devotion, and it was a saying of his, that ejaculatory prayer was like arrows in the hands of the mighty; happy is the man who hath his quiver full of them. He was scrupulously careful in admitting persons to church communion. Church purity was one of the great objects of his life. He was persuaded there are many rules in the word of God, by which it may be judged, who are saints, and by which those, who admit others to gospel ordinances, are to be guided so as to separate between the precious and the vile.

* Winthrop. † Mather.

This is no more than every sect, and indeed all individuals, claim for themselves. The only difference is, they do not all fix on the same standard for admission to their communion, but all have their limits, beyond which they do not, and will not, pass to receive members to their communion.

He thought too much caution could not be used, where some persons think very little is necessary. His own words are: "The officers and brethren of the church are but men, who judge by the outward appearance; therefore their judgment is fallible, and hath been deceived, as in the reception of Annanias, Saphira, and Simon Magus. Their duty is to proceed, as far as men may by rule, with due moderation and gentleness to try those who offer themselves for fellowship, whether they be believers or not. When they have done all, hypocrites will creep in." He was remarkable for diligence in his studies; this was noticed by the Indians, who used to call him *the big study man*.

Mr. Davenport continued at New Haven till 1667, when, such was his vigour, though in his 69th year, such his fame in the churches, that he was invited to Boston to succeed a Cotton, a Norton, and a Wilson. He continued in his new situation only till March 15th, 1670, when by an apoplexy, he was called from his labours in the 72d year of his age.

The following account of this plantation is from one of our early writers.* "The government of New Haven, although the younger sister of the four, yet she is as beautiful as any of this brood of travellers, and *most* minding the end of her coming hither, to keep close to the rule of Christ both in doctrine and discipline; and it were to be wished her elder sister would follow her example to nurture up all her children accordingly."

* Wonderworking Providence.

CHAP. XI.

History of Connecticut continued; Character of Rev. Mr. Thomas Hooker.

The first settlers in New Haven had all things common; all purchases were made in the name and for the use of the whole plantation, and the lands were apportioned to each family, according to their number and original stock.

At their first election, in October, 1639, Mr. Theophilus Eaton was chosen governor for the first year. Their elections, by agreement, were to be annual, and the word of God their only rule in conducting the affairs of government in the plantation.

The confederation of the New-England colonies, formed and entered into by the four principal colonies of Massachusetts, Plymouth, Connecticut, and New Haven in 1643, continued in force till the time of Sir Edmund Andros, 1686, and were of great utility, both for defence against the aboriginals, and for harmonizing the public councils in church and state. At the time of this confederation the colonies of Connecticut and New Haven consisted of only three towns each.

The general court of New Haven this year established it as a fundamental article, that none be admitted as free burgesses but church members, and that none but such should vote at elections. They also ordained, that each town choose from among themselves judges who were professors of religion, to be a court, to have cognizance of all civil actions not exceeding twenty pounds; and of criminal cases where the punishment was, sitting in the stocks, whipping, and fining not exceeding five pounds. There was liberty of appeal from this court to the court of magistrates. The court of magistrates consisted of all the magistrates throughout the colony, who were to meet twice a year at New Haven, for the trial of all capital causes. Six made a quorum.

The general court was to consist of the governor, deputy governor, magistrates, and two representatives from each town. The annual election of officers was at that time established, and has ever since continued.

The unsettled state of the colony had prevented their establishing a code of laws. To supply this defect, the general court ordered "that the judicial laws of God, as they were delivered to Moses, and as they are a fence to the moral, being neither typical nor ceremonial, nor having any reference to Canaan, shall be accounted of moral equity, and generally bind all offenders, and be a rule to all the courts in this jurisdiction, in their proceedings against offenders, until they be branched out into particulars hereafter."

About this time a war broke out between the Mohegan and Narraganset Indians. A personal quarrel between Onkus, sachem of Mohegan, and Sequesson, sachem of Connecticut, was the foundation of the war.*

In consideration of the success and increase of the New-England colonies, and that they had been of *no charge* to the nation, and in prospect of their being in future very serviceable, the English parliament, March 10, 1643, granted them an exemption from all customs, subsidies and other duties, until further order.

In 1644, the Connecticut adventurers purchased of Mr. Fenwick, agent for lord Say and Seal, and lord Brook, their right to the colony of Connecticut, for £1600.

In 1647, died Mr. Thomas Hooker, a pillar of Connecticut colony, and a great light of the churches in this western

* Winthrop.

world. He was born at Marfield, in Leicestershire, 1586. He was educated at Emanuel college, Cambridge, in England, where he was afterwards promoted to a fellowship, in which office "he acquitted himself with such ability and faithfulness, as commanded universal admiration and applause." It was in this period of his life, that he had such deep convictions of his own lost state, and exposedness to the wrath of God, as filled his mind with anguish and horrour. With the singer of Israel he was ready to exclaim, "While I suffer thy terrours, O Lord, I am distracted."

After enduring this spirit of bondage for a considerable time, he received light and comfort, and his mind became powerfully and pleasantly attached to religious contemplations. It was now his custom, when retiring to rest at night, to select some particular promise of scripture, which he repeated and reflected upon in his waking hours. In this he found so much comfort and improvement, that he advised others to adopt the same course. He now determined to be a preacher of the gospel, and soon entered on the business in the vicinity of London. He was immediately distinguished for his ministerial talents, especially for comforting persons under spiritual troubles. Being disappointed as to a desired settlement at Dedham, he became a lecturer at Chelmsford, and an assistant to Mr. Mitchel, the incumbent of the place. This was in 1626. His lectures were soon thronged, and remarkable success attended his preaching. A reformation followed, not only in the town, but in the adjacent country. By a multitude of inns in the town, which are the ruin of any place, the people of Chelmsford had become notorious for their intemperance, and profanation of the sabbath. By the influence of Mr. Hooker's ministry, these vices were banished, and the sabbath visibly sanctified by the people.

This great blessing was continued to them but a short time. In about four years his difficulties, on account of his nonconformity, were so great, that he gave up his pulpit, and retired to a school, which he kept in his own house. Though his best employment was gone, happily his *influence* was not lost. This was all exerted for the benefit of the christian cause. He engaged the serious ministers in his vicinity to establish a monthly meeting for prayer and fasting, and theological conferences. By his influence several pious young ministers were settled around him, and others more confirmed in the system of genuine gospel truth. So great was his popularity at the time of his being silenced, that no less than forty-seven *conforming* ministers of the neighbourhood, who might have been expected to be in opposition to him, petitioned the bishop of London in his behalf. They say, that "they esteem and know the said Mr. Thomas Hooker to be for doctrine orthodox; for life and conversation, honest; for diposition, peaceable, and in no wise turbulent or factious." These powerful mediators could not prevail.

About the year 1630, he was bound over in a bond of £50 to appear before the high commission court, which bond he thought proper to forfeit by the advice of friends, a number of whom raised the money in his behalf. He then fled to Holland; on the passage the vessel in the night struck on a shoal of sand. Mr. Hooker, with remarkable confidence, assured them that they should all be preserved, and they were soon remarkably delivered. In Holland he preached two years at Delft. He was then called to Rotterdam, where he was employed with the celebrated Dr. Ames, between whom there was a mutual esteem and affection. Dr. Ames declared, that though he had been acquainted with many scholars of different nations, yet he had never met with Mr. Hooker's equal, either for preaching or disputation.

But not finding the satisfaction which he wished among the Dutch, and a number of his friends in England inviting him to accompany them to America, he returned to his native country to prepare for his voyage across the Atlantic. Soon was the news of his arrival spread, and the officers of the bishop were in pursuit of him. At one time they knocked at the door of the chamber where he and Mr. Stone were in conversation. Mr. Stone went to the door. The officer demanded whether Mr. Hooker was not there. "What Hooker?" replied Stone, "Do you mean Hooker who once lived at Chelmsford?" The officer answered, "Yes, he." "If it be he you look for," said Stone, "I saw him about an hour ago at such a house in the town; you had best hasten there after him." The officer took this evasion for a sufficient account, went his way, while Mr. Hooker concealed himself more securely till he went on board at the Downs; this was in 1633. Mr. Stone and Mr. Cotton were on board the same ship.

Mr. Hooker arriving at Cambridge, was received with open arms by those of his friends, who had come over the year before, when he uttered these words, "Now I live, if ye stand fast in the Lord." But multitudes following them, Newtown became too narrow for them; accordingly, in 1636, they removed to the fertile spot on the delightful banks of Connecticut river, which they called HARTFORD. There he was deservedly considered as the father and oracle of the colony. As a preacher he was remarkably animated and impressive; not only his voice, but his eyes, his hands, his every feature, spoke the holy ardour of his soul. All was life and reality in his descriptions. It was not that theatric flourish, which is exhibited by men panting for admiration, but that zeal, which is kindled by a coal from

God's altar. His moving addresses flowed from his own
exquisite relish of divine things; and an impassioned desire
of promoting them in the hearts of others. His success,
like his services, was eminent. A single instance or two
may be mentioned. A profane man once, for his diversion,
said to his companions, "Come let us go and hear what
bawling Hooker will say to us." For their sport they all
went to Chelmsford lecture. Soon conviction seized the
mind of the man. The word of God was "quick and powerful," and he retired with an awakened and distressed conscience, and by the subsequent instructions of Mr. Hooker,
he became a hopeful disciple of Jesus Christ; and afterward followed him a thousand leagues, that he might enjoy
his preaching.

At another time one of his opposers hired a person to play
on a fiddle in the porch or churchyard; but Mr Hooker's
vivacity and zeal were not in the least abated; when the
man went up to the door to hear what he said, his attention
was caught; conviction followed; he directly made his confession to Mr. Hooker, and ever after lived a devout life.
He had a surprising talent of reaching the consciences of
his hearers in the application of his discourses.

When at the land's end, he took his last view of England, saying "Farewell, England, I expect now no more
to see that religious zeal, and power of godliness, which I
have seen among professors in that land." He said that
adversity had slain its thousands; but prosperity its ten
thousands. He feared that those, who had been zealous
christians in the fire of persecution, would be cold in the
lap of peace. So exact were his observations of Providence, so attentive was he to the signs of the times, so confident of the answer of prayer, that "the secret of the Lord
was with him;" and the people in some instances viewed
him as a prophet. As a man of prayer, he was distinguished.

He would say, that "prayer was the principal part of a minister's work; by this he was to carry on the rest." Accordingly, he devoted one day in every month to private prayer and fasting, besides many such days, which he kept publicly with his people. It was his opinion, that if professors neglect these duties, iniquities will abound, and the love of many wax cold. His prayers in public were more fervent than lengthy; they were adapted to the occasion; as he proceeded, his ardour increased; and the close of his prayer was often a rapture of devotion. His people were often surprised with the remarkable answers to his prayers.

Though irascible in his natural make, he acquired a remarkable command of his temper. He was ready at all times to sacrifice his own apprehensions to the better reasons of others. The meanest of his brethren and children were treated by him with endearing condescension. An example occurs. Mr. Hooker, immediately after a neighbour of his had sustained some damage, met a boy notorious for such mischief, and began to accuse and chide him. The boy denied the charge. Mr. Hooker continued his angry lecture. "Sir," said the boy, "I see you are in a passion. I'll say no more to you," and ran off. Upon inquiry, Mr. Hooker found the boy could not be proved guilty; he therefore sent for the boy, and humbly made his confession; which with the good counsel he gave him made a lasting impression upon the mind of the lad. Yet when he was in the pulpit he appeared with such astonishing majesty and independence, it was pleasantly said of him, *He would put a king in his pocket.* Judges, and princes, and peasants equally shared in his solemn reproofs.

He had a remarkable talent of solving cases of conscience, and for this purpose he set apart one day in a week for any of his people to come and propose their scruples and difficulties. Though his own preaching was generally very practical and experimental, he wisely advised young ministers when first settled, to preach the whole system of divinity for their own benefit, as well as that of their people. He had a most happy method of governing his church. He would propound nothing to them till it had been previously considered by some of the principal brethren; if at any time he saw an altercation beginning in the church, he would delay the vote till another opportunity, before which he would visit, and generally gain over those, who had objected to the measure. He would say, "the elders must have a church in a church, if they would preserve the peace of the church." It was his desire to live no longer than he could perform the work of his place. His last sickness was short, during which he said little. Being asked his opinion on some important things, he replied, "I have not that work now to perform; I *have* declared the counsel of the Lord." One of his friends observed to him that he was going to receive his *reward*. "Brother," said he, "I am going to receive *mercy*." When the awful moment arrived, he closed his own eyes, and gently stroking his forehead, with a smile in his countenance, he gave a little groan, and expired, July 7, 1647.

The colony of Connecticut expressed their disapprobation of the use of tobacco, in an act of their general assembly at Hartford in 1647, wherein it was ordered, "That no person under the age of twenty years, nor any other that hath already accustomed himself to the use thereof, shall take any tobacco, until he shall have brought a certificate from under the hand of some who are approved for knowledge and skill in physic, that it is useful for him; and also that he hath received a license from the court, for the same. All others who had addicted themselves to the use of tobacco were, by the same court, prohibited taking it in any company, or at their labours, or on their travels, unless they were ten miles at least from any house, or more than once a day though not in company, on pain of a fine of *six pence* for each time; to be proved by one substantial evidence. The constable in each town to make presentment of such transgressions to the particular court, and, upon conviction, the fine to be paid without gainsaying."

Massachusetts and New Haven colonies were more severe with the Quakers, than Connecticut or Plymouth. Of the four, Connecticut was the most moderate. Severe laws were passed against them by the general court at New Haven, 1658.

Had the pious framers of these laws paid a due attention to the excellent advice of that sagacious doctor of the law, Gamaliel, they would perhaps have been prevented from the adoption of such severe and unjustifiable measures. This wise man, when his countrymen were about to be outrageous in persecuting the apostles, addressed them in the following words, which merit to be engraved in letters of gold: "*Refrain from these men, and let them alone; for if this counsel or this work be of men, it will come to nought; but if it be of God, ye cannot overthrow it; lest haply ye be found even to fight against God.*"* This divine maxim was but little attended to in times of persecution. Our ancestors seem to have left it to posterity to make the important discovery, that persecution is the direct method to multiply its objects. It must be acknowledged that they were men, that they did not rise superiour to *all* the prejudices and errors of the age in which they lived. Still they ought to be ranked among the best men of their age.

These people, who have been so much censured and ridiculed, had, perhaps, as many virtues as their posterity. And it would be wise in the moderns, who stand elevated upon the shoulders of their ancestors, with the book of their

* Acts, Chap. v.

experience spread before them, to imitate their virtues and to veil their faults.

The colonies of Connecticut and New Haven from their first settlement increased rapidly; tracts of land were purchased of the Indians, and new towns settled from Stamford to Stonington, and far back into the country, when in 1661, Major John Mason, as agent for the colony, bought of the natives all lands, which had not before been purchased by particular towns, and made a public surrendry of them to the colony, in the presence of the general assembly. Having done these things, the colonists petitioned king Charles II. for a charter, and their petition was granted. His majesty, on the 23d of April, 1662, issued his letters patent under the great seal, ordaining that the colony of Connecticut should forever hereafter, be one body corporate and politic, in fact and in name confirming to them their ancient grant and purchase, and fixing their boundaries as follows, viz. "All that part of his majesty's dominions in New-England, in America, bounded east by Narraganset river, commonly called Narraganset Bay, where the river falleth into the sea; and on the north by the line of Massachusetts plantation; and on the south by the sea, and in longitude, as the line of the Massachusetts colony, running from east to west, that is to say, from the said Narraganset Bay on the east, to the South Sea on the west part, with the islands thereunto belonging." This charter has ever since remained the basis of the government of Connecticut, which was originally the earl of Warwick's patent, 120 miles of two degrees in breadth, and extending from Narraganset Bay across the continent. Connecticut charter comprehended the same. But court construction in 1664, limited the 120 miles to the seacoast, instead of the two meridional degrees. New Haven people had actually made an emigration and settlement under lord Say and Seal at Delaware, near Philadelphia, in 1655, evidently showing that it was the original understanding that the earl of Warwick's patent extended two degrees in breadth below Massachusetts. But for the gratification of the duke of York, this was arbitrarily taken from the purchasers of lord Say and Seal's title, and erected into the colonies of New-York, New-Jersey, and Pennsylvania, by the duke.

Such was the ignorance of the Europeans, respecting the geography of America, that their patents extended they knew not where. Many of them were of doubtful construction, very often covered each other in part, and have produced innumerable disputes and mischiefs in the colonies, some of which are not settled to this day.

At the close of the revolution, Connecticut ceded all her charter claims west of Pennsylvania, to Congress,* reserving only a tract the width of the state of Connecticut, and 120 miles in length; bounded east, on the western line of Pennsylvania, and north by lake Erie, containing nearly *four millions* of acres. This cession was accepted by Congress, which established to Connecticut her title to these lands. The legislature of Connecticut, in 1793, granted to the sufferers in the several towns that were burnt during the war, a tract of half a million of acres, on the west end of this reservation; and in the summer of 1795, sold the remainder, consisting of about 3,300,000 acres, to Oliver Phelps, William Hart, and associates, for 1,200,000 dollars. This sum, by an act of the legislature of Connecticut, passed in June, 1795, is appropriated to the *support of schools* in the several societies constituted by law, within the state: and also, in such societies as may request it, and by leave of the general assembly, for the *support of the christian ministry and the public worship of God*.

* See resolves of Congress for Sept. 14, 1786.

The colony of New Haven, though unconnected with the colony of Connecticut, was comprehended within the limits of their charter, and, as they concluded, within their jurisdiction. But New Haven remonstrated against their claim, and refused to unite with them, until they should hear from England. It was not until the year 1665, when it was believed that the king's commissioners had a design upon the New England charters that these two colonies united.

In 1672, the laws of the colony were revised, and the general court ordered them to be printed; and also, "that every family should buy one of the law books."

In 1750, the laws of Connecticut were again revised, and published in a small folio volume of 258 pages. Dr. Douglass observes, "that they were the most natural, equitable, plain, and concise *code* of laws, for plantations, hitherto extant."

There has been a revision of them since the peace of 1783, in which they were greatly and very judiciously simplified.

The years 1675 and 1676 were distinguished by the wars with Philip and his Indians, and with the Narragansets, by which the colony was thrown into great distress and confusion. The inroads of the enraged savages were marked with cruel murders, with fire and devastation.

Connecticut has ever made rapid advances in population. There have been more emigrations from this, than from any of the states, and yet it is full of inhabitants. No person qualified by law is prohibited from voting. He who has the most merit, not he who has the most money, is generally chosen into public office. As proof of this, it is to be observed, that many of the citizens of Connecticut, from the humble walks of life, have risen to the first offices in the state, and filled them with dignity and reputation. That base business of electioneering, which is so directly calculated to introduce wicked and designing men into office, is yet but little known in Connecticut. A man who wishes to be chosen into office, acts wisely for that end when he keeps his desires to himself.

Connecticut had but a small proportion of citizens, who did not join in opposing the oppressive measures of Great Britain, and was active and influential, both in the field and in the cabinet, in bringing about the revolution. Her soldiers were applauded by the commander in chief, for their bravery and fidelity.

The revolution, which so essentially affected the government of most of the colonies, produced no very perceptible alteration in the government of Connecticut. While under the jurisdiction of Great Britain, they elected their own governors, and all subordinate civil officers, and made their own laws. Connecticut has ever been a republic, and perhaps as perfect and happy a republic, as ever existed. She has proceeded in her old track, both as to government and manners; and, by these means, has avoided some of those convulsions, which have rent other states into violent parties, producing opposition, insurrection and war.

At the anniversary election of governor and other public officers, in all the New England states excepting in Rhode Island, a sermon is preached, which is published at the expense of the state. On these occasions a great concourse of respectable citizens, particularly of the clergy, are collected from every part of the state.

Connecticut, as well as Massachusetts, has been highly distinguished in having a succession of governors, eminent both for their religious and political accomplishments.

CHAP. XII.

Settlement of Rhode-Island; this colony refused admittance into the confederation; Narraganset Indians surrender their country to the king of England; Roman Catholics; Charter surrendered.

MOTIVES of the same kind with those, which occasioned the settlement of several other states, gave birth to Rhode-Island. The emigrants from England, who came to Massachusetts, though they did not perfectly agree in religious sentiments, had been tolerably united by their common zeal against the ceremonies of the church of England. But when they were removed from ecclesiastical courts, and possessed a charter allowing liberty of conscience, they fell into disputes and contentions among themselves.

The true grounds of religious liberty were not understood by any sect. While all disclaimed persecution for the sake of conscience, a regard for the public peace, and the preservation of the church of Christ from infection, together with the obstinacy of the heretics, was urged in justification of that, which, stripped of all its disguises, the light of nature, and the laws of Christ, in the most solemn manner condemn.

Mr. Roger Williams, a Puritan minister, came over to New-England in 1631, and settled at Salem, assistant to the Rev. Mr. Skelton. His settlement was opposed by the magistrates, because he refused to join with the church, at Boston, unless they would make a public declaration of their repentance for maintaining communion with the church of England, while in their native country. In consequence Mr. Williams removed to Plymouth, where he remained assistant to Mr. Smith three years, or as others say, two, and others, not one; when he disagreed with some influential characters in that town, and by invitation returned to Salem and succeeded Mr. Skelton, lately deceased. His settlement was still opposed by the magistrates, who charged him with maintaining, "That it is not lawful for a godly man to have communion in family prayer, or in an oath, with such as they judge unregenerate;" therefore he refused the oath of fidelity, and taught others to follow his example; "that it is not lawful for an unregenerate man to pray; that the magistrate has nothing to do in matters of the first table; that there should be a general and unlimited toleration of all religions; that to punish a man for following the dictates of his conscience was persecution; that the patent which was granted by king Charles was invalid, and an instrument of injustice which they ought to renounce, being injurious to the natives, the king of England having no power to dispose of their lands to his own subjects."* On account of these sentiments, and for refusing to join with the Massachusetts churches, he was at length banished the colony, as a disturber of the church and commonwealth.

He left his house, wife and children at Salem in the winter. Fortunately for Mr. Williams, he had cultivated an acquaintance with the Indians, and learned their language. Before he left the colony, he had privately treated with Canonicus and Osamaquin, two Narraganset sachems, for a tract of land within their territories, provided he should be under the necessity of settling among them. These circumstances, together with the advice of governor Winthrop, induced him, with four of his friends, after his banishment, to direct his course toward Narraganset Bay.

He and his companions established themselves first at Secunk or Seekhonck, now Rehoboth. But that place being

* H. Adams.

within the bounds of Plymouth colony, governor Winslow, in a friendly manner, advised them to remove to the other side of the river, where the lands were not covered by any patent. Accordingly, in 1636, they crossed Seekhonck river, and landed among the Indians, by whom they were hospitably received, and thus laid the foundation of a town, which, "from a sense of God's merciful providence to him in his distress," Mr. Williams called PROVIDENCE. Here the little colony were soon after joined by a number of others, and though they were secured against the Indians by the terror of the English, yet, for a considerable time, they suffered much from fatigue and want; but they enjoyed liberty of conscience, and the consolation of having 'provided a refuge for persons persecuted for conscience sake.''

Unhappy religious dissentions still prevailed in Massachusetts; and from a zeal for the purity of the faith, governor Winthrop strove to exterminate the opinions, which he disapproved. For this purpose, on the 30th of August, 1637, a synod was convened at Newtown, (now Cambridge) to whom eighty erroneous opinions were presented; these were debated and unanimously condemned. At a court holden at the same place, the following October, Wheelright, Mrs. Hutchinson, and Underhill, the leading characters, who had embraced these errors, were banished, and several others were censured for seditious conduct. A number, who had signed a seditious petition to the general court, in which they charge them with having condemned the truth of Christ, who refused to retract, were disarmed. Of these, fifty eight belonged to Boston, six to Salem, three to Newbury, five to Roxbury, two to Ipswich, and two to Charlestown.

The subsequent election of civil officers was carried by a party spirit, excited by religious controversy; but the orthodox party maintained the ascendancy, and Mr. Winthrop was re-elected governor. Those who were banished by the court, joined by a number of their friends, left the colony, and went in quest of a new place for settlement. They first proceeded to Providence, where they were kindly received by Mr. Williams, and with whom they remained for some time.

In March, 1638, two sachems, by virtue of their authority, and in consideration of fifty fathoms of white beads, sold to Mr. Coddington (one of the most respectable of these exiles) and his associates, the great island of Aquidneck, and the other isles in Narraganset bay, except two, which had been previously sold. The natives soon after agreed, upon receiving ten coats and twenty hoes, to remove before the next winter. The largest island was soon after called Rhode-Island. Having thus acquired a title and possession on considerations, which gave satisfaction to the original owners, they here established themselves; and copying the conduct of their neighbours, they formed a similar association for the purposes of civil government. Though the numbers associated were few, yet the soil being fruitful, and the climate agreeable, many persons soon resorted where they found protection, and the island, in a few years, became so populous, as to send out colonists to the adjacent shores. The colony elected Mr. Coddington their judge and chief magistrate. This gentleman came to America in 1630, and settled at Boston as a merchant. After his removal to Rhode-Island, he embraced the sentiments of the Friends, and became the father of that denomination of Christians in that colony. Their yearly meeting was held in his house, till his death, in 1688. Mr. John Clarke was another principal character among the exiles; for the sake of enjoying liberty of conscience, he voluntarily abandoned the colony of Massachusetts, and settled in Rhode-Island, where in 1644 he founded a Baptist church.

The first settlement on Rhode-Island was made at the north end, and called Portsmouth. In 1639, another settlement was begun at the southwest part of the island, on a fine harbour, which they called Newport. From the convenience of this harbour, the fertility and pleasantness of the island, and the wealth of the first settlers, this place had a rapid growth, and in a few years became the capital of the colony. The government, which they established was of the democratic kind. The chief magistrate and four assistants were invested with part of the executive powers; the remainder, with the legislative authority, was exercised by the body of the people in town meetings.

The colonies at Providence and Rhode-Island, at different periods, received large accessions from the denominations of Baptists and Friends, from the other colonies. This colony was settled on a "plan of entire religious liberty; men of every denomination being equally protected and countenanced, and enjoying the honours and offices of government."

The inefficacy of a voluntary government, and the want of a patent to legalize their proceedings, was soon experienced at Providence and Rhode-Island. Accordingly in the year 1643, they sent Mr. Roger Williams to England, as their agent, to procure for them a charter from the crown. On his arrival at London, he found that king Charles I. had been driven from his capital; he of course applied to those, who had assumed the power. Sir Henry Vane, his former associate and friend in America, received him kindly, and aided his views. In March, 1644, through the earl of Warwick, then governor and admiral of all the plantations, he obtained from parliament "a free and absolute charter of civil incorporation of Providence plantations in Narraganset Bay," investing the inhabitants with the requisite authority to govern themselves, according to the laws of England.

Mr. Williams was well received by some of the leading members of Parliament, and when he was about to embark for America, they gave him a letter of recommendation to the governor and assistants of Massachusetts, in which they represented the merits of Mr. Williams, and advised to the performance of all friendly offices toward him. This letter had the effect to ameliorate the differences, which had subsisted between Mr. Williams and the Massachusetts colony; and there was afterwards a profession of christian love and mutual correspondence between them. Yet while Mr. Williams retained what were deemed dangerous principles, the governor and assistants of Massachusetts thought it inexpedient to grant him liberty of "ingress and egress," lest the people should be drawn away with his erroneous opinions.

When in 1643, the dangers and necessities of the New-England colonies induced them to think of forming a confederacy for their mutual support and defence, Providence and Rhode-Island plantations were desirous of uniting in the plan; but Massachusetts, disliking their religious sentiments, opposed their motion, and refused them a seat in the convention for forming the confederacy. Thus forsaken of their neighbours, they found it necessary to devise other means of safety. They accordingly cultivated the friendship of the neighbouring sachems with assiduity and success, and in a short time acquired such an influence with them, as to procure from the Narraganset chiefs in 1644, a formal surrender of their country to king Charles I. in right of his crown, in consideration of his protecting them against their enemies. This territory was afterwards called the *King's Province.*

The people of these plantations, thus empowered to manage their own affairs, in the true spirit of democracy, convened an assembly in May, 1647, composed of the body of freemen, in the several plantations. Several salutary regulations were adopted. The executive power, by this assembly, was vested in a President. This form of government, so agreeable to their inclinations and views, they did not long enjoy in tranquillity. It was suspended in October, 1652, by an order of the council of state for the commonwealth. The parliament wished to establish here those plans of reformation, which they attempted in Massachusetts, and which they actually effected in Virginia and Maryland. But Providence and Rhode-Island, deriving advantage from the distractions, which soon after ensued in England, resumed its form of government. This it continued to enjoy without interruption, till the Restoration.

That event gave great satisfaction to these plantations. They immediately proclaimed Charles II and not long after sent Mr. Clarke, as their agent, to the court of that monarch, to solicit for a patent, which was deemed in New-England so essential to real jurisdiction; and in Sept. 1662, he obtained the object of his wishes. Yet, owing to the opposition of Connecticut, the present charter was not finally passed till July, 1663. The emigrations, beforementioned, from Massachusetts, and the subsequent settlements at Providence and Rhode-Island, were recapitulated; "which being convenient for commerce," says the patent, "may much advance the trade of this realm, and greatly enlarge the territories thereof;" and being willing to encourage the undertaking of his subjects, and to secure to them the free enjoyment of their civil and religious rights, which belonged to them as Englishmen, he conferred on them ample liberty in religion, and special privileges with regard to jurisdiction. The patentees, and such, as should be admitted free of the society, were incorporated by the name of "The governor and company of the English colony of Rhode-Island and Providence." The supreme or legislative power was invested in an assembly; the constituent members were to consist of the governor, the assistants, and such of the freemen, as should be chosen by the towns; but the governor, or deputy governor, and six assistants, were to be always present. Thus constituted, the assembly was empowered to make ordinances, and forms of government and magistracy, for the rule of the lands and inhabitants; so that they should not be repugnant, but agreeable to the laws of England, considering the nature of the place and people; to erect such courts of justice for determining all acts within the colony, as they should think fit; to regulate the manner of elections to places of trust, and of freemen to the assembly; to impose lawful punishments, pecuniary and corporal, according to the course of other corporations within the realm; and to pardon such criminals, as they should think fit. That the inhabitants might be religiously and civilly governed, a governor, deputy governor; and ten assistants, were appointed for the management of their affairs; and they were authorized to execute the ordinances beforementioned, which every one was commanded to obey.

The governor and company were enabled to transport such merchandise and persons, as were not prohibited by any statute of the kingdom; and "paying such customs as are, and ought to be paid for the same." They were empowered to exercise martial law, and, upon just causes, to invade and destroy the native Indians and other enemies. There was granted to the governor and company, and their successors, "that part of the dominions of the crown, in New-England, containing the islands in Narraganset bay, and the countries and parts adjacent; to be holden of the manor of East Greenwich, in common soccage." The inhabitants of those territories and their children, were declared fully entitled to the same immunities, as if they had resided or had been born within the realm; and to guard against the experienced oppressions of Massachusetts, they were enabled to pass and repass through any other English colonies, and to traffic with them. But with this proviso, that nothing should hinder any subjects whatsoever from fishing on the coasts of New-England.

Such was the substance of the charter of Rhode-Island, and such were the privileges conferred by it. The government of this province was administered to the satisfaction of Charles II. during the remainder of his reign. By the charter of this Province, "None were at any time thereafter to be molested, for any difference in matters of religion;" yet the *first* assembly that convened under this charter, in March, 1663, enacted a law declarative of their privileges, in which they say, "that all men of competent estates, and of civil conversation, *Roman Catholics only excepted*, shall be admitted freemen, or may choose or be chosen, colonial officers." By this act, persecution of the Roman Catholics immediately commenced, by depriving them of the rights of citizens, in violation of their charter privileges. This is a remarkable fact in the history of a people, who have been zealous for universal freedom of opinion in matters of religion.

Upon the accession of James II. to the throne, the colonists of Rhode-Island and Providence immediately transmitted to him an address, in which they acknowledged their subjection to him, pledged themselves to obey his authority, and asked, in return, for the protection of their chartered privileges. This address did not, however, avail to protect them against the plans of reform in New-England, resolved on by the British court. Articles of "high misdemeanor were exhibited to the lords of the committee of foreign plantations, against the governor and company of the colony of Rhode-Island and Providence," in which, among other things, they are charged with neglecting to keep an authentic record of their laws; with refusing to permit the inhabitants to have copies of them; with rasing or cancelling their laws as they please, without consent of the assembly, and with administering the government and justice, without taking the legal oaths. These charges were referred to the attorney general, July, 1685, with orders immediately to issue a writ of *quo warranto* against their patent. The governor and company were served with a regular notice of the process, which had been issued against them, and they were put upon their defence; they declined standing a suit with their king. In full assembly, they passed an act formally surrendering to his majesty their charter, with all the powers it contained. This act, it is said, "was afterwards made way with, agreeably to a common practice."*

The governor and company afterwards assembled, and on serious consideration of the suit instituted against them, agreed upon an address to his majesty, in which they pray, that their charter privileges, civil and religious, might be continued; that "all things wherein they have been weak and short, through ignorance, may be remitted and pardoned." They conclude, by "prostrating their *all* at his majesty's feet, with entire resolution to serve him with faithful hearts." Such servile language was improper for freemen to use, or for the ruler of a free people to receive. It failed of its intended effect. No sooner was the address received, than the committee of the colonies, with the approbation of the king, ordered, that Sir Edmund Andros, the governor of Massachusetts, should demand the surrender of their charter, and govern them in the manner the other colonies of

* Chalmers.

New-England were governed. At the same time they were assured of his majesty's protection, and of his determination to exercise no other authority over them, than what was common to the other plantations. Accordingly, in December, 1686, Andros formally dissolved the government of Rhode-Island, broke their seal, assumed the reins of government, and selected five of the citizens, and formed them into a legislative council. This state of things continued scarcely two years, when the revolution of 1688, put an end to the tyrannic authority of Andros, in this and the other colonies. Their charter was resumed, and has ever since continued to be the basis of their government.

CHAP. XIII.

War with the Pequot Indians.

THIS is a dismal section of our history. The time has been, when pious christians had so lost sight of their Saviour's precepts and examples as to engage in unnecessary war. Excepting this war of extermination, which lasted but a few days, our forefathers lived about fifty years in peace with the Indians; and had they as christians duly considered the importance of peace, the preciousness of human life, and that war partakes of the spirit of murder, and had they taken suitable care to dispense perfect justice to their red brethren, to soothe, to satisfy, and instruct them, probably this, and the subsequent wars might have been prevented. Prudence and good sense may persuade these people, and preserve their friendship. "The differences we have had with them have generally been more owing to *us* than to them."* Did not truth and impartiality forbid, we

* Du Pratz.

could wish this chapter erased from the volume. The reader may, however, gain some benefit; he may learn how dreadful is a spirit of war; he may learn how far good men, while ignorant and under the influence of an erroneous conscience, may fall short of that temper which is required in the gospel. While you shudder at the narrative of blood and murder, you may with new fervour pray the God of peace, to hasten the day, when "nations shall learn war no more," when Jesus shall reign a thousand years of peace.

In 1634, the Indians murdered Capt. Stone and Capt. Norton, with six others, in a bark sailing up Connecticut river. The next year they killed part of a crew, who had been shipwrecked on Long Island. In the year 1636, at Block Island, they killed Mr. Oldham. To obtain satisfaction for these injuries, the governor and council of Massachusetts sent ninety men, who sailed under the command of captains Endicott, Underhill, and Turner. They had commission to put to death the men of Block Island, but to spare the women and children, to make them prisoners, and take possession of the Island. Then they were to visit the Pequots, and demand the murderers of Capt. Stone, and the other English; and a thousand fathom of wampum for damages, and some of their children for hostages. Force was to be employed, if they refused. They arrived in September at Block Island; the wind being northeast, and a high surf, it was difficult landing. About 40 Indians gave a shot from their bows, and fled. The island was covered with bushes, but had no good timber. They traversed it for two days, burned two villages of wigwams, and some corn, of which there was about 200 acres, and then retired.

Thence they directed their course for Connecticut river; where they took twenty men, and two shallops, to assist them, and returned to Pequot river, (now the Thames) "landing in much danger, the shore being high, ragged rocks." Three hundred natives were soon assembled, who trifled with the demand of Endicott, encouraging him, yet delaying to observe his demand, when he assured them he had come for the purpose of fighting. They immediately withdrew; when they had proceeded beyond musket shot, he pursued them; two of them were killed, and others wounded; the English burned their wigwams, and returned. The next day they went on shore the west side of the river, burned their wigwams, spoiled their canoes, and returned to Narraganset, and thence to Boston.

After the troops left Pequot river, the twenty men of Saybrook lay wind bound, when they undertook to fetch away the Indians' corn. Having carried one load, and supplied themselves a second time, the Indians assaulted them; they returned the fire, which was continued most of the afternoon. One of the English was wounded. Two days after, five men at Saybrook were attacked in the field, one was taken prisoner, the others fled, one having five arrows in him. A fortnight after, three men in the same neighbourhood were fowling, two of whom were taken prisoners.

October 21, Miantonomo, the sachem of Narraganset, came to Boston with two sons of Canonicus, another sachem, "and twenty sanops." Twenty musketeers met him at Roxbury. The sachems declared, that they had always loved the English, and desired firm peace with them; that they would continue the war with the Pequots and their confederates, till they were subdued, and desired that we would do so; that they would deliver our enemies to us or kill them; and desiring that if any of theirs should kill our cattle, that we would not kill them, but cause them to make satisfaction. This was the substance of the treaty established. They were also to return fugitive servants, to furnish guides for our troops when they marched against the Pequots, and they were not to approach our plantations, during the war, without some Englishman or known Indian.

About this time the governor of Plymouth wrote to Massachusetts, that *they* had occasioned a war by *provoking* the Pequots, casting a reflection on the late expedition. It was replied, that they could not safely pursue them without a guide, that they went not to make war, but to obtain justice, that they had killed thirteen men, and burned sixty wigwams, which was sufficient satisfaction for four or five, whom they had murdered. About the middle of October, a bark coming down Connecticut river, one Tilly, the master, went on shore to kill fowls, and was taken prisoner. They cut off his hands and feet, after which he lived three days. At the same time, they killed another man in a canoe.

The next spring the colony of Connecticut declared their dislike of the Pequot expedition, expressing their hope, that Massachusetts would continue the war, and offered assistance. Capt. Underhill, with twenty men, was sent to Saybrook to defend it against the Dutch and Indians. In May, the Indians at Weathersfield killed six men, and three women, and took two maids prisoners, and killed twenty cows.*

The Indians becoming more daring, and the danger increasing, it was universally resolved to make a vigorous effort to repel the evil. Their success in flying from the English at Groton, had greatly encouraged them. They boasted of this at Saybrook fort, that they had deluded the English, that their God "was all one flye," that "the Englishman was all one squaw."

Massachusetts raised one hundred and sixty men,† beside forty‡ previously sent to Narraganset; Mr. Stoughton was

* Winthrop.   † Mather.   ‡ Winthrop.

the commander, and Mr. Wilson, of Boston, their chaplain, "to sound the silver trumpet of the gospel before them." These two were designated by lot, with public invocation of God. Connecticut raised ninety men, under the command of Capt. Mason. Captain Underhill joined the expedition with nineteen of the garrison. Uncas, the sachem of the Mohegans, lent his assistance.

On their way to the Pequot country, from Saybrook they sent out a party of Indians, who met seven Pequots, of whom they killed five and took one; him they tortured, and set all their heads on the fort; so contagious are malignant passions. This was done, because they had tortured some of our men taken captive.

The army sailed from Connecticut river, passed Pequot, or the Thames, and entered the Narraganset or Mistick. They were joined by five hundred Narraganset Indians; but as the army marched to the intended scene of action, these daring sons of war fell in the rear or fled. So terrible was the name of Sassacus, who was in one of the two forts where the Pequots had assembled, and which the English designed immediately to assault: "Sassacus," they said, "was all one a God, nobody could kill him." The army silently moved by the light of the moon toward the nearest fort. Wequash, their guide and spy, brought them word, that the Pequots in the fort were all asleep. Seeing the English vessels pass them in the course of the day, supposing they had returned home in terror, they had sung and danced with joy till midnight, and were now buried in deep sleep. Captain Mason approached the east side and Underhill the west side of the fort; a dog barked; the centinel awoke: he cried, *Wannux, Wannux*, i.e. English, English; the troops soon entered the fort, which consisted of trees set in the ground, two winding passages being left open; a dreadful carnage followed. Instantly the guns of the English were directed to the floors of the wigwams, which were covered with their sleeping inhabitants. Terrible was the consternation to be roused from their dreams by the blaze and thunder of the English musketry; if they came forth, the English swords waited to pierce them; if they reached the pallisadoes, and attempted to climb over, the fatal balls brought them down; their combustible dwellings, crowded together, were soon in flames; many of them roasted and burned to death, rather than venture out; others fled back to their burning houses, and were consumed, to escape the English swords.* The English endeavoured to save the women and children alive; which the men observing, in anguish and dying terror, cried. *I Squaw, I Squaw*, in hopes of finding mercy; but their hour was come. Their dwellings being wrapped in fire, the army retired and surrounded the fort: to escape was impossible; like a herd of deer they fell before the deadly weapons of the English. The earth was soon drenched in their blood and covered with their bodies. In a few minutes, five or six hundred of them lay gasping in their blood, or silent in death. The darkness of the forest, the blaze of the dwellings, the rivulets of blood, the ghastly looks of the dead, the groans of the dying, the shrieks of the women and children, the yells of the friendly savages, presented a scene of sublimity and horror indescribably dreadful.

The same morning, May 20, 1637, their pinnaces arrived with provisions in Pequot harbour to relieve their necessities. They were in the country of their enemies; the mighty Sassacus and his garrison were near, ready to fall upon them; they were parched with thirst, and fainting with hunger. But they directed their march for Pequot harbour, which they considered six miles distant. On the way they

* Trumbull.

were assailed by three hundred savages, furious as bears bereaved of their whelps. Being repelled with courage, they retired; when they found their slaughtered friends at the fort, their grief and madness were indescribable; they stamped the ground; they tore their hair; they roared and howled like wolves of the forest.

The Massachusetts troops, under Captain Stoughton, did not arrive till the latter part of June. By the assistance of the Narragansets, they surrounded a swamp and took eighty captives; thirty of them were men, all of whom excepting two sachems, they killed. Those who had escaped from the Connecticut forces retired to the fort of Sassacus; they upbraided him with their misfortunes; they separated; they were scattered over the country. All the other tribes exulted in their fall, attacked and killed them wherever they found them, or sent them to the English as prisoners, or, having killed them, sent their heads and limbs.

Captain Stoughton and his company pursued a party beyond Connecticut river, but not finding them, he returned to Pequot river, where he heard of a hundred; he marched, found and killed twenty-two men, took two sachems and a number of women and children, thirty of whom were given to the Narragansets, forty-eight were sent to Boston, who were placed in different families.

A few days after, Capt. Stoughton being joined by Capt. Mason and troops of Connecticut, sailed for New Haven with eighty men. They killed six Indians, and took two. At a head of land east of New Haven, now Guilford, they beheaded two sachems, and called the place Sachem's Head, which name it still retains. A Pequot prisoner had his life given him on condition of his finding Sassacus; he found him, and brought the intelligence to the English; but Sassacus suspecting the mischief, with Mononotto, another famous chief, fled to the Mohawks. In a swamp, three miles west of Fairfield, eighty of their men and two hundred women and children had concealed themselves. Capt. Stoughton by information from a Pequot spy, whom he had employed, discovered them; Lieutenant Davenport and two or three others endeavouring to enter, were badly wounded. A fire was kept up for several hours, when the Indians desired a parley and offered to yield. They came forth in small numbers, during the afternoon, in which time two hundred women and children had resigned themselves, with the sachem of the place; but night coming on, the men would not come out, and declared they would fight; accordingly, a constant firing was kept up all night. Toward morning, it being very dark, the Pequots crept silently out of the swamp and fled. So terminated the Pequot war, and Pequot nation. Saesacus, with twenty or thirty attendants, had fled to the Mohawks, who treacherously violating all the laws of hospitality, slew them, being hired as it was supposed by the Narragansets. A part of the skin and hair of Sassacus they sent to Massachusetts. So vanish the tribes of men in sad succession. In the course of a few months one of the most formidable nations, then in New-England, was swept away; eight or nine hundred of them had been killed; many were fugitives in the forests, and a remnant, to save themselves from cruel deaths by their own countrymen, submitted to the English. Captain Stoughton, on his way home, landed once more at Block Island, had an interview with the natives, who submitted themselves tributaries to the English.

In August, the troops returned to Boston, having lost but two of their number, both of whom died with sickness, A thanksgiving was observed through the colonies on account of their complete victory over their enemies.

The day previous to the dreadful storming of the fort at Mistick, had been kept as a day of fasting and prayer. This or some other circumstances attending that bloody scene, wonderfully impressed the mind of *Wequash*, the guide of the English, with the power of the Englishman's God. He went about the colony of Connecticut with bitter lamentations, that he did not know Jesus Christ, the Englishman's God. The good people faithfully instructed him concerning the religion of the gospel; after which he made a most serious profession; he forsook his savage vices, went up and down the country preaching Christ to his benighted countrymen; he bore a thousand abuses from them, and finally submitted to death for his religion.

CHAP. XIV.

Earthquake; Uncas visits Gov. Winthrop; Hampton settled; Harvard College founded; Indian plot at Kennebec; settlement of Rowley; character of Rev. Ezekiel Rogers.

The year 1638 was remarkable for a great earthquake throughout New England. This earthquake, as did that also of 1627, which was equally violent and extensive, constituted a remarkable era, that was long remembered and referred to by the pious inhabitants of these infant colonies.

This year, Uncas, from Mohegan, made governor Winthrop a visit at Boston; in his polite address, after delivering his present, laying his hand on his heart, he said, "This heart is not mine, but yours; I have no men, they all yours; command me at y difficult service, and I will perform it; I will not believe any Indian's words against the English; if any man kill an Englishman, I will put him to death, let him be ever so dear to me." The governor gave him "a fair red coat, provision for his journey, and a letter of protection, when he departed highly gratified."*

In 1638, Hampton, in New-Hampshire, was settled; its Indian name was Winnecumet; a church was gathered, and a minister chosen the same year. Among the ministers of Hampton, was the Rev. Daniel Gookin, ordained in 1710.

In 1639, the college at Cambridge was founded. As soon as our pious and enlightened ancestors, the first settlers of New-England, had erected for themselves, comfortable dwellings, provided necessaries for their support, reared convenient places for the worship of God, and settled the civil government, their next object was to establish an institution of science for the benefit of their "posterity, dreading an illiterate ministry," when the learned ministers they then enjoyed should sleep in the dust.† Two years before, in 1636, the general court had voted £400 for the establishment of a public school; but this year the Rev. JOHN HARVARD, a worthy minister of Charlestown, died, and bequeathed one half of his estate, amounting to above 1800 dollars, to this infant seminary. Thus endowed, the school was erected into a college, and assumed the name of its principal benefactor, HARVARD; and Newtown, in compliment to the college, and in memory of the place where many of our fathers received their education, was called CAMBRIDGE.‡ In 1640, the legislature granted the income of Charlestown ferry, as a perpetual revenue to the college, and the same year the Rev. Henry Dunster was appointed the first president, a preceptor or professor having previously had the instruction of the youth.

The first commencement was attended two years after, when nine students took the degree of bachelor of arts.

* Gov. Winthrop.   † New-England's First Fruits.
‡ Rev. Mr. Holmes's History of Cambridge.

Most of the legislature were present, and dined in the college with the scholars for their encouragement, which gave content to all.* The next year the general court, which had previously committed the government of the college to all the magistrates, and the ministers of the three nearest churches, with the president, passed an act by which all the magistrates and the teaching elders of the six nearest towns, with the president, were appointed forever the governors of that seminary. They met for the first time in December, and chose a treasurer.

In 1650, the college received its first charter from the general court, appointing a corporation consisting of seven persons, a president, five fellows, and a treasurer, to have a perpetual succession by election to their offices. Their style is, *The President and Fellows of Harvard College.* To this body was committed all the estate of the college; they have the care of all donations; the board of overseers continue a distinct branch; united, they form the legislature of the college.

In 1669, when the hearts of good men were roused to seek the spiritual welfare of their pagan neighbours, a brick edifice, thirty feet long, and twenty wide, was erected at Cambridge, for an Indian college. Numbers began to prepare for college in the school; several entered; but death and other events interposed, so that only one ever attained academical honours. The design was prudent and noble, but Providence frowned on the execution.

The executive government consists of the president, three professors, four tutors, a librarian and regent. The divinity professorship was founded in 1722, and the mathematical professorship four years after, both by the noble generosity of Mr. Thomas Hollis, of London, merchant. The pro-

* Winthrop.

fessorship of Hebrew, and other oriental languages, was founded in 1765, by the Hon. THOMAS HANCOCK, Esq. The professorship of Rhetoric and Oratory, founded by the late NICHOLAS BOYLSTON, Esq. of Boston, and that of Natural History by private subscription, have lately come into operation. Professors on these four cations deliver public lectures to all the students assembled, beside giving more private instructions to each class separately. Happy would it be for all the colleges had they such professorships. A foundation is laid in part for a professorship of natural religion, moral philosophy, and civil polity, from the estate of the late Hon. JOHN ALFORD, Esq. of Charlestown, which is not yet in operation. The late governor BOWDOIN gave £400 to the university, the interest of which is to be applied in premiums, for the advancement of useful and polite literature among the residents and graduates of the college.

In the year 1782, three medical professorships were established, viz. a professorship of anatomy and surgery; a professorship of the theory and practice of physic; a professorship of chymistry and materia medica. The funds of the two first were left by the late Dr. Ezekiel Hersey, of Hingham, his brother, the late Dr. Abner Hersey, of Barnstable; and the late Mrs. Sarah Derby, widow of Dr. Hersey, of Hingham; afterward the wife and widow of the late Richard Derby, Esq. of Salem. The late Dr. John Cummings, of Concord, added to the fund for the professor of the theory and practice of physic. The fund for the professor of chymistry and materia medica, was left by the late William Erving, Esq. All these professorships take the names of their founders.

For a number of years before the revolution, there were, generally, in the university from 180 to 190 undergraduates. During the war, the numbers were much less; since the war, they have been gradually increasing, and in 1804,

P

there were 220 undergraduates: in 1808, about 200; and in 1820, nearly 300. Indigent students are much assisted in their education.

In 1639, a printing office was set up at Cambridge by Mr. Daye, at the charge of Mr. Glover, who died on his passage to America. The first thing here printed was the freeman's oath; the next an almanack made for New-England by Mr. Pierce, mariner; the next the Psalms, newly turned into metre, now obsolete, though once used in all the churches; and called the *New-England Psalms*.

At Kennebec, this year, the Indians, being in want of food, determined to kill the English at the Plymouth trading house there, and seize the provisions. A number of them, to execute the business, entered the house in their usual manner; Mr. Willet the master being engaged in reading the Bible, his countenance more solemn than at other times, and not looking at them, nor noticing them, as they expected, they instantly retired and told their companions, their plot was discovered; who inquired how that was possible; they replied, that it was certain from Willet's countenance, and they supposed he had discovered it by the book he was reading; so the Plymouth people escaped without harm.[*]

In the spring of this year Rowley was settled by Mr. Ezekiel Rogers, and about twenty families, most of them possessing good estates.

This religious people then considered it a great privilege to settle so near Ipswich, four miles distant, on account of being able to attend the lectures of both towns. They were very industrious, were the first in North-America,[†] who made cloth, and built the first fulling mill in New-England. It stood just above the head of the tide on mill river, where it is now continued. A cedar tenter post, which they brought out of England is now perfectly sound.

[*] Winthrop.   [†] Johnson.

No less diligent were this people in attending the ordinances of the gospel, and in gathering a church. Almost every individual among them was considered "meet to be a living stone," in the temple of the Lord. In 1644, churches were to be gathered at Andover and Haverhill; but the magistrates and ministers notified, desired that "from the remoteness of those towns, and their scarcity of houses," the meeting might be at Rowley, to which they both consented.*

Their minister, Mr. Rogers, was born at Weathersfield, in England, 1590. His father, Mr. Richard Rogers, "was a man who walked with God," who would sometimes say, *I should be sorry if every day were not to me as my last day.* Ezekiel very early showed a sparkling wit, a correct judgment, and a capacity for learning. At thirteen years of age he was "capable of preferment at the university." At twenty, he took the degree of master of arts. Leaving college, he became a chaplain in the religious family of Sir Francis Barrington. Here he was conversant with people of the first rank.

Mr. Rogers was celebrated both for his prayers and sermons; his strains of oratory were delightful. After he had lived five or six years in the family of Sir Francis, he bestowed on him the benefice of Rowley, in Yorkshire. He hoped that the evangelical and zealous preaching of Mr. Rogers would awaken that drowsy neighbourhood. His church standing in the centre of several villages, a great assembly attended his preaching.

But while others were enlightened and encouraged, Mr Rogers had little comfort in his own mind. He had many fears, and great distresses respecting his own *experience* of those truths, which he preached to others. He feared he

* Winthrop.

was himself a stranger to that faith, repentance, and conversion, which he pressed upon others. He trembled lest his own heart was not duly impressed with those pathetic expressions by which he affected and moved others. His affliction was increased by not having any serious friend in that part of the kingdom, to whom he could communicate the spiritual trouble of his mind. So deeply was his heart wounded, that he resolved to take a journey into Essex county to consult with a cousin, who was minister at Dedham. When he arrived, it was a lecture day. Entering the assembly, he to his surprise found the sermon perfectly adapted to his state of mind; all his doubts were as fully resolved, as if he had previously laid his heart open to the preacher. His fears vanished, and he returned to his ministry with new courage, and remarkable success attended his labours.

His animated discourses often exhausted his strength, for though his spirit was lively, his body was feeble. This led him to the study of physic, in which he had considerable skill. By the violent motion of riding on horseback he once burst a blood vessel, but by retiring to his chamber, and avoiding all company for about two months, he recovered.

After a public ministry at Rowley of about 20 years, like many other good ministers, he was deprived of his pulpit, and his people of him, by the arm of authority. A number of his neighbours being on the wing for New-England, he joined with them, and arrived in 1638, and notwithstanding the pressing invitations he received from his Yorkshire friends, who had previously settled in Connecticut, he chose to fix his residence near his kinsman Rogers, who lived at Ipswich.

Five years after his settlement at Rowley, in Massachusetts, he was appointed to preach the election sermon; this rendered him famous through the Commonwealth.

While he was praised abroad, he was venerated at home; his ministry was highly approved and greatly successful among his own people. Regeneration and union to Jesus Christ by faith, were the great points on which he principally insisted in his preaching. When speaking on these topics, he had a remarkable talent of penetrating the souls of his hearers, and unveiling the very secrets of their hearts. His sermons and his prayers often remarkably expressed the feelings and exercises of his people. Amazed they heard their minister represent with exactness their thoughts, their desires, their motives, and their whole characters. They were sometimes almost ready to exclaim, Who hath told him all this?

His conversation with his people was serious and instructive. With the youth he took great pains, especially with those, who had been commended to him by their dying parents. He was a tree of knowledge laden with fruit, which children could reach. Sometimes a dozen of them would visit him together, when he would admit them singly into his study, and examine them, how they walked with God, how they spent their time, what religious books they read, whether they faithfully prayed to God. Then would he admonish them carefully to avoid those temptations to which they were most exposed, and dismiss them. If he heard of any contentions, among his people, he would send for the parties, and examine the grounds of their complaints; so great was his influence, that he generally quenched the sparks of discord before they burst forth in open flame. A traveller, passing through the town, inquired of him, if he were the person who *served* there. He replied, "I am, sir, the person, who *rules* here."

The latter part of this good man's life was a dreary winter of sufferings. He buried his wife, and all his children. A second wife was soon snatched from his arms. The night of his third marriage, his house was burned with all his goods, and an excellent library, which he had brought from England. Having rebuilt his house, he soon after fell from his horse, and so bruised his right arm, that it became entirely useless; he afterwards wrote with his left hand. His great spirit spoke in the style of lamentation. In a letter to a minister in Charlestown, two or three years before his death, after inquiring respecting the success of his ministry, and the piety of his children and household, he mourns that his young people are little affected, that they strengthened one another in evil by example and counsel. He says, "I tremble to think what will become of this glorious work, which we have begun, when the ancients shall be gathered unto their fathers." "I fear grace and blessings will die with them. All is hurry for the world, every one for self, and not for the public good. It hath been God's way not to send sweeping judgments, when the chief magistrates are godly. I beseech all the Bay ministers to call earnestly upon the magistrates; tell them their godliness is our protection. I am hastening home; I am *near* home; you too are not far off; O the weight of glory that is ready waiting for us, God's poor exiles. We shall sit next to the martyrs and confessors. Cheer up your spirit with these thoughts, and let us be zealous for God and Christ."

He closed his labours and life, Jan. 23, 1661, in the seventieth year of his age.[*] His library he gave to Harvard college; his house and lands he gave to the town for the support of the gospel ministry. A part of the land was bequeathed on the condition his people supported a pastor and teacher according to the early custom of the country; but they have long since neglected to do this, and the corporation of Harvard college, to whom the land was forfeited,

[*] Mather

made their rightful claim, and obtained it. So that Mr. Rogers is numbered among the distinguished benefactors of the university. Still in the first parish of Rowley the rent of the lands, left them by Mr. Rogers, has lately been more than the salary of their minister. The west parish of Rowley, and about half of Byfield, which belonged to Rowley, received their proportion of the donation, when they were incorporated in separate societies.

CHAP. XV.

Emigration ceased; settlement of Woburn; Confederation of the colonies; Eastham settled; character of Mr. Treat; Gov. Winthrop's speech; his character.

In 1640, in consequence of a change of affairs in the mother country, emigration to New-England ceased. It was estimated at the time, that about 4000 families, consisting of 21,000 souls, had arrived in 298 ships, and settled in this new world. Since this period, the current of emigration has been from New-England. The expense of removing these families was estimated at £192,000 sterling, which, including what they paid to the council of Plymouth and to the sachems of the country, was a dear purchase of their lands.

In 1642, the town of Woburn was settled. As a specimen of the manner in which other towns were settled, we give a more particular account of this. The town was laid out four miles square, and granted to seven men, "of good and honest report," on condition that they, within two years, erected houses there, and proceeded to build a town. These seven men had power to give and grant lands unto persons desirous of sitting down with them. Each one had meadow and upland granted him, according to his stock of cattle, and capacity of cultivating the soil. The poorest man had six or seven acres of meadow, and twenty-five of upland; an eye being had to future settlers, for whom lands were reserved. No man was refused on account of his poverty, but after receiving his portion of land, had assistance in building a house. But such as were of a turbulent spirit, were not allowed to "enjoy a freehold, till they should mend their manners." The seven men, to whom the town was granted, laid out the roads as might best accommodate the lands, as to civil and religious privileges. Accordingly, those who received land nearest to the meetinghouse, had a less quantity at home, and more at a distance. In this manner about sixty families first settled in Woburn.

Equally circumspect and wise were their religious arrangements. As soon as they had a competent number to support a minister, they considered themselves as "surely seated, and not before, it being as unnatural for a right New-England man to live without an able ministry, as for a blacksmith to work his iron without a fire." This people, therefore, like others, laid their "foundation stone" with earnestly seeking the blessing of heaven in several days of fasting and prayer. They then took the advice of the most orthodox and able christians, especially the ministers of the gospel, not rashly running into a church state before they had a prospect of obtaining a pastor to feed them with the bread of life. They chose to continue as they were, in fellowship with other churches, enjoying their christian watch, till they had the ordinances administered among them. But they soon obtained "Mr. Thomas Carter of Watertown, a reverend, godly man, apt to teach the sound and wholesome truths of Christ," to preach for them. They then formed into a church, on the 24th of the 6th month, after Mr. Symes of Charlestown "had continued in preaching and prayer about the space of four or five hours." The other ministers present were Messrs. Cotton and Wilson of Boston, Mr. Allen of Charlestown, Mr. Shepherd and Mr. Dunster of Cambridge, Mr. Knowles of Watertown, Mr. Allen of Dedham, Mr. Eliot of Roxbury, and Mr. Mather of Dorchester.*

After public worship, the persons intending to be formed into a church stood forth, one by one, before the congregation and the ministers, "and confessed what the Lord had done for their souls, by his spirit, under the preaching of the gospel, and the events of his providence" that all for themselves might "know their faith in Christ;" the ministers or messengers present, asking such questions as they thought proper; and, when satisfied, giving them the right hand of fellowship. Seven were thus formed into a church, who in ten years had increased to seventy-four.

On the 22d of the ninth month, Mr. Carter was by a council ordained their pastor, "after he had exercised in prayer and preaching the greater part of the day." When a person desired to join with the church, he visited his minister, "declaring how the Lord had been pleased to work his conversion;" if the minister found the smallest ground of hope, he propounded him to the *church;* after which, "some of the brethren, with the minister, examined him again, and reported their opinion to the church." After this, all the congregation "had public notice" of his designs and he "publicly declared to *them* the manner of his conversion." If any were, "through bashfulness, unable to speak for edification, less was required of them." Women were never called to speak publicly. All this was done "to prevent the polluting of the ordinance by such as walk scandalously, and to prevent men and women from eating and drinking their own condemnation." "After this manner

* Mather.

had the other churches of Christ their beginning and progress" in New-England.

Exposed to foreign and domestic enemies, four of the New-England colonies, viz. Massachusetts, Plymouth, Connecticut, and New-Haven, confederated for mutual defence. Rhode-Island was denied the privilege of joining this confederacy. The articles of union were agreed on and ratified, May 19th, 1643, and were in substance as follows:

"The united colonies of New-England, viz. Massachusetts, Plymouth, Connecticut, and New-Haven, enter into a firm and perpetual league, offensive and defensive.

Each colony to retain a distinct and separate jurisdiction; no two colonies to join in one jurisdiction, without the consent of the whole; and no other colony to be received into the confederacy without the like consent.

The charge of all wars, offensive and defensive, to be borne in proportion to the male inhabitants between 16 and 60 years of age in each colony.

Upon notice from three magistrates of any colony, of an invasion, the rest shall immediately send aid; Massachusetts 100, and each of the other, 45 men; and if a greater number be necessary, the commissioners to meet and determine upon it.

Two commissioners from each government being church members, to meet annually the first Monday in September; the first meeting to be held at Boston, then at Hartford, New-Haven, and Plymouth, and so yearly in that order, saving, that two meetings successively be held at Boston.

All matters wherein six shall agree, to be binding upon the whole; and if there be a majority, but under six, the matter in question to be referred to the general court of each colony, and not to be obligatory unless the whole agree to it.

A president for preserving order, to be chosen by the commissioners each year out of their number.

The commissioners shall have power to establish laws, or rules, of a civil nature, and of general concern, for the conduct of the inhabitants, viz. relative to their behaviour toward the Indians, to fugitives from one colony to another, and the like.

No colony to engage in war, except upon a sudden exigency, (and in that case to be avoided as much as possible) without consent of the whole.

If a meeting be summoned upon any extraordinary occasion, and the whole number of commissioners do not assemble, any four who shall meet may determine upon a war when the case will not admit of delay, and send for the agreed proportion of men out of each jurisdiction, but not less than six shall determine the justice of the war, or have power to settle bills of charges, or make levies for the same.

If any colony break any article of the agreement, or in any wise injure another colony, the matter shall be considered and determined by the commissioners of the other colonies."

In 1644, Eastham, on Cape Cod, was settled by a number of the more respectable people of Plymouth. The year before, several members of the church became dissatisfied with their situation. Though at the time of their selecting the spot, they had most favourable ideas of the soil, they had now discovered that it was one of the most barren parts of the country. Many from this circumstance had left the place, and others were asking dismissions. This induced the church to consider seriously whether it were not best for all to remove in a body. So cordially united was this band of brothers, that the idea of separation was inexpressibly distressing. Many meetings of the church were held on the subject, and various were their opinions. Some appeared to be determined on a removal: others thought nothing was wanting, but a contented mind, to make them happy where they were, suggesting that it was not a fear of poverty, but a desire of riches, that excited any to remove; still, though not convinced, they finally yielded to the others, rather than lose their society, and it was unanimously agreed to remove, if a suitable place could be found.

Seldom has there been a more striking display of the social and benevolent feelings of the heart, than in this resolve. Here they had found a secure asylum for twenty-three years; here most of them were contented and happy; here they had cleared the forest and fenced fields, planted gardens, and erected houses; yet they voluntarily resolve to sacrifice all, to plunge into the forest anew, to enjoy the society of their neighbours. Several places were proposed, and repeated examinations made; but no better place for a town and capital of the colony could be found; the majority therefore gave liberty to those who were disposed to form a new settlement at Nauset, which they called Eastham. Mr. Thomas Prince was the leader of this settlement, and was afterward many years governor of the colony.

A church was soon formed; but they were not able to support a minister till 1672, when the Rev. Samuel Treat was ordained: he is entitled to a high rank among the first ministers of New-England. Not only his own people, but the Indians, commanded his affections and unwearied labours. For a long course of years, he prosecuted with sacred zeal the work of converting the pagans around him. He had four assemblies under his care, to whom he preached as often as it was practicable, and their teachers of their own tribe, who instructed them in his absence, visited him every week to be further instructed and prepared for their public labours. Under his influence they not only formed themselves into religious societies, and observed religious appointments, but they had schools, elected magistrates, instituted courts, and were very much civilized. Mr. Treat spoke and wrote their language with the greatest facility. At his funeral, the Indians entreated the favour of carrying the corpse in their turn; thus expressing their tender affection for the man, who had so long broke to them the bread of life.

Mr. Treat was the oldest son of the governor of Connecticut, who was the father of twenty-one children. He graduated at Harvard college in 1669. Mr. Treat was a sound Calvinist.[*] He was a son of thunder in the pulpit, believing that a great part of mankind will be moved by nothing but the terrors of the Lord.

With all his excellencies, Mr. Treat was a bad speaker. Having once preached for his father-in-law, Mr. Willard, of Boston, the people were so disgusted, that a number of them entreated Mr. Willard never to admit him into the pulpit again; he made them no reply, but asked Mr. Treat to lend him his sermon. A few weeks after, Mr. Willard preached the same sermon to his people; they listened with rapture; they were charmed; they flew to their minister to obtain a copy for the press. An impressive fact to show the great importance of pulpit eloquence. Mr. Willard had a melodious voice and a graceful delivery.

In 1645, New-England was remarkably prosperous, and licentiousness, in some instances, followed. Some people of Hingham broke the peace; governor Winthrop sent them to prison. Several of the inhabitants, who petitioned in their behalf, were cited to the court; they appealed to parliament, and offered to find bail to stand by its award. They were fined and imprisoned, but governor Winthrop, against whom

[*] See his character in a well written account of Eastham in the Collections of the Historical Society.

their complaints were principally directed, was desired to leave the seat of justice, and stand at the bar for trial. With dignity he descended, and after the trial made the following noble speech.

"Gentlemen, I will not look back to the past proceedings of this court, nor to the persons concerned; I am satisfied, that I was publicly accused, and that I am now publicly acquitted; but give me leave to say something on the occasion that may rectify the opinion of the people from whom these distempers of the state have arisen. The questions, which have troubled the country of late, have been respecting the authority of the magistrate, and the liberty of the people. Magistracy is certainly an appointment of God, and I entreat you to consider, that you choose your rulers from among yourselves, and that we take an oath to govern you according to God's laws, and the laws of our country, to the best of our skill; if we commit errours not willingly, but for want of ability, you ought to bear with us; nor would I have you mistake your own liberty. There is liberty of doing what we *will*, without regard to law or justice; this liberty is indeed inconsistent with authority; but civil, moral, *federal* liberty, consists in every one's enjoying his property, and having the benefit of the laws of his country: this is what you *ought* to contend for with the hazard of your lives; but this is very consistent with a due subjection to the civil magistrate, and paying him that respect, which his character requires."

This admirable address had the most happy effect. It fixed Mr. Winthrop in the affections and esteem of the people and court. By this well timed condescension he became more powerful than ever.* This good man descended from a respectable family, who were attached to the religion

* Hannah Adams

of the reformation. His grandfather, Adam Winthrop, was an eminent lawyer and lover of the gospel. His father was of the same profession and character. Governor Winthrop was born, June 12, 1587, and was bred to the law, though he had a strong inclination for divinity. So conspicuous were his merits, that he was made a justice of the peace at the age of eighteen. He was distinguished for his hospitality, his piety, and his integrity. Being chosen governor before the colony embarked for America, he sold an estate worth six or seven hundred pounds sterling per annum; and in the 43d year of his age, he arrived at Salem, June 12, 1630, and within five days travelled through the trackless woods to Charlestown. The same autumn he passed over the river to Boston, which became his permanent residence. He was an example to the people, not only of temperance and piety, but of frugality, denying himself those indulgences and elegances to which his fortune and office entitled him, that he might be an example to others, and have more liberal means of relieving the needy. He would often send his servants on some errand at meal-times, to see how his neighbours were provided, and if there was a deficiency, he would supply them from his own table. He sent for a neighbour, who had stolen wood from his pile, and bid him come and welcome through the winter; and then pleasantly asked his friends, if he had not put a stop to the man's stealing.

A democratic influence prevailing, he was left out of office, in 1634, and the two following years. In the administration of justice, he was considered by some as too mild. He once returned an angry, provoking letter he had received, saying, "I am not willing to keep by me such a matter of provocation." Soon after, in time of scarcity, the letter writer sent to buy one of his cattle; he begged him to accept it as a gift. But with all this gentleness of nature, he was firm and valiant for the truths of the gospel, exposing himself to abuse and disgrace in their support.*

He had not so high an opinion of democratical government, as some other gentlemen.† When the people of Connecticut were forming their constitution, he warned them of this danger, and wisely remarked in his letter, that "the best part of a community is always the *least*; and of that best part the wiser is still *less;* wherefore the old canon was, choose ye out *judges*, and thou shalt bring the matter before the judge."

Having expended a large portion of his great estate for the advantage of the colony, having exhausted his strength in cares and labours in their service, he felt the decays of a premature old age, years before his decease. A cold, succeeded by a fever, put an end to his life and eminent services, March, 26, 1649, in the 63d year of his age. He anticipated the serious event with calm resignation to the will of God. He left five sons; one of them was afterwards governor of Connecticut, and his posterity are still respectable.

CHAP. XVI.

Character of the natives who inhabited New-England.

The Indians were polytheists, or believed in a plurality of Gods.‡ Some they considered as local deities; yet they believed there was one supreme God, the Creator of the rest, and of all creatures and things. Him they called Kichtan. They believed that once there was no sachem nor king, but Kichtan, who was the self existent creator of the Heavens and governor of mankind. One man and

* See Chap. 21, of Synods, First Part. † Belknap. ‡ Wood.

woman they supposed were first created, who were the parents of all men. They believed that good men, at death, ascended to Kichtan, above the heavens, where they enjoyed their departed friends and all good things; that bad men also went and knocked at the gate of glory, but Kichtan bid them depart, for there was no place for such; whence they wandered in restless penury. Never man saw Kichtan, but old men told them, and told them to tell their children, and to tell them to teach their posterity these things, and lay the like charge upon them. This supreme being they held to be good, and prayed to him when they desired any very great favour, sometimes meeting together to cry to him for plenty and victory, at the same time singing, giving thanks, feasting, dancing, and hanging up garlands as memorials of favours received.

Another power they worshipped, whom they called *Hobbamock*, or *Hobbamoqui** This being resembles the devil, mentioned in scripture. To him they prayed to heal their wounds and diseases. When found curable, he was supposed the author of the complaints; when they were mortal, they were ascribed to Kichtan, whose diseases none are able to remove; therefore, they never pray to him in sickness. Their priests and chief warriors, Powahs and Panieses, pretended often to see Hobbamock in the shape of a man, fawn, or eagle, but generally of a *snake*, who gave them advice in their difficult undertakings. The duty and office of the Powah, was to pray to Hobbamock for the removal of evils; the common people join or say, amen; sometimes breaking out with them in a musical tone. In his prayer, the Powah promised skins, kettles, hatchets, beads, and other valuable things, as sacrifices, if his request should be granted. Sometimes they sacrificed their own infant children to

* Publications of the Historical Society.

him. Women, in remarkably hard travail, which seldom
happened, sent for the Powah. When the English arrived,
their religion was declining. The natives said that within
their remembrance, Kichtan had been much more addressed.

The Narragansets were distinguished for their sacrifices.
They had a spacious temple, and stated times for their public assemblies; a fire was kindled in the temple, into which
the Powahs cast the most valuable riches of the people
voluntarily brought by them, as skins, beads, hatchets, and
knives. The Indians north, though not disposed to imitate
their example, admired this supposed piety, imagining it the
reason that the plague or yellow fever had not raged there,
which had depopulated their country.

The *Panieses* seem to have been a singular kind of aris-
tocracy in a community of warriors. They were selected
from their companions in childhood, and trained to sufferings, and daring exploits, men of stature and strength, courage and wisdom. They were the counsellors of the king,
surrounded his person in battle, and though painted and dis-
figured, were always known, in scenes of blood and death,
the terror of their foes.

Horrible were the severities or penances they inflicted
on themselves. They abstained from pleasant meat, and
observed a variety of rules, that Hobbamock, or the devil,
might appear to them. They drank the juice of bitter herbs
till they disgorged it into a vessel, then drinking it again
and again till they were overcome and scarcely able to
stand: they bruised and tore their flesh to make themselves
acceptable to the devil, that he might appear to them.
Their Powahs were dexterous fellows, and probably adepts
in the secens of legerdemain. According to the report of
the Indians, they could make water burn, rocks move, trees
dance, change themselves into blazing men. What is more

marvellous, they could burn an old tree to ashes in the winter, when there was not a green leaf in the whole country, put the ashes into water, and take thence a green leaf which you might handle and carry away. They could change a dry snake skin into a living snake, to be seen, felt, and heard. Fine showmen these!

Bows and arrows were their principal weapons in war. Their captains had long spears, on which, if victorious, they bore home the heads of their chief enemies, slain in battle, it being their custom to cut off the heads, hands and feet of their slaughtered enemies, which were carried to their families as tokens of their victories. Always when they engaged in war, they painted their faces with a variety of colours, to disguise themselves, and appear more terrible. They wore to battle their most costly jewels and dress, to remind themselves that they fought not only for wives and children, but their goods and possessions. Their battles were rude assaults, without discipline or order.

The country was divided into small tribes or kingdoms, the son, or nearest relative, inheriting the government of the father. Their laws were few, but their kings were greatly beloved and revered. Some of these might be called emperors, having a number of kings under their direction. Plotting against the life of the king, and murder, were punished with death. The malefactor was arraigned before the king and his nobles; if condemned by a jury, the executioner entered, blindfolded the victim, set him in public view, and with a club beat out his brains. They had no prisons, whipping posts, nor stocks; these are the appendages of civilized society. The kings took care of the aged, the widow, and fatherless. The sachems married none but of royal rank; their concubines might be from inferiour families; these were put away at pleasure, but the wife retained her rank and the government of the other women during life.

Every kingdom had its known limits. The common people were generally content with one wife. In marriage the consent of the king was required, who as priest joined their hands, "never to part till death," unless she prove an adultress. Hospitality is the cardinal virtue of savages, from the line to the poles. In New-England, travellers generally lodged in the house of the king. When they arrived they gave information how long they would tarry, and provision was made for them, accordingly. Though their fare was scanty for themselves, they were generous to their own countrymen, or the English, who called upon them; sometimes lying abroad, that the stranger might sleep in their cottage. They ate sitting on the ground, or rather reclining in the Turkish manner, with their victuals on the earth, without plate, napkin, knife or fork, without bread, salt or drink.

Hunting and fishing were their principal employments. Deer and other animals they shot with arrows. Sometimes they built two hedges, a mile or two distant at one end, gradually approaching together at the other, where only a narrow gap was left open; there they placed themselves, killing every creature as it passed through. Here they sometimes set a curious species of trap, or terrible snares, formed by bending down young trees, which would spring with force sufficient to raise the largest animal. An English mare having once strayed away, was caught, and like Mahomet's fabled coffin, raised between the heavens and earth, in one of these snares; the Indians arriving, and seeing her struggling on the tree, cried, "Good morning, what cheer, what cheer. Mr. Englishman's squaw horse." Having no better epithet than woman horse; but being afraid of her "iron feet," they ran and told the English where they could find their *squaw* horse hanging on a tree.

They perfectly understood when and where to seek for fish of every kind in their particular season. Seals were favourites, the oil being in high esteem. Their bows, and arrows, and cords were nicely made; their canoes were of birch bark, in which they would venture into a rough sea, or of logs burned hollow, and smoothed with clam shells, the outside being hewed with stone axes.

They were great gamesters, often losing every particle of property they possessed, yet being as cheerful and good-natured as those, who won all. They often played town against town, and sometimes they played kingdom against kingdom; the people of one nation meeting those of another, to run, play ball, &c. On these occasions they always painted themselves, so as not to be known, that if any injury was done, mischief should not follow from revenge.

Their children very young were taught to swim and to manage the bow. They were grave in their deportment, and not loquacious; but emphatical in their expressions, and impressive in their manner. The Frenchman, say they, has a *good tongue*, but a *false heart;* the Englishman *all one speak, all one heart.* An Indian once hearing an English woman scold at her husband, her rapid expression exceeding his apprehension, he fled from the house, but stopping at the next neighbour's, he described the dismal scene, by telling them she cried, *Nan Nana, Nan Nana, Nan Nana, Nan,* saying, the husband was a great fool to *hear* her so much, and *chastise* her so little. Domestic jars were unknown among them. They smiled and were cheerful, but never laughed loud, and never quarrelled with one another. Their apparent insensibility under pains and wounds is well known; yet had they awful apprehensions of death. That they should be surprised and amazed at the arts and implements of civilized men is not incredible.

The first ship they saw, was supposed to be a walking island, the masts to be trees, the sails, white clouds, the explosion of their artillery, thunder and lightning. Attempting to go on board to pick strawberries, they were saluted with a broadside. They cried out, "So big walk, so big speak, and by and by kill." At the first windmill they saw, they were alarmed and afraid to approach. They considered the first ploughman as a wizard, and told the man he was almost a devil. They readily believed the history of the Old Testament, of the creation, fall, and deluge, but when told of a *Saviour*, they cried out *Pocatnie*, *i.e.* is it possible?

They were a healthy, stout race of men, living sometimes an hundred years; but when sick, and all hope of recovery was past, then their bursting sobs and sighs, their wringing hands, their flowing tears, and dismal cries and shrieks, were enough to excite sympathy and tears from marble eyes. After the corpse was brought to the grave, they wept and mourned, and so again when it was laid in the grave, and after it was buried they often shed tears for a long time; sometimes for a year, morning and night, they poured forth many groans, and raised many "Irish like howlings." In time of mourning, their faces were painted black. They believed in a paradise far southwest, at the portal of which lay a great dog, preventing the entrance of wicked souls. They buried the arms, and much of the treasure of the deceased with him; one to affright the dog, the other to purchase peculiar privileges. The wicked they conceived pass to the dark abodes of Hobbamocko, where they were tortured according to the opinions of *ancient* pagans.

Their dress, when they wore any, was of the skins of beasts; often wearing nothing but a short apron before.

The Powahs are their physicians, who roar and howl over them with many magical ceremonies. A hot house and cold bath were one of their principal remedies; the method was, to sit in a hot house an hour, which was a cave terribly heated, and then plunge into some brook or pond. When they had burned the wood near them, they removed to another place; and when the English first came to this country, the Indians supposed it was for wood. Their division of time was by sleeps, moons, and winters. By being abroad so much, they had some knowledge of the stars, and what is surprising, they called Charles' Wain *Paukunna-waw*, or the bear, the name given it by Europeans.

Their women, as is common among savages, performed almost all the drudgery of the family. They built the houses, covering them with mats, so that they were warmer than those of the English; not a drop of rain, not a breath of wind penetrated them. Some of these were fifty or sixty feet long. These were to be removed from place to place at the command of the husbands. Every year they had their fishing place, their hunting place, and their planting place, where the house remained the longest.

The women planted, and hoed, and harvested all the corn, brought home all the fish and game, dressed, and cured, and cooked it: but like Arab wives, ate not till their husbands had done. They were modest in their dress, and chaste in their conduct.

On this account, and several others, as anointing their heads, giving dowries for their wives, observing a feast of harvest, offering sacrifices, and grievous mournings for their dead, they have been supposed descendants of Abram.* There are doubtless several striking points of resemblance between the Israelites and Indians; but a further acquaint-

* Roger Williams, Mr. Eliot.

ance with the History of man, shows that customs very similar are common in every corner of the globe, among those nations, who are in the savage state of society.

Many of their savage customs are laudable and humane. When any are sick, their friends resort to them, and often remain till death or recovery. When they recover, on account of the expense they have been at, their friends send them provisions and other comforts. The aged are treated with great respect; their names are all significant, and are changed according to character and circumstances. To which we may add, if the year proved dry, they had great and solemn meetings from all parts to supplicate their gods, and beg for rain. These devotions they continued sometimes ten days, a fortnight, and three weeks, or till rain came. When a field was to be cleared, or any great work accomplished, all the neighbours, men, women, and children, freely lent their assistance; fifty or an hundred were sometimes seen labouring together. The ties of brotherhood were so strong, that sometimes when a person had committed murder and fled, his brother was executed in his stead. It was common for a man to pay the debts of his deceased brother. Their virgins were distinguished by a modest falling down of their hair over their eyes. Their affection was very strong for their children, who by indulgence were saucy and undutiful. A father would sometimes, through grief and rage for the loss of a child, stab himself. Sometimes they would, by break of day, call up their wives and surviving children and families, to make lamentation, with abundance of tears, crying out, "O God, thou hast taken away my child; thou art angry with me; O, turn thine anger from me, and spare the rest of my children." If they received any good in hunting, fishing, or agriculture, they acknowledged it came from God. If they met with a fall, or any accident, they would say, God was angry with them. When they observed any distinguished excellence, they would say, it was a god. At the architecture, the husbandry, and other arts of the English, they often exclaimed, "you are a god, or they are gods," implying that all excellencies are in God. After the season of harvest and hunting, they had anniversary religious festivals. Do not some pretended christians blush at these things?

Their strongest profession of honesty and integrity was, *my heart is good*, implying that all goodness was in the heart.*

CHAP. XVII.

The society for propagating the gospel; the faithful labours of the New-England ministers to instruct the natives in the religion of Jesus Christ.

In 1650, a society in England, instituted for propagating the gospel, began a correspondence with the commissioners of the United Colonies, who were employed as agents for the society. In consequence, exertions were made to christianize the Indians. The Rev. Mr. Eliot, minister of Roxbury, had distinguished himself in this pious work. He had established towns, in which he collected Indian families, taught them husbandry, the mechanic arts, and a prudent management of their affairs, and instructed them with unwearied attention in the principles of the christian religion. For his zeal and success he has been called the *Apostle of New-England.*

He began his labours about the year 1646. being in the forty-second year of his age. The first pagans, who enjoyed

* Roger Williams.

his labours, resided at Nonantum, now the east part of Newton. Waban, a principal chief there, became a convert, and was distinguished for his piety. Being encouraged by the success of his first attempt, he soon after opened a lecture at Neponsit, within the present bounds of Dorchester. These two lectures he continued several years without any reward or encouragement, but the satisfaction of doing good to the souls of men. Beside preaching to them, he formed two catechisms, one for the children, the other for adults. They readily learned these, seriously attended his public lectures, and very generally prayed in their families, morning and evening.

After a number of years, certain individuals in England, affected by his pious and disinterested labours, raised some generous contributions for his encouragement; he gratefully received these, declaring that he never expected any thing. By such timely aid he was enabled to educate his five sons at college. All these were distinguished for their piety, and all, excepting one, who died while a member of college, were preachers of the gospel. His eldest son preached several years to the Indians at *Pakemit*, now Stoughton, and at Natick, and other places. Other ministers, in different parts of New England, by the example of Mr. Eliot, zealously engaged in the missionary work. Messrs. Bourne and Cotton in Plymouth colony, studied the Indian language, and preached at Martha's Vineyard, and other places. At Martha's Vineyard and Nantucket, Mr. Mayhew and son entered on the work; and in Connecticut Messrs. Pierson and Fitch preached Jesus and the resurrection to the heathen in their vicinity.

That the natives might have the word of life in their own language, which alone was able to make them wise unto salvation, Mr. Eliot translated the bible for their use. The New-Testament was published in 1661, and the whole bible soon after. The expense was borne by the society for propagating the gospel in New-England. Beside this, he translated and composed several other books, as a primer, a grammar, singing psalms, the practice of piety, Baxter's call, and several other things. He took care that schools should be opened in the Indian settlements, where their children were taught to read; some were put into schools of the English, and studied Latin and Greek. A building was erected for their reception, and several of them sent to Cambridge college. The legislature instituted judicial courts among the natives, answering to the county courts of the colony. In these courts, one English judge was united with those chosen by the natives. They had rulers and magistrates elected by themselves, who managed their smaller matters.

The first church of christianized pagans was gathered at Natick; they had two instructors of their own body, when the English preachers could not attend. In 1670, they had between forty and fifty communicants. The second praying town was Pakemit, or Punkapaog, now Stoughton; their first teacher was of their own number, William Ahawton, "a pious man, of good parts." The second church of Indians was at *Hassanamessit*, now Grafton; their teacher's name was Takuppa-willin, "a pious and able man, and apt to teach." They had a meeting house built after the English manner; their communicants were sixteen, their baptized persons thirty.

At *Okommakummessit*, or Marlborough, was a society, with a teacher. *Wamesit*, or Tewksbury, was the fifth praying society; their teacher was called Samuel, who could read and write. Annually a judicial court was held there. Here Mr. Eliot used to go and preach at that season, on account of the strangers, who resorted there. In 1674, after he had been preaching from Matth. xxii. concerning the marriage of the king's son, at the wigwam of Wannalancet, near the falls, this man, who was the oldest son of the sachem or king, who had always been friendly to the English, but openly rejected the gospel, after sermon, rose and said, "Sirs, you have been pleased, for four years, in your abundant love, to apply yourselves particularly to me and my people, to exhort, press and persuade us to pray to God. I am very thankful to you for your pains. I must acknowledge, I have all my days used to pass in an old canoe, and you exhort me to change and leave my old canoe, and embark in a new canoe, which I have always opposed; but now I yield myself up to your advice, and enter into a new canoe, and do engage to pray to God hereafter." He ever after persevered in a christian course, though on this account several of his people deserted him. The sixth society gathered from the Indians, was at Nashobah, now Littleton: their teacher was called John Thomas. In this place, and at Marloborough, the Indians had orchards set out by themselves. Mungunkook, or Hopkinton, was the next place where a christian society was gathered; the families were twelve, their teacher was Job.

Several years after, seven other societies of praying Indians, with Indian teachers, were formed further west. One in Oxford, one in Dudley, three in different parts of Woodstock, which then was claimed by Massachusetts, one in Worcester, and one in Uxbridge. Several other places about the same time received christian preachers. The places mentioned received teachers selected from the natives, who had been instructed by Mr. Eliot. The whole number of those called praying Indians, in these places, was about 1100.

But the gospel was preached with still greater effect in Plymouth colony. The Rev. Mr. Bourne had under his care, on Cape Cod and its vicinity, about 500 souls; of whom about 200 could read, and more than 70 could write. He had formed one church of 27 communicants; 90 had been baptized. Beside these, Mr. Cotton of Plymouth preached occasionally to about half a hundred on Buzzard's Bay. Mr. Mayhew and son began to instruct the Indians of Martha's Vineyard, in 1648 or 9. They were remarkably successful. The greatest part of them were soon considered as praying Indians. On this island and Chappaquiddick, were 300 families; on the latter, sixty, of whom fifty-nine were praying families. On Nantucket was a church, and many praying families. In 1694, there were on this island three churches and five assemblies of praying Indians. In 1685, the praying Indians in Plymouth colony were 1439, beside children under 12 years of age. At one time, in different parts, were 24 congregations. In Connecticut and Rhode-Island, but little success attended the gospel among the Indians. The sachems of Narraganset and Mohegan violently opposed their people's hearing the gospel. The Rev. Mr. Fitch of Norwich, took great pains, gave some of the Mohegans lands of his own, that they, who were disposed to hear the gospel, might be nearer him, and also freed from the revilings of their companions; at one time he had about 30 under his care.

The legislatures of the several colonies enacted salutary laws for restraining the evil conduct of the natives; means were also furnished for their receiving presents or rewards for distinguishing themselves in what was laudable. In Connecticut, the legislature in 1655, having appointed a governor over the Pequots, gave him the following laws, to which the people were to subject themselves. They shall not blaspheme the name of God, nor profane the sabbath. They shall not commit murder, nor practice witchcraft, on pain of death. "They shall not commit adultery, on pain of severe punishment. Whoever is drunk shall pay ten shillings, or receive ten stripes. He that steals shall pay double damages."

CHAP. XVIII.

Quakers persecuted; apology for our forefathers; synod of 1662; Character of Capt. Standish.

THE persecution of the Quakers commenced in 1656. In 1661, an order was received from the king, requiring that neither capital nor corporeal punishment should be inflicted on the Quakers, but that offenders should be sent to England. During this persecution, several were executed. On the subject of the New-England persecutions, the author of the European settlements in North-America judiciously remarks; "Such is the manner of proceeding of religious parties toward each other, and in this respect the people of New-England were not worse than the rest of mankind; nor was their severity any just matter of reflection upon that mode of religion which they profess."* Religious intolerance is now very generally reprobated, and it is hoped the time has already arrived, when no people can be found, who think "that by killing men for their religion, they do God good service."

By order of the general court, a synod of the New-England churches convened at Boston, September, 1662. The people were at this time much divided in opinion on the two following questions, which were submitted to the synod for their decision, viz. 1st, "Who are the subjects of baptism?" 2d. "Whether, according to the word of God, there ought to be a consociation of churches, and what should be the

* Burke.

manner of it?" The general court ordered the result of this synod to be printed; and it may be seen at large in Dr. Mather's Magnalia, and in Neal's History of the Puritans.

In 1656, at a very advanced age, died Capt. Standish, the military commander, the WASHINGTON of Plymouth colony. A man so conspicuous and celebrated in his life, ought not to be forgotten when dead. It is impossible to have any adequate view of the establishment and rise of Plymouth colony, without entering familiarly into the character of this hero, of that little band of pilgrims. He descended from a family of distinction, and was heir apparent to a great estate, unjustly detained from him, which compelled him to depend on himself for support. He was small in stature, but of an active spirit, a sanguine temper, and strong constitution. These qualities led him to the profession of arms. Having been in the service of queen Elizabeth, in aid of the Dutch, after the truce he settled with Mr. Robertson's people in Leyden. He was in the first company who came over in 1620; he commanded the first detachment for making discoveries after their arrival; he was chosen military commander on the first settlement of their military concerns. Generally, in the subsequent excursions and interviews with the natives, he was the first to meet them, accompanied by a small number of his own choosing. During the terrible sickness of the first winter, when two or three died in a day, and the living were scarcely able to bury the dead, Capt. Standish retained his health, and kindly nursed the sick. On the 29th of January, he was called to see his beloved wife expire.

When *Corbitant*, one of the petty sachems of Massasoit, meditated a revolt, captain Standish, with 14 men, surrounded his house in Swansey; but he being absent, they informed his people, they should destroy him, if he persisted in his rebellion. This so alarmed the chief, that he entreated the mediation of Massasoit, and accordingly was admitted, with eight other chiefs, to subscribe his submission to the English.

In 1622, when he had fortified Plymouth, he divided his men into four "squadrons," appointing every individual his post. In case of fire, a select company mounted guard with their backs to the fire, to watch for approaching enemies. Being sent on a trading voyage to Matachiest, between Barnstable and Yarmouth, in February, 1623, a severe storm compelled him to leave his vessel, and sleep in a hut of the Indians; being impressed with an idea of their design to kill him, he made his people keep guard all night, by which he escaped the snare they had laid for him. In the morning it was found that goods had been stolen in the night from the shallop; he, with his party, surrounded the house of the sachem, and the things were restored.

Often was the providence of God conspicuous in his preservation. The next month, at Manomet, a creek in Sandwich, where he went for corn, he was not received with their usual cordiality; two Indians from Massachusetts were there, one had an iron dagger, and derided the Europeans because he had seen them, when dying, "cry, and make sour faces like children." An Indian of the place who had formerly been his friend, appearing now very friendly, invited the captain to sleep with *him*, because the weather was cold. Standish accepted his hospitality, and passed the night by his fire; but sleep had departed from his eyes; he was restless, and in motion all night, though his host seemed solicitous for his comfort, and "earnestly pressed him to take his rest." It was afterwards discovered that this Indian intended to kill him if he had fallen asleep.

Weston's people, who settled at Wessagusset, lived without religion or law. This rendered them contemptible in the view of savages, who soon began to insult and abuse them. The company pretended to satisfy the Indians for a theft, not by punishing the thief, but by hanging a decrepid old man, who had become burdensome to them. This settlement was composed of a set of needy adventurers. But before they knew their own danger, the governor of Plymouth had learned from Massasoit the plot of the natives for their destruction, and sent Capt. Standish to their relief. He had made choice of eight men, refusing to take more. Arriving at Wessagusset, now Weymouth, he found the people scattered, and in imminent danger, yet stupidly insensible of the destruction which was ready to burst upon them. Standish was careful not to excite the jealousy of the natives till he could assemble the people of the plantation. An Indian brought him some furs, whom he treated "smoothly," yet the Indian reported that he "saw by the captain's eyes, that he was angry in his heart." This induced *Pecksuot*, a chief of courage, to tell *Hobbamock*, Standish's Indian guide and interpreter, that he "understood the captain was come to kill him, and the rest of the savages there; but tell him," said he, "we know it, but fear him not; neither will we shun him, let him begin when he dare, he shall not take us at unawares." Others whetted their knives before him, using insulting gestures and speeches. Among the rest, Wittuwamat, a daring son of war, whose head the government had ordered Standish to bring to Plymouth, boasted of the excellence of his knife, on the handle of which was a woman's face. "But," said he, "I have another at home, with which I have killed both French and English; that has a man's face; by and by these two must be married." Further said he of his knife, "By and by it shall *see*, by and by it shall *eat*, but not *speak*."

Pecksuot, being a man of great stature, said to Standish, "though you are a great captain, yet you are but a little

man, and though I be no sachem, yet I am a man of great
strength and courage." The captain had formed his plan,
and was therefore silent. The next day, seeing he could
get no more of them together, Pecksuot, and Wittuwamat,
and his brother, a young man of eighteen, and one Indian
more, being together, and having about as many of his own
men in the room; he gave the *word*, the door was fast; he
seized Pecksuot, snatched his knife from him, and killed
him with it; the rest killed Wittuwamat, and the other Indian. The youth they took and hanged. Dreadful was the
scene; incredible the number of wounds they bore; without
any noise, catching at the weapons, struggling and striving
till death. At another place he and his men killed one
more. Capt. Standish then returned to Plymouth, carrying
the head of Wittuwamat, which was set up on the fort.
The news of this exploit spread terror through the surrounding tribes; amazed and terrified, they fled to the
swamps and desert places, which brought on diseases and
death to many. One of the sachems said, "The God of the
English was offended with them, and would destroy them in
his anger."

Some reflected on Capt. Standish, as being more of a
hero than a christian in this affair; but if there were any
fault, it certainly rested with the good magistrates of Plymouth; Standish only obeyed their orders; they deliberately
and coolly sanctioned the most bloody part of his conduct,
by setting up the head of Wittuwamat as a public spectacle.
All military exploits are dreadful.

In 1625, he was sent an agent for the company to England. The plague was raging in London, and he met with
difficulty in accomplishing his business; but the next year
he returned with goods for the colony, bringing the melan-
choly news, that Mr. Cushman and Mr. Robinson were
numbered with the dead.

A company of the baser sort had set down at Quincy; under one Morton, they had deposed their commander, sold arms to the natives, and invited fugitives from other places. Capt. Endicott, from Salem, gave them a small check, and cut down their *liberty pole*. Capt. Standish subdued them. Being sent for the purpose, and finding reasoning vain, he took them prisoners and carried them to Plymouth; thence they were sent to England. Previous to this, in 1624, the people of Plymouth had erected fishing flakes at Cape Ann. A company from the west of England, the next year, took possession of them. Capt. Standish was sent to obtain justice. His threats were serious, and the people of Cape Ann assured the company they were dead men, unless they satisfied the captain, for he was always punctual to his word. The company then built another stage or flake, in a more advantageous situation, which the Plymouth people accepted: thus harmony was restored.

A tradition in the family says, that a friendly native once came and told the captain, that a particular Indian intended to kill him; that the next time he visited the wigwam, he would give him some water, and while he should be drinking, the Indian would kill him with his knife. The next time the captain had occasion to go to the place, he remembered his trusty sword. He found a number of savages together, and soon had reason to believe the information, which had been given him. It was not long before the suspected Indian brought him some drink; the captain receiving it, kept his eye fixed on him while drinking. The Indian was taking his knife to make the deadly stab, when Standish instantly drew his sword and cut off his head at one stroke; amazed and terrified, the savages fled, and left our warrior alone.

After the year 1628, we hear no more of the military exploits of this valorous commander. Whether a constant series of vigorous exertion for so many years, had impaired his health, and rendered him unfit for active service, as it is said he was afflicted with the stone and strangury in his advanced years; or whether he became tired of such dreary, dangerous excursions, it is perhaps impossible now to ascertain. Certain it is, he did not in the least degree lose the confidence of the people. During his whole life, he was constantly elected one of the principal officers of the growing commonwealth: he was one of the magistrates or judges of the superiour court of the colony as long as he lived. When, "in regard of many appearances of danger towards the country," a council of war was appointed in 1652, "vested with full power to issue warrants to press men, and to give commissions to chief officers," the venerable Standish was among "the first three." In 1653, we find him acting in this council; and once more we may see him clothed in his coat of mail. In 1654, Cromwell called on New-England for troops to subdue the Dutch of New-York. Massachusetts ordered 500 to be furnished. Capt. Standish received the command of those raised in Plymouth colony. A part of his commission, probably his last, was in these words: "We having raised some forces, over which we do constitute our well beloved friend, Capt. Miles Standish, their leader and *Commander in Chief;* of whose approved fidelity and ability we have had *long* experience."

He was now probably seventy years of age. He had been engaged in the wars in the Netherlands, which ended about 1609. It is not probable that he left his native country before he was twenty-one; how long he continued in the army we know not, but probably he was twenty-five when he joined Mr. Robinson's congregation after the peace; it is not probable that a younger man would have been made a military commander in 1620; this will make him just seventy. He lived two years after this, dying in 1656, at

Duxbury, where he had a tract of land, which is now known by the name of the Captain's Hill. He had one son, Alexander, who died in Duxbury; a grandson of his, deacon Joseph Standish, settled in Norwich, Connecticut, a great grandson of whom is the junior compiler of this volume. A house of deacon Standish was burned, in which was destroyed the sword of the captain, with which was fought the first battles of New-England. They are certainly deceived, who imagine they have it in possession. His name will be long venerated in New-England. He was one who chose to suffer affliction with the people of God, who subdued kingdoms, and put to flight the armies of the aliens.

CHAP. XIX.

Comet; Philip's War; life and character of captain Church.

The people of New-England were surprised by the appearance of a comet, from the 17th of November, 1664, till the 4th of February following. They deemed it ominous (as they afterwards did the Aurora Borealis,) of some calamity, which was shortly to befal them.

In the year 1675, a war with the Indians, by the name of *Philip's war*, broke out, which endangered the existence of the colony. Some doubted whether the Indians would not succeed in the total extirpation of the English. This distressing war lasted more than a year.

This was the first hostile attack from the natives, which had been really alarming to the country. In 1637, the troops of Massachusetts and Connecticut had destroyed the Pequots. In 1643, there were some disturbances with the Narragansets; but matters were settled without shedding blood. In 1646, a plot was formed by Sequesson, a sachem near New-Haven, to assassinate the magistrates of that colony; but he effected nothing. In 1647, there were some transient difficulties with the Narragansets and Mohegans. The next year, the Narragansets hired the Mohawks to assist them against the Mohegans, but were detected. The following year, some persons were murdered by the Indians at New-Haven and Long Island.

In the year 1653, the public mind was agitated, a general panic seized the country, from an apprehension that there was a conspiracy of the Indians through the country to cut off the English. These rumours and terrors of the day appeared, afterward, to have had no just foundation.

In 1657, Alexander, the son of Massasoit, invited the Narragansets to join with him in revolting from the English. General Winslow went with only ten men, and brought him to Plymouth, where, though he was treated very civilly, his vexation and madness threw him into a fever, of which he died. His brother Philip succeeded him, and renewed his covenant with the English in 1662; yet, in 1671, he commenced hostilities against the English, but was soon subdued, and promised never to begin war again, before he had made complaint himself to Plymouth colony. Except these slight difficulties, for almost forty years the English had enjoyed peace with the Indians.

In 1675, John Sausaman, an Indian whom the English had employed as a missionary to instruct his brethren, informed the governor of Plymouth, that Philip, with several other tribes, was plotting the destruction of the English. Soon after this, Sausaman was found murdered; three Indians were arrested, tried, convicted, and hung for the murder. Philip, now more offended, sent away his women, armed his men, and robbed several houses in the vicinity of his own dwelling. June 24, 1675, the colony observed, as a day of humiliation and prayer. As the people of Swansey were returning from public worship, the Indians, lying in ambush, fired a volley, killed one man and wounded another. Two men, who went for a surgeon, were shot; and at the same time, in another part of the town, six other persons were killed. Immediately a company of horse and foot marched from Boston, and another company of foot from Plymouth, and arrived the 28th near Philip's seat; twelve men the same evening reconnoitered his camp, were fired upon, one was killed, and one wounded; the next morning a resolute assault was made, when the savages fled, leaving their camp and their country to the conquerors.

The troops of Massachusetts then marched into the country of the Narragansets, to renew the treaty with them, sword in hand, and engage them not to join in the war with Philip. This they effected, and returned home. Philip fled to the Nipmuck Indians, in Worcester county, who were persuaded to assist him. August 2, captains Wheeler and Hutchinson went into that country to renew a treaty with them, according to an appointment; but the Nipmucks, instead of attending the treaty, from an ambush fired on them, killed eight men, and mortally wounded captain Hutchinson. The rest fled to Quaboag, where all the inhabitants had collected in one house.

Immediately they were surrounded by a host of enemies, Nipmucks, and Philip, with the men who had fled with him. They soon burned every house in the place, except the one in which the people and soldiers were collected. Here they directed their whole force; upon this cottage they poured a storm of musket balls for two days; countless numbers pierced through the walls, yet only one person was killed;* with long poles they thrust against it brands and

* Fisk, Hubbard, Mather.

rags dipped in brimstone; they shot arrows of fire; they loaded a cart with flax and tow, and with long poles fastened together, they pushed it against the house. Destruction seemed inevitable. The house was kindling, the surrounding savages stood ready to destroy the first that opened the door to escape. In this awful moment of terror, God sent a "mighty" shower of rain, which extinguished the kindling flames. August 4, Major Willard came to their relief, and raised the siege, destroying many of the enemy.

The Indians went to Deerfield and burned most of the houses; the next day they were at Northfield, where they killed eight men; Capt. Beers went, with thirty-six men, to bring off the inhabitants; on his march he was assaulted by the enemy, himself and twenty of his men were killed. September 18, Capt. Lathrop, with a number of teams and eighty young men, the flower of Essex county, went to bring a quantity of grain from Deerfield; on their return they stopped to gather grapes at Muddy Brook; when, instantly, 7 or 800 hundred Indians rushed upon them, and dreadful was the slaughter; confined among the trees, resistance was almost in vain; 70 sons of New-England fell and were buried in one grave; never had the country seen such a bloody hour. Captain Mosely, hearing the report of the guns, flew to the scene of action, with a few men, renewed the conflict, killed ninety-six of the enemy, and wounded forty, losing only two of his own men.

The enemy soon after burnt 32 houses in Springfield. The general court, then sitting in Boston, appointed a committee, who, with the ministers of the vicinity, might suggest what were the sins, which brought these heavy judgments, and what laws could be enacted for the prevention of those sins. Their report was received October 19, and measures were taken to carry the design into effect. The same day, at Hatfield, the New-England troops obtained a decisive victory over the enemy. Seven or eight hundred of them assaulted the town, but were repulsed in such a vigorous manner, that they fled in every direction; numbers of them were drowned in attempting to cross the river; others reached the Narraganset country before they rested. The English, on this important day, lost but one man. Those in Narraganset retired to a small piece of dry land, in a great swamp, seven miles west of the south ferry that goes over to Newport. Here they collected stores, and built the strongest fort they ever had in this country. A circle of pallisadoes was surrounded by a fence of trees, a rod in thickness. The entrance was on a long tree over the water, that only one person could pass at a time. This was guarded in such a manner that every attempt to enter would have been fatal. By the help of Peter, an Indian prisoner, but now a necessary guide, one vulnerable spot was discovered; at one corner the fort was not raised more than 4 or 5 feet in height, but here a block-house was erected, so that a torrent of balls might be poured into this gap.

Gen. Winslow, with 1500 men from Massachusetts, and 300 from Connecticut, with 160 Indians, having arrived near the place about 1 o'clock, after travelling 18 miles without refreshment or rest, discovered a party of the enemy, upon whom they instantly poured a shower of balls; the Indians returned the fire and fled into the fort. The English pursued, and without waiting to reconnoitre, or even to form, rushed into the fort after them; but so terrible was the fire from the enemy, they were obliged to retire. The whole army then made a united onset; hardly were they able to maintain their ground; some of their bravest captains fell. In this awful crisis, while the scale of victory hung doubtful, some of the Connecticut men, who were in the rear on the opposite side, where was a narrow place destitute of pallisadoes, leaped over the fence of trees, and fell on the rear of the enemy. This decided the contest. They were soon totally routed.

As they fled, their wigwams were set on fire. Instantly 600 of their dwellings were in a blaze. Awful was the moment to the poor Indians. Not only were they flying from their last hope of safety, and from their burning houses; but their corn, their provisions, and even many of their aged parents and helpless children, perished in the terrible conflagration. They could behold the fire, they could hear the last cries of their expiring families; but could afford them no relief. Seven hundred of their warriors they had left dead on the field of battle; 300 more afterward died of their wounds.* They had been driven from their country, and from their pleasant firesides: now their last hopes were torn from them; their cup of sufferings was full.

Sad was the day of victory to the English. Six brave captains fell before their eyes; 80 men were killed or fatally wounded; 150 were wounded who recovered. Twenty fell in the fort, 10 or 12 died the same day, on their march back to their camp, which they reached about midnight; it was cold and stormy, and the snow deep; several died the next morning, so that this day, December 20, they buried 34 in one grave. By the 22d, 40 were dead, and by the end of January, 20 more. Of the 300 from Connecticut, 80 were killed or wounded. Of their 5 captains, 3 were killed, and 1 so wounded, that he never recovered. In the fort they had taken a large number of prisoners, about 300 warriors, and as many women and children. It was supposed that 4000 Indians were in the fort when the assault was made.

The Indians never recovered the loss of this day. The destruction of their provisions in the fort was the occasion of great distresses in the course of the winter. But a thaw

* Hubbard.

in January, gave them some relief, when a party fell on Mendon, and laid it in ashes. In February, they received some recruits from Canada, when they burned Lancaster, and took forty captives, among whom was Mrs. Rowlandson, the minister's wife, he being on a journey to Boston to obtain soldiers for their defence. Marlborough, Sudbury and Chelmsford soon felt the terror of their arms. February 21, they penetrated as far as Medfield, burned half the town, and killed about 20 of the inhabitants; in 4 days they were in Weymouth, on the seashore, and in the same month, they dared to enter Plymouth, and to destroy 2 families. Had they been so disposed 50 years before, instead of 2 families, they might easily have destroyed the whole colony. In March they were in Warwick, and burned the town. They were pursued by Capt. Pierce, with 50 English and 20 Indian soldiers, but he was overpowered by numbers, himself and 49 of the English, with 8 of the Indians, being slain, after they had killed 140 of the enemy. The same day, Marlborough was in flames, and several people were killed at Springfield.

While detached parties were thus carrying terror through the towns in the oldest settlements of the colony, others were ravaging further west. In March, 1676, Northampton was assaulted, 5 persons killed, and 5 houses burned. They soon attacked Sudbury, and burned Groton; exclaiming to the garrison, "we have burned your meeting-house; what will you do for a house of prayer?"

In some of these skirmishes, the christian Indians were very helpful, and displayed great presence of mind. In the action in which Capt. Pierce was killed, one of them fled and concealed himself behind a rock, but observing that he was discovered, and that an enemy lay ready to fire on him the moment he should move, he took a stick and gently raised his hat in sight; the other instantly fired a ball through it; when, dropping his hat, he rose and shot his adversary. At the same time, another Indian saved himself and the only Englishman, who was saved, by running after him with his hatchet, as if he intended to kill him. Another rescued himself by this stratagem. He besmeared his face with wet gunpowder, by which the enemy mistook him for one of their own party, who were painted black.

Wandering parties of the enemy still continued their depredations. The 28th of March, they burned 40 houses in Rehoboth, and the next day 30 in the town of Providence. In April they did mischief in Sudbury and Andover. At Sudbury about a dozen persons were killed; and Captain Wadsworth, going to their assistance, was suddenly assaulted by 500 of the enemy, when he, Capt. Bruklebank, and more than 50 of their men, were slain. Five or six of this company were made prisoners, who were scourged, tortured and killed in the most cruel manner.

This was a most distressing time in New-England. The war had been raging almost a year; the towns all over the country had been in a constant state of alarm and terror; the enemy appearing in different and distant places at the same moment. The season of planting was at hand; to neglect this service would produce a famine; to call home their troops would be only to invite the enemy to destroy them. Parties must be sent out, garrisons must be manned; the labours of the field must be performed. In this crisis a spirit of prayer was remarkably conspicuous through the country. Fervent supplications were offered by the churches of New England.

About this time their Powah told the Indians *nothing more could be done;* a spirit of dissention and discouragement seized them; they had been driven from their best planting ground the year before, and from their most considerable fishing places, hunger and sickness followed, which was very mortal. In their difficulties they acted without system or energy. To complete their miseries, the Maquas fell upon them with incredible fury. They were now routed in every part of the country. Troops from Connecticut, which colony had been preserved from their cruelties, took and killed above 60 at one time, and 44 at another. Capt. Denison commanded one of these parties. Among his captives was the terrible Nanunttenoo, son of Miantonimoh. A Pequot first arrested him; a young Englishman soon came up and asked him some questions; his reply was, "You too much child; no understand matters of war. Let your captain come; him I will answer." When he was told that he was to be put to death, "he said he liked it well, that he should die before his heart was soft, or he had said any thing unworthy of himself." They were repulsed from Bridgewater, a town which lost not a man in this war. Near Medfield and Plymouth their parties were put to flight; another party above Northampton, on Connecticut river, was vanquished, and 100 of them killed. Immediately after, Capt. Turner with a party killed 300 of them, himself and 30 of his men being slain on the field of battle. They were driven from Hadley, Hatfield, and Rehoboth. June 29, 1676, was a day of public thanksgiving through the colony, to bless God for the comfortable prospect, that their troubles were drawing to a close.

About this time, the Maquas fell upon Philip, and killed 50 of his men. The occasion of their hostilities was singular, and tends to develope the character of Philip, who was a deep politician, with a heart glowing with love of his country, and burning with indignation against the prosperous strangers, who were extending themselves over the inheritance of his fathers.

Philip, after his flight from Mount Hope, had visited the Maquas; and to rouse their vengeance against the English to make a common cause of the war, had murdered several of their people from time to time, and persuaded them it was the English. But in one instance, not effectually executing his business, the bruised Indian revived, returned home, and accused Philip as the murderer. Thus Philip himself was the means of turning the fury of the Maquas from the English against himself and his people. The despairing monarch fled to his former dwelling, a most unfortunate, unhappy man, deserted by his allies, assaulted by a powerful neighbour, on whose help he had depended; his own people discouraged and scattered, suffering and dying, strangers triumphing in his distresses, and seizing his possessions. Had his father possessed his foresight and courage, perhaps his posterity might long have enlivened the palace at Mount Hope.

About this time the churches in Plymouth colony set apart a day to renew their covenant with God and one another. The next day major Bradford, with the Plymouth forces, after escaping an ambush, obtained a victory without losing a man. July 21, the Connecticut troops, in Narraganset, took and killed 180 of the enemy, without the loss of a man. In the Plymouth colony, 200 submitted to the English; and a party, assaulting Taunton, was repulsed without any loss. At this time Capt. Church distinguished himself; in one week, with a small party of 18 English and 22 Indians, he fought 4 battles, killed and took 79 of the enemy, without losing one of his own men. July 25, from Dedham and Medfield 36 Englishmen and 90 christian Indians took 50 prisoners, without any loss of their own party. Two days after, Sagamore John, with 180 Nipmucks, submitted to the English. Four days after this, a company from Bridgewater fell upon a company of Indians, who snapped their guns, but all missed fire; they fled, excepting 10, who were killed, and 5 made prisoners. The 1st of August,

Capt. Church took 23 more; the next day he arrived at Philip's head quarters, where he took and killed 130 more; Philip fled, leaving his family. Capt. Church pursued, and found him in a swamp: attempting to fly, an Indian shot him through the heart. His head was sent to Plymouth, where it arrived on the day they had devoted to solemn thanksgiving. So fell one of the most valiant captains of the New World; and so will the arts of civilized men always triumph over the simple savage. In a few weeks Capt. Church subdued several hundred more.

The same success attended the colony at the eastward. In September, 400 Indians were made prisoners at *Quocheco;* one half being found accessories in the war, were sold; the other half were set at liberty. Peace soon followed. One of their warriors, taken prisoner, observed; "You could never have subdued us, but, striking his breast, the Englishman's God makes us afraid here."

Never has New England seen so dismal a period as the war with Philip. About 600 men, the flower of her strength, had fallen in battle, or been murdered by the natives. A great part of the inhabitants were in mourning. There were few families who had not lost some near relative. In Massachusetts, Plymouth, and Rhode-Island, 12 or 13 towns had been utterly destroyed, and others greatly damaged. About 600 buildings, chiefly dwelling houses, had been burned; a large debt had been contracted, and vast quantities of goods, cattle, and other property had been destroyed. About every eleventh family had been burned out, and an eleventh part of the militia through New-England had been slain in the war.* So costly is the inheritance we have received from our valiant forefathers. The land we sow has been stained with their blood.

* Trumbull.

In this war, which threatened the existence of New England, Mr Benjamin Church was a distinguished commander, and his memory deserves the notice of posterity. He was born in Duxbury in 1639. His father, Joseph Church, with two brothers were among the early settlers of Plymouth colony. In 1674. Benjamin removed to Seconet, now Little Compton, the first English settler in the place. Being in the neighbourhood of Philip, his influence was of vast importance in counteracting the designs of that cunning foe, at the commencement of hostilities. Philip sent 6 men to Awashonks, squaw-sachem of Seconet, to engage her in the intended war. According to the custom of the savages, when any matter of great importance is to be decided, she called her subjects to a great dance, and invited Mr. Church to attend. He found several hundred Indians assembled, and Awashonks herself in "foaming sweat" leading the dance. She immediately sat down, called her nobles around her, ordered Mr. Church to be invited into her presence, and, after compliments were past, informed him of the message received from Philip. Mr. Church repelled the charge that the English meditated war, and made a favourable impresssion on her and most of her people. Though the agents of Philip were very daring, and Little Eyes, one of her council, joined with them, she desired Mr. Church to visit the Plymouth government on her behalf. Promising to see her soon, he set off, and at Pocasset, now Tiverton, he met Peter Nunnuit, husband of the Queen of Pocasset, who told him that Philip had held a dance of several weeks, that the young men from all parts of the country were eager for war, and Philip had promised them that next Lord's day, when the English would be at public worship, they might kill their cattle and plunder their houses. The next morning Church was in Plymouth, and the governor ordered the captains to march with the greater part of their companies, and rendezvous at Taunton. Church, with a detachment of English and friendly Indians, was in front. On the sabbath the Indians began their depredations, and soon proceeded to indulge their thirst for Englishmen's blood.

At Swanzey they killed 10 persons, beheading, dismembering and mangling them in a most horrid manner. The garrison of the place was roused; a party of horse pursued the enemy, but fell into an ambush; a chief officer was wounded, and the troop fled. Church hallooed, and stormed, and told them it was a shame to leave a man wounded among the enemy. Two returned with him, but before they reached the man, he fell lifeless from his horse. While the two men bore him away, Church pursued his horse, going off to the enemy. Having taken it, he called to his company to come and renew their pursuit. The enemy soon saluted him with a volley; yet providentially every shot missed him; though one of his company across the river was wounded. The troops marched down upon the Neck. At Keekamuit they took down the heads of eight Englishmen, raised upon poles according to the savage custom. They soon found that Philip had crossed the river, with all his people, to Pocasset. A council of war determined to build a fort. Church was much disgusted at the business of "building a fort for nothing, to cover the army from nobody," being impatient to cross the river and kill Philip. This he declared was the surest way of maintaining Mount Hope. He was more restless, because he had promised the Queen of Seconet to visit her. At length Capt. Fuller received orders to cross the river with 6 file of men, and to take Capt Church as second. The same day they passed to Rhode Island, and in the night crossed to the Pocasset shore. Concealing themselves in two parties, one of them, "being troubled with the epidemical plague of loving tobacco," kindled a fire to smoke it, by which the enemy discovered them and fled. Church had ordered their breakfast from the island, but the man employed forgot his duty, and "their only provisions were a few cakes of rusk," which Church had in his pocket, divided among them. He then, at his own request, took a part of the men, and went in search of the enemy. They proceeded towards Seconet, and passed down Punkatees neck. By the side of a wood, they were saluted by a volley of 50 or 60 guns; yet not a man was hurt. Retreating to a field, they were surprised by observing a hill above them apparently moving, being covered with Indians, running in a circuit to surround them. In fair view, on Rhode Island, were collected a company of horse and foot. Church ordered his men to strip off their coats, that their brethren on the island might recognize them by their white shirts; he ordered three guns to be distinctly fired, in hopes they would come to his relief. A part of his men he ordered to take a wall; but before they reached it, the enemy, concealed on the other side, assailed them with a shower of bullets. All now endeavoured to shelter themselves behind a small bank, and a piece of fence, where they were attacked from every rock, stump, tree or fence within sight. A store house, which overlooked them, the enemy seized, which seemed to threaten their last hope: but, piling up stones before them, they maintained the contest. A boat arriving from Rhode Island was kept at a distance by the incessant fire of the Indians. Church desired them to send their canoe, and take him and his men on board; but his arguments were weak, compared with the whizzing of the bullets. Some of the men began to cry out, "For God's sake, come and take us off; our ammunition is spent." Lest the enemy should hear and learn their weakness, Church fiercely ordered the boat to send the canoe, or be gone, or he would fire upon them. Away went the boat; the Indians renewing the battle with increasing fury. Some of the English were discouraged and spoke of saving themselves by flight. Their captain convinced them that this was impossible, and encouraged them to persevere. "I have," says he, "observed so much of the remarkable and wonderful providence of God in so far preserving you, that I am encouraged to believe, with much confidence, that God will yet preserve you, that not a hair of your head shall fall to the ground; be patient; be courageous; be prudently saving of your ammunition; and I doubt not you will yet come off well." His little army were roused, and determined to take their lot with him.

As one of them was setting a flat stone before him, it was struck by a ball, which greatly alarmed the fellow. Capt. Church turned this to his advantage. "Observe," said he, "how God directs the bullets; the enemy could not hit you when in the same place; yet they could hit the stone as soon as it was raised." While they were fighting for their lives, the woods trembling with the roar of the musketry, the shouts and yells of the savages, and a dismal night coming on, a sloop was descried coming down the river, near Gold Island. Golding, the captain, came to an anchor, though his sails, colours and stern were instantly filled with bullet holes. Church was the last that went in the canoe; but recollecting that he had left his hat and cutlass at a well, he declared the enemy should not have them. Having brought off those things, as he went on board two bullets struck the canoe; another lodged in a stake opposite to his breast, and a fourth "grazed the hair of his head." So closed an action of 6 hours, 20 men, fainting with hunger, against 300 ferocious savages. A deliverance, of which the captain always spoke in the most devout and grateful manner. The next day they returned to Mount Hope; whence Mr. Church went to Rhode Island for provisions, and learned from an

Indian where were the head quarters of Weetamore, squaw sachem of Pocasset. On his return, a party was sent to attack the Queen; but, after marching 2 miles, the commanding officer was discouraged, and declared, that if he knew he should destroy all the enemy by the loss of one man, he would not make the attempt. Church was vexed, offered to lead the way, and *hazard the brunt*, to no purpose, tartly adding: "Pray sir, lead your company to yonder windmill on Rhode-Island; there will be no danger of being killed, and we shall have less trouble to supply them with provisions." Still the officer would return; and, after receiving more men, was transported to Fall river in Freetown, to visit Weetamore. Capt. Church and Capt. Hunter, an Indian and one more, were sent on discovery. They soon came upon three of the enemy. Hunter wounded one, which he found was his kinsman. The captive desired favour might be shown to his squaw, but asked none for himself, "excepting the liberty of taking a whiff of tobacco." While he was taking his "whiff," his kinsman dispatched him with one blow. So is man the prey of man; the victim of selfishness and cruelty. Neighbours and brothers destroy each other. Such are the bitter fruits of sin. The quarters of Weetamore were soon discovered; she and her people fled, and ours returned to Mount Hope.

Soon after, a great part of Dartmouth was covered with desolation; but Capt. Eels and Earl took 160 prisoners, promising them good treatment; yet, in spite of them and Capt. Church, who all argued and plead and begged, those in higher office carried them to Plymouth, and transported them out of the country. About this time Philip fled to the Nipmucks, in Worcester county.

Capt. Church attended Gen. Winslow as a volunteer in the Narraganset expedition, waxed valiant in fight, rushed into the fort, was badly wounded by two balls, and though unable to stand, refused to be carried off, till the enemy were driven from their shelter. In vain he exerted his influence to prevent the fort, the dwellings and the stores from being set on fire. Had he succeeded, the wounded might have been comfortably lodged, and many lives preserved. In three months his wounds were so far healed, that he accompanied Gen. Winslow into the Nipmuck country, though so lame that he needed the assistance of two men to mount his horse.

Soon after his return, he removed his family from Duxbury to Rhode-Island, for their greater security, intending to engage in agricultural labour; but he no sooner took a tool in his hand, than he cut off one finger, and badly wounded another. He pleasantly said, he thought he was wrong in leaving the war, and would return to war again. Accordingly, he went to Plymouth, agreed with the government, and returned to raise men. Passing Seconet Point, he spoke with some Indians on the rocks, and appointed an interview with Awashonks, and some of her principal men. At Rhode Island he requested *a permit* to hold the treaty. They told him he was mad, that the rogues would certainly kill him. At length they consented he should go, and take only two friendly Indians with him; but they would give him no written permit. Buying a roll of tobacco and a bottle of rum, he visited his family, who were almost overwhelmed with apprehensions of danger; yet he obtained their consent, and, committing his wife, his babes and himself to the divine protection, he proceeded on his embassy. Landing at Seconet, he was kindly received by the queen and a few attendants, according to previous appointment. But walking from the water to find a convenient place to sit down, a great body of Indians, who had been concealed in the tall grass, rose up and surrounded them, armed with hatchets, guns, and spears; their faces painted, and hair trimmed in style of war. The sight was terrible, and doubtless our gentleman was surprised; yet he retained his presence of mind, and calmly said to the queen, "When people treat of peace, they lay aside their arms." Perceiving that the savages looked surly, he added, "they might only carry their guns at a small distance for formality." Thus he managed them, by showing neither fear nor jealousy. Laying aside their guns, they sat down. He then affably drank, and circulated his rum and tobacco. They soon engaged "that they would submit to the government of Plymouth, and serve them in what they were able, if their lives might be spared, and none of them transported out of the country." They were soon ordered to Sandwich, where Church visited them, after going to Plymouth for liberty of employing them as soldiers. Arriving at Sandwich, he and his attendants were conducted to a shelter, open on one side, where Awashonks and her chiefs soon paid him a visit, and the multitude made the air ring with their shouts. Near the open side of the shelter, a huge pile of dry pine was soon raised, which, after supper, was set on fire. The Indians gathered round. Awashonks, with her oldest people, kneeling down, formed the first circle, next to the fire. All the stout men, standing up, made the next; the rabble surrounded them in another circle. The chief warrior then stepped between the circles and the fire with a spear in one hand, and a hatchet in the other, dancing round, and fighting the fire. Calling over the tribes of Indians, who were hostile to the English, at the mention of each tribe, he would draw out and fight a new firebrand. Finishing the fight with the brand, he would bow and thank it. So he proceeded, naming and fighting all the tribes and nations. Sticking down his weapons, he retired, and a second performed the same dance, fighting with new fury. When half a dozen chiefs had thus acted their parts, the captain of the guard told Mr.

Church, they had been making soldiers for him, that this was "all one swearing them." Having in this manner engaged all the stout men, Awashonks and her captains came to Mr. Church, and said, "Now we are all engaged to fight for the English. You may call forth all or any part of us, at any time, as you have occasion, to fight the enemy." They then presented him with a fine firelock. He accepted their offer, took a number of their men, and the next morning before light, marched for Plymouth, where, July 24, 1676, he received a commission and reinforcement to fight the enemy. In the night he marched into the woods, and before day was at Middleborough. He soon discovered and took a large party of Indians. The compensation of the troops was half the prisoners and arms taken; the Indian soldiers had the loose plunder. The same week, near Munponset pond, he took another large party.

He soon became the favourite of the public, and the government gave him authority to raise or dismiss troops at his pleasure, to commission officers, to pardon his captives, Philip and a few notorious murderers excepted, and to march where he pleased in New-England. He soon took Little Eyes and his party, who had revolted from Awashonks, when she joined the English. Some of the Indians reminded him that this was the rogue that threatened to kill him at the dance before the war, and intimated that this was a good time to be revenged. Church told them, that christians did not seek revenge. He treated Little Eyes kindly, who expressed much gratitude.

Soon after, while pursuing the enemy, they found their track separated. The English agreed to pursue one; the Indians the other, though they at first objected, saying they should not feel *safe* without *him*. The English had not marched far before they saw across a swamp a company of Indians gathering whortleberries. Church ordered 2 men,

Philip's chief captain, calling to his men to stand and fight on. He and a great part of his company escaped. About 130 were taken and killed. In the morning the little army met, and the fall of their mighty enemy was proclaimed, at which they gave three huzzas. His body was drawn to the upland, having no covering but his small clothes and stockings. Capt. Church observed, that as he had caused many an Englishman to lie unburied, therefore not a bone of him should be buried. He then ordered an Indian to behead and quarter him. The Indian taking his hatchet, thus addressed Philip: "You have been one very great man. You have made many a man afraid of you. But so big as you be, I will chop you in pieces."

Capt. Church now visited his family, and returned to Plymouth. Tidings soon came that Anawon was spreading terror in Rehoboth and Swanzey. Again the government applied to Capt. Church. As soon as it was known, that he had engaged, men were not wanting, who declared they would go with him while there was an Indian in the woods. So important are men in a community, who possess the public confidence. It being the latter part of the week, he went to Rhode-Island with his company to keep the sabbath, and be near the scene of action on Monday morning. This christian commander, with his company, sacredly observed the duties of the sabbath. The God of the sabbath gave him remarkable success. But his pious design at this time was interrupted. On the morning of Lord's day, a post was sent him that the enemy were passing from Prudence Island to Pappasquash neck, on the west side of Bristol. He immediately marched; but when he and 15 or 16 Indians had crossed the ferry to the main, the wind and waves were so boisterous, that the canoe could not cross again. With this handful of tawney troops he proceeded, and that night took 10 prisoners. His lieutenant having arrived, the next day he took several more prisoners, one white man and five Indians being with him. Among them were a man and woman directly from Anawon. They informed him that this famous chieftain, who had made so many mothers childless, was in Squannaconk swamp, in the southeast part of Rehoboth, with 50 or 60 of Philip's best soldiers. The moment was important. He took counsel. He asked the prisoner from Anawon, whether he could reach him that night. The Indian replied, if he travelled "stoutly" he might "by sunset." He inquired of his Indians whether they would go with him. They said they were always ready to obey him, but added, "Anawon is a great warrior; he was a valiant soldier of Woosamequin, the father of Philip. He has been Philip's chief captain during the war. He is a cunning man, of great resolution. He has declared he would never be taken alive by the English. His men are daring fellows, some of Philip's best soldiers. We fear he cannot be taken by so few. It will be a great pity, after the great things you have done, captain, now to throw away your life." Church replied, that he believed Anawon was a subtle and valiant warrior, but he had long sought him in vain; that he was unwilling to lose this opportunity; that his lieutenant and men were at a distance, and that he had no doubt but the same God, who had so often protected, would still assist them. They replied, *We will go*. Church then asked his white man what he thought. "Sir," said he, "I am never afraid to go any where, when *you* are with me." Having sent a captive to his lieutenant, with orders to conduct his prisoners to Taunton, and meet him the next morning on the Rehoboth road, he asked the old Indian from Anawon, if he would be his pilot. He consented, and they moved on. Just at sunset, the old man, who went before, sat down. He said that Anawon at that time sent out his scouts to see if the coast was clear. At

Philip's chief captain, calling to his men to stand and fight on. He and a great part of his company escaped. About 130 were taken and killed. In the morning the little army met, and the fall of their mighty enemy was proclaimed, at which they gave three huzzas. His body was drawn to the upland, having no covering but his small clothes and stockings. Capt. Church observed, that as he had caused many an Englishman to lie unburied, therefore not a bone of him should be buried. He then ordered an Indian to behead and quarter him. The Indian taking his hatchet, thus addressed Philip: 'You have been one very great man. You have made many a man afraid of you. But so big as you be, I will chop you in pieces."

Capt. Church now visited his family, and returned to Plymouth. Tidings soon came that Anawon was spreading terror in Rehoboth and Swanzey. Again the government applied to Capt. Church. As soon as it was known, that he had engaged, men were not wanting, who declared they would go with him while there was an Indian in the woods. So important are men in a community, who possess the public confidence. It being the latter part of the week, he went to Rhode-Island with his company to keep the sabbath, and be near the scene of action on Monday morning. This christian commander, with his company, sacredly observed the duties of the sabbath. The God of the sabbath gave him remarkable success. But his pious design at this time was interrupted. On the morning of Lord's day, a post was sent him that the enemy were passing from Prudence Island to Pappasquash neck, on the west side of Bristol. He immediately marched; but when he and 15 or 16 Indians had crossed the ferry to the main, the wind and waves were so boisterous, that the canoe could not cross again. With this handful of tawney troops he proceeded, and that night took 10 prisoners. His lieutenant having arrived, the next day he took several more prisoners, one white man and five Indians being with him. Among them were a man and woman directly from Anawon. They informed him that this famous chieftain, who had made so many mothers childless, was in Squannaconk swamp, in the southeast part of Rehoboth, with 50 or 60 of Philip's best soldiers. The moment was important. He took counsel. He asked the prisoner from Anawon, whether he could reach him that night. The Indian replied, if he travelled "stoutly" he might "by sunset." He inquired of his Indians whether they would go with him. They said they were always ready to obey him, but added, "Anawon is a great warrior; he was a valiant soldier of Woosamequin, the father of Philip. He has been Philip's chief captain during the war. He is a cunning man, of great resolution. He has declared he would never be taken alive by the English. His men are daring fellows, some of Philip's best soldiers. We fear he cannot be taken by so few. It will be a great pity, after the great things you have done, captain, now to throw away your life." Church replied, that he believed Anawon was a subtle and valiant warrior, but he had long sought him in vain; that he was unwilling to lose this opportunity; that his lieutenant and men were at a distance, and that he had no doubt but the same God, who had so often protected, would still assist them. They replied, *We will go*. Church then asked his white man what he thought. "Sir," said he, "I am never afraid to go any where, when *you* are with me." Having sent a captive to his lieutenant, with orders to conduct his prisoners to Taunton, and meet him the next morning on the Rehoboth road, he asked the old Indian from Anawon, if he would be his pilot. He consented, and they moved on. Just at sunset, the old man, who went before, sat down. He said that Anawon at that time sent out his scouts to see if the coast was clear. At dark they returned; at which time he rose to proceed. Church asked him if he would take a gun and fight for him. In a most affecting manner he bowed very low and said, "I pray you not to impose such a thing on me, as to fight my old friend Capt. Anawon. But I will go with you and help you, and as you have given me my life, I will lay hands on any man, who shall offer to hurt you." They soon heard a noise, when Church and two Indians, crawling forward to the edge of a precipice, saw the enemy in full view before them. They were in 3 companies. Anawon, his son, and several chiefs, had cut down a tree under the rocks, and against it set up a row of bushes to form a shelter. Great fires were burning without, pots and kettles were boiling, and spits turning loaded with meat. Their arms stood near, covered with a mat. Returning to his company, Capt. Church ordered his pilot and daughter, as they would be received without notice, to descend first, with their baskets on their backs. He and his friends followed in their shadow, letting themselves down by the bushes in the cracks of the rocks. Church, with his hatchet in his hand, first reached the arms at the feet of Anawon. The old chieftain, starting up on end, cried out, *Howah*, and in despair fell back silent. Church sent his Indians to the other companies to inform them their chief was a prisoner, and warn them to submit. They obeyed. "What have you for supper?" said Church to Anawon; "I am come to sup with you." Anawon ordered his women to provide supper, and asked Church whether he would have cow beef or horse beef. He replied that cow beef would be the most pleasant. Supper was soon ready; after which, as he had not slept for two days and a night, Church told his men if they would let him sleep two hours, they should rest the whole night after. But his situation was too interesting for sleep; his men, however, he soon perceived were all in a sound slumber. He and

Anawon were the only persons awake in all the camps. So does elevation of character and a sense of responsibility, fill the heart with anxious care. While the Indian chief recollected the deeds of his valour in the service of three kings, and exulted in the destruction of villages, the sighs of his prisoners, and the blood of a thousand battles, the chains of his own captivity sunk deep into his soul; the fall of his prince, the ruin of his country, the utter extinction of his tribe, filled his heart with the agony of horror and desperation. For an hour the two captains lay looking at each other, when Anawon arose, and walked off, as Church supposed for some necessary purpose; but, soon finding him out of sight and hearing, he began to be alarmed, took all the arms to him, crowded himself under young Anawon, so that the father must have endangered his son in attempting to kill him. But the old man soon returned, and falling on his knees said, "Great captain, you have killed king Philip, and conquered his country. I believe that I and my company are the last, who war against the English; so I suppose the war is ended by your means. These things, therefore, are yours. They are the royalties of king Philip, with which he adorned himself when he sat in state. I think myself happy in presenting them to Capt. Church, who has so fairly won them." Then opening the pack, he pulled out a belt, nine inches broad, curiously wrought with black and white wampum, in various figures of flowers, birds, and beasts; also another wrought in the same manner, worn on the head of the warrior, hanging down his back, from which two flags waved behind him. A third with a star on the end hung round his neck down to his breast. These and two horns of glazed powder, and a red cloth blanket, constituted the royal dress of king Philip. They spent the night in free conversation. Anawon gave a narrative of his mighty successes in former wars, when he fought under

Woosamaquin. In the morning they marched to Taunton. Church and Anawon, with half a dozen friendly Indians, went to Rhode-Island, while the troops and other prisoners were sent to Plymouth, where Church soon followed them. News soon came that Tispaquin, with his company, was doing mischief near Sippican, now Rochester. He was a celebrated Powah, or conjurer. The Indians said bullets would not kill him. Church pursued, and soon took a number of prisoners, who belonged to him. Leaving two squaws, he directed them to tell their chief on his return, that Capt. Church had carried his wife and children to Plymouth, and if he would follow them, he should be his soldier, intending to employ him against the Indians at the eastward. The chief and his company soon resigned themselves to the people of Plymouth. Church was then at Boston, and on his return was extremely afflicted to find that Tispaquin and Anawon were beheaded.

The next January, Capt. Church ranged the woods, and took several straggling parties. This closed the Indian wars of the ancient colony of Plymouth. Several tribes continued friendly. They have always been treated kindly, supplied with missionaries and schoolmasters, and, though dwindled to remnants, they continue to this day.

Peace being restored to his country, Capt. Church settled at Bristol. Afterwards he removed to Fall-river, (now Freetown) and thence removed to Seconet, (Little Compton.) In each of these places he acquired a good estate. But in 1689, the Indians at the eastward commenced hostilities. Church received a major's commission, and with 250 men, landed at Casco, and soon obtained a victory near the town. He ranged the woods far and wide, visited the garrisons at Black Point, Spurwink, Blue Point and Kennebec, put suitable officers in those places, and returned home. The next year, in September, with 350 men, he drove the enemy from Androscoggin and Maquait. In 1692, major Church accompanied Gov. Phips to Pemaquid, where the governor, with two companies, erected a fort, while major Church went to Penobscot, drove off the savages, and took considerable plunder of corn and fur. Returning to the governor, they sailed to the Kennebec. The governor proceeded to Boston, but sent major Church up the river, who soon gained a victory, and pursued the enemy to Teconit falls, took the fort there, destroyed great quantities of their corn, returned to Pemaquid, and thence home. So distinguished were his talents, that he had no competitor. In 1696, the governor again applied to him, and he sailed to Penobscot, exploring the islands, and ascending the river; thence he proceeded to Nova-Scotia. The French and Indians fled from their settlements, and he brought away a rich booty of warlike stores and provisions.

The last military adventure of our christian hero was in 1704, when, having received a colonel's commission, and the command of ten companies, he sailed for the eastward. At Green Island he took a few prisoners. At Penobscot he took or killed every Indian and Frenchman, that could be found. Among the captives was a daughter of Casteen, whom they kindly treated, though her father had been such a bloody foe of New-England. Thence they proceeded, and drove the French and Indians from Passamaquoddy. Sailing across the bay, they took Menas, a town in Nova-Scotia. On his return, Col. Church touched at various places on the main and the islands, and found that the enemy were all gone. He was informed that the French priests had told the Indians, it was impossible for them to live in the same country with the English, and advised them to remove to the Missisippi, promising to go and live and die with them. According to this advice of the French, who had excited them to quarrel, and were the occasion of their ruin and our sufferings, the Indians left their homes, their provisions and their country, to the victorious English.

Col. Church was a man of good stature, well proportioned, hardy and active. He possessed a correct judgment, remarkable presence of mind, and dignity of manners. His generous, affable, and obliging temper secured the love and esteem of his acquaintance. He was a serious and devout member of the church in Bristol. He daily worshipped God in his family, read and expounded the scriptures. He sanctified the sabbath, and regularly attended the ordinances of the gospel. The morning before his death he rode two miles to condole with his only sister, mourning the death of her only son. After a pious conversation, he bid her farewell in a most affecting manner, telling her he should never see her again, till he met her in heaven. On his return, his horse fell, a blood vessel broke, he was taken up speechless, and in twelve hours expired, in the 78th year of his age. His memory is held in grateful remembrance, and his posterity are respectable.

CHAP. XX.

Sufferings of the Colonists; Synods of New-England.

At this time the colonists were afflicted with various calamities. While they were contending in a bloody war with the natives for their lives and their property, complaints were making in England, which struck at their government. An inquiry now commenced, which issued in the loss of their charter. At the same time Great-Britain and Ireland were suffering under a prince, hostile to civil and religious liberty; and connected, as New-England was, with the mother country, she could not but share, in a greater or less degree, in the evils of such a government. Add to these, the small pox spread through the country, and uncommon losses had been sustained by sea, during the wars against the French and Dutch.

In this state of things, a synod was convened by order of the general court, in May, 1679, which was called the Reforming Synod. They inquired what were the provoking sins of the times, and what the duties to be done to recover the divine favour. The effects were happy on morals and religion. Previous to this, in 1637, a Synod had met at Cambridge for the suppression of Antinomian, and other errors. Eighty errors were presented, examined and condemned. Great was the good, which they effected. In the years 1647, and 8, another synod met at Cambridge, and established that Platform, which has ever since remained the professed directory of the churches in Massachusetts, in government and discipline. In 1679, a Synod unanimously approved this Platform, "desiring that the churches may continue stedfast in *the order of the gospel*, according to what is therein declared from the word of God."—This Platform has been considered as an authority in judicial decisions, on questions of an ecclesiastical nature.

Several years after the death of Mr. Hooker, a violent contention arose in the church of Hartford, "upon some nice point of congregationalism." The governor, and other principal characters taking a zealous part in the controversy, the flame soon spread to neighbouring churches, and finally through the whole colony. In 1654 or 5, a council was called to settle the dispute; but their opinion was little regarded, as they were supposed previously to have taken sides in the contest. Another council was therefore called from Massachusetts, in 1656, but their labours for peace were equally unsuccessful.

At this period, when the churches were in a state of general agitation, a large and respectable part of the christian community, came forward and advocated that all persons of regular lives should be admitted to full communion, and that all baptized persons should be treated as members of the church; and some insisted, that all who had been members of regular ecclesiastical *parishes* in England, and supported public worship, should be allowed the privileges of full communion. A list of grievances was introduced to the legislature on account of their being denied, as they stated, their just rights and privileges by the ministers and churches. The *churches* had chosen their ministers; this was considered, by the *congregation*, as a great grievance, as they had an equal concern for themselves and families, and bore their share in supporting them. These points were warmly agitated through the colony. The times were altered. The people, who first settled the country, were generally pious professors of religion; but many of their children, and others, who had more recently immigrated here, made no profession of religion, and their children were not baptized.* These people, as all the honours and offices of the country were in the *church*, were engaged to obtain the privileges of church membership. These were joined by a more serious party, who saw no other way to remedy distressing evils, which they devoutly deplored.

The first planters had a numerous posterity, and themselves had generally become grand parents. These excellent and godly fathers of the land, with the deepest distress, saw their grand children excluded from the ordinances of baptism, and the blessings of the church. Many of them appeared sober, were desirous of renewing their baptismal covenant, and submitting to the discipline of the church;

* Trumbull.

"yet they could not come up to that experimental account of their regeneration, which would sufficiently embolden their access to the other sacrament." It became the study of the aged, how they might continue their descendants under the watch of the church, "that they might be in a fairer way to receive the grace of God." That they might be under the government of the Shepherd, the Lord Jesus Christ, they had brought their lambs into this forlorn wilderness. Yet, with their ideas of church purity, they feared, that if all persons were admitted, not guilty of censurable scandal, a worldly part might bring things into a disagreeable state.*

The magistrates of Connecticut, observing the civil community, as well as the church, to be in danger from the paroxysm commencing, procured a draught of the questions, which disturbed the public mind, and sent them to the magistrates of Massachusetts, with a request that several of the ablest ministers of each colony might deliberate, and give them an answer. "Accordingly, letters from the government procured an assembly of the principal ministers of New-England, at Boston, June 4, 1657, who by the 19th of the month, presented an elaborate answer to 21 questions."* Among other things, referring to the state of children born in the church, they assert, "That it is the duty of those come to years of discretion, baptized in their infancy, to own the covenant; that it is the duty of the church to call them to this; that if they refuse, or are scandalous in any other way, they may be censured by the church. If they understand the grounds of religion, and are not scandalous, and solemnly own the covenant, giving up themselves and their children to the Lord, baptism may not be denied their children."*

* Mather.

The practice here recommended, in regard to baptized children, was not adopted by all the churches. Opposition was made to it, in such manner and extent, that the general court considered it expedient to call a synod of all the churches to meet in Boston, in the spring of 1662. Two questions, embracing the subjects, then agitated in the churches, were submitted by the general court to the decision of this synod, viz. 1st, "Who are the subjects of baptism? 2d, Whether, according to the word of God, there ought to be a *consociation* of churches, and what should be the manner of it." The first of these questions was answered by the synod, in seven propositions, "briefly confirmed by the scriptures." These propositions, having been approved by the general court, and never been since disapproved by any public act of the churches, are, from their importance, here inserted at length.

1. "They that according to scripture are members of the visible church, are the subjects of baptism.

2. "The members of the visible church according to scripture, are confederate visible believers, in particular churches, and their infant seed, i.e. children in minority, whose next parents, one or both, are in covenant.

3. "The infant-seed of confederate visible believers, are members of the same church with their parents, and when grown up, are personally under the watch, discipline and government of that church.

4. "These adult persons, are not therefore to be admitted to full communion, merely because they are and continue members, without such further qualifications, as the word of God requireth thereunto.

5. "Church members, who were admitted in minority, understanding the doctrine of faith, and publicly professing their assent thereto; not scandalous in life, and solemnly owning the covenant before the church, wherein they give

up themselves and their children to the Lord, and subject themselves to the government of Christ in the church, their children are to be baptized.

6. "Such church members, who either by death, or some other extraordinary providence, have been inevitably hindered from public acting, as aforesaid, yet have given the church cause in judgment of charity to look at them as so qualified, and such, as had they been called thereunto, would have so acted; their children are to be baptized.

7. "The members of orthodox churches, being sound in the faith, and not scandalous in life, and presenting due testimony thereof; these occasionally coming from one church to another, may have their children baptized in the church whither they come, by virtue of communion of churches: But if they remove their habitation, they ought orderly to covenant and subject themselves to the government of Christ in the church where they settle their abode, and so their children to be baptized. It being the churches' duty to receive such into communion, so far as they are regularly fit for the same."

On the subject of *consociation*, the synod subscribed to a profession made in the English churches: "That it is a most abhorred maxim, that a single society of men, professing the name of Christ, should judge them of the same body and society, and yet exempt themselves from giving account, or being censurable by any other, either christian magistrate above them, or neighbour churches about them."

They answered the question concerning the consociation of churches in the affirmative, and in 8 propositions prescribed the *manner* of it.

They approved the consociation of churches, as the faithful use of the gifts, which Christ has bestowed on them for his glory, and their mutual good and edification. They declared it the duty of churches consociated, among other things, "to

give an account to one another of their public acts, when
regularly desired, to strengthen one another in their administration of discipline, to lend aid in case of divisions and
contentions, in ordinations, in the removing or deposing elders, in doubtful and difficult questions; also to rectify mal-
administrations, and to admonish one another when need
requires. They recommend it to the churches thus to unite
in consociation.

The result of this synod was presented to the general
court in Oct. 1662, who thought "meet to commend it to
the consideration of all the churches and people in their jurisdiction."

Several learned and pious clergymen dissented from the
result of the synod, respecting baptism, among whom were
president Chauncey, Mr. Increase Mather, and Mr. Davenport, who all wrote against it. Other able men wrote in
favour of it.

The practice now, as from the beginning, has men of the
first rank for piety, talents, and respectability, both for and
against it. The subject has been very ably discussed. It
has never been considered, on either side, an article essential to the communion of churches, and is a point on which
all good men agree to differ.

In 1679, the reforming synod met in Boston, Sept. 10.
The people had for some time suffered the afflictive provi-
dences of heaven. Droughts had turned the land to powder and dust; blasts had destroyed the wheat of the field;
fire had spread devastation in the mart of commerce; pestilence had walked through the towns; ships of the merchant
had been cast away, or returned without their accustomed
profits; the yell of savage bands had terrified the rural village; their murderous arrows had clothed widows and or-
phans in the garments of mourning. Serious people were
deeply impressed; particular churches exerted themselves

to promote a reformation; ministers were roused to exert themselves in the cause of righteousness. Under these circumstances, the general court were induced to call upon the churches to send their elders and messengers to meet in synod, for the discussion of two questions, "What are the provoking evils of New-England? What is to be done that these evils may be reformed?" Before they convened, the churches observed a day of fasting and prayer, to seek direction from God. Mr. John Sherman, and Mr. Urian Oaks were chosen moderators of the synod.

Respecting the first question, the synod voted, that the provoking sins of New-England were a great decay of the power of godliness; also, pride, manifested in violating order, and a spirit of contention; that the rising generation were not mindful of the obligations resulting from their baptism; that a profanation of God's name, sabbath breaking, want of family religion, in daily prayer, and reading the scriptures; intemperance, and uncleanness, "temptations to which are common in naked arms, and necks, and naked breasts," violation of promises, and inordinate zeal for the world, shown in individuals, by forsaking their churches for greater farms, or more valuable merchandise, who ought to remember, that when Lot left Canaan and the church for better accommodations in Sodom, "God fired him out of all," opposing the work of reformation; selfishness; and undervaluing the gospel of Christ, "are matters of the Lord's controversy." That as several of them were sins not punished by human laws, therefore there were special reasons to expect, that God himself would punish them.

As to the second question, "What is to be done for the reformation of these evils?" they voted, that if all, who were above others, would become exemplary; if the people would publicly declare their adherence to the faith and discipline of their fathers; if no persons were admitted to church com-

munion, without a public profession of their faith and
repentance; if a strict discipline were maintained in the
churches; if there were a full supply of church officers, pastors, teachers, and ruling elders; if these officers were duly
supported; if the laws of the commonwealth were faithfully
executed; if there were an explicit renewal of covenant in
the churches; if schools were strictly inspected and supported, and the people cried fervently for the rain of righteousness, there would be a reformation of the evils deplored.
This synod was followed with many of the good effects,
which were desired and expected by its friends.

The next year, May 12, 1680, another synod met in Boston, to adopt a confession of faith. Mr. Increase Mather
was chosen moderator. "The confession of faith, consented
to by the congregational churches of England, which was
nearly the same which was agreed to by the reverend assembly at Westminster, and afterward by the general assembly of Scotland, was approved, with a few variations, as the
faith of New-England. The synod chose to use the confessions of faith adopted in Europe, "that so they might, not
only with one heart, but with one mouth, glorify God and
our Lord Jesus Christ."*

The fathers of the Plymouth colony had adopted the articles of the church of England, and the confession of faith,
professed by the French reformed churches;† or, in other
words Calvinism, as the articles of their faith, or the substance of their creed. In the synod of New-England, 1648,
there was a unanimous vote expressive of the same
opinions.

In the synod of 1680, is a language explicit on the most
discriminating points. "In the unity of the godhead there
be three persons," say they, "of one substance, power and
eternity." "God from all eternity did, by the most wise

* Mather. † Hazard.

and holy counsel of his will, freely and unchangeably ordain whatsoever comes to pass. By the decree of God, for the manifestation of his glory, some men and angels are predestinated unto everlasting life, and others foreordained unto everlasting death." The first pair "being the root, and by God's appointment standing in the room of all mankind, a corrupt nature is conveyed to all their posterity." "The Lord Jesus Christ, the eternal God, hath fully satisfied the justice of God, and hath purchased reconciliation, and an eternal inheritance." "God hath endued the will of man with that natural liberty and power of acting upon choice, that it is neither forced, nor by any absolute necessity of nature, determined to do good or evil." "Works done by unregenerate men, although for the matter of them they may be things, which God commands, yet because they proceed not from a heart purified by faith, nor are done in a right manner according to the word, nor to a right end, the glory of God; they are therefore sinful, and cannot please God, nor make a man meet to receive the grace of God." "The works of creation and providence, with the light of nature, make no discovery of Christ, much less do they enable men, destitute of revelation, to attain saving faith or repentance."

In 1703, the trustees of the college in Connecticut wrote a circular letter to the ministers of the colony for a general synod. The proposal was acceptable, and the churches and ministers met in a consociated council, and adopted the Savoy and Westminster confessions of faith, and drew up certain rules of discipline, preparatory to a general synod.

In 1708, a synod was convened at Saybrook, composed of ministers and delegates from the colony, with two or more messengers from a convention of the churches in each county. They drew up that system of church government and discipline, called the *Saybrook Platform*. It was passed into a law, and became the constitution of Connecticut churches. A distinguishing feature of this Platform is the negative it gives the ministers to the vote of the church: but this authority is seldom exercised.

In 1724, the convention of ministers petitioned the general court to call a synod; but the attorney and solicitor general, gave it as their opinion, that it was not lawful for a synod to meet without authority from the king, and the design was laid aside.*

Such is a general view of the synods in New-England, and such were the occasions and effects of their meetings. These are sketches of the platforms and confessions of faith adopted by them. The doctrines above enumerated were considered orthodox by our excellent ancestors both before and after they came to this country. No convention since, no consociation, no synod, nor general council, has adopted any other systems of doctrine and discipline; therefore, such may now be considered the discipline and orthodoxy of the New-England churches.

CHAP. XXI.

Loss of Charter; state of New-England; Andros arrives; tenor of his administration; William and Mary proclaimed; Indian war; Expedition against Canada and Nova-Scotia; New Charter.

In June, 1683, articles of high misdemeanor were exhibited by Edward Randolph, the public accuser of those days, against the governor and company of Massachusetts. In consequence, a writ of *quo warranto* was ordered; and Randolph was appointed to carry it to New-England. To give

* Chalmers.

importance to the messenger, and to his message, both of which were extremely obnoxious to the people of Massachusetts, a frigate was ordered to convey him to Boston. To prevent alarm in the colony, a declaration accompanied the *quo warranto*, that it should affect no private rights. When he arrived, the general court deliberated on the critical state of their affairs. The governor and a majority of the assistants resolved to submit to the royal pleasure, and transmitted an address to that effect. But the representatives, supported by the decisive influence of the clergy, refused their assent. All was ineffectual to preserve the charter. In Trinity term, 1684, judgment was given for the king, by the high court of chancery, against the governor and company of Massachusetts, "that their letters, patents, and the enrolment thereof be cancelled."

Thus ended the ancient government of Massachusetts by legal process. The validity of these proceedings was afterwards questioned by high authority. The house of commons at a subsequent period resolved, "that those *quo warrantos* against the charter of New-England were illegal and void."

Amidst all her disputes with the mother country, New-England greatly flourished. Agricultural pursuits were successful, manufactures and commerce were extended, and population and wealth increased, because "the rough hand of oppression had not touched the labours of the inhabitantst or interrupted the freedom of their pursuits." If, for a shor, time, the splendour of New-England independence was obscured by the clouds of royal authority, it soon blazed forth never to be extinguished.

Ten months passed after the dissolution of the charter, when it was thought necessary to establish a temporary government for the preservation of order. During this period, James II. ascended the throne of England, and was proclaimed in Boston, April, 1685, with "sorrowful and affected pomp." In September following, a commission was issued, appointing a president and a council, composed of the most loyal of the inhabitants, of the government of Massachusetts, New-Hampshire, Maine and Narraganset, till the chief governor should arrive. Col. Dudley, a native of Massachusetts, was appointed president.

The people reluctantly submitted to a power which they could not oppose; declaring, that "though they could not give their assent to it, they should demean themselves as loyal subjects, and humbly make their addresses to God, and in due time to their gracious sovereign, for relief." Counsellors were nominated by the king; no house of representatives was mentioned in the commission; still, to reconcile the minds of the people to the intended introduction of a governor general, the courts of justice were allowed to remain on their original plan; juries were continued; former laws and customs were observed.*

Before a year of governor Dudley's administration had expired, (December, 1686) Sir Edmund Andros arrived in Boston from New-York, where he had been governor, being now appointed captain general, and vice admiral of Massachusetts, New Hampshire, Maine, Plymouth, Rhode-Island and Connecticut, during pleasure. In 1688, New-York and New-Jersey were added to his jurisdiction. He, with four of his council, was empowered to grant lands, with such quit rents as the king should appoint. Like all tyrants, from Nero to those of the present day, Sir Edmund began his administration with professions of high *regard for the public welfare.*

In the fall of 1689, he went to Hartford, where the assembly were sitting, and demanded the charter, declaring their

* Hutchinson.

government dissolved. Remonstrances were made, and the business delayed till evening; when, tradition says, the charter was brought into the assembly, and laid on the table; candles were extinguished, but lighted again. The charter could not be found. All was quiet and peaceable. The charter had been taken by Capt. Wadsworth, and concealed in a hollow oak tree, which is standing at this day.* Still Sir Edmund seized the reins of government; turned out the old, and appointed new officers, civil and military.

Numerous were the oppressions of this tyrant. The press was restrained, liberty of conscience infringed, and exorbitant taxes levied.† The charter being vacated, it was pretended all titles to lands were destroyed; farmers, therefore, who had cultivated their soil for half a century, were obliged to take new patents, giving large fees, or writs of intrusion were brought, and their land sold to others. To prevent petitions or consultations, town meetings were prohibited, excepting one in a year for the choice of town officers. Lest the cries of oppression should reach the throne, he forbid any person to leave the country without permission from the government. But the resolute Dr. Increase Mather escaped the watchful governor, his guards and emisaries; crossed the Atlantic, and spread before the king the complaints of New-England. But relief came not till the revolution.

When the report reached Boston, that the Prince of Orange had landed in England, joy beamed in every eye. Though the governor imprisoned the man who brought the Prince's declaration; though, by a proclamation, he commanded all persons to prepare for an invasion from Holland; though magistrates and the more considerate men were determined quietly to wait the issue; yet the indignant spirit of the

* 1820. † Trumbull.

people could not be restrained. On the morning of April 18th, the public fury burst forth like a volcano. The inhabitants of Boston were in arms; the country flocking to their assistance. Andros and his associates fled to a fort; resistance was vain; he was made a prisoner, and sent to England. The charges exhibited against him not being signed by the colonial agents, he was dismissed, and this tyrant, thus indignantly driven from New-England, was appointed governor of Virginia.

Mr. Bradstreet, the late governor, with those who had been magistrates under the charter, assumed the government, taking the name of the "Council of Safety," till new orders should arrive from England. These were shortly after received from king William, who, with his queen, Mary, were proclaimed in Boston, May, 29th, 1689, with more ceremony, than had ever been known in that colony on the like occasion. The revolution in Boston was popular in New-Hampshire, but they found themselves in a very unsettled state. After waiting in vain for orders from England, they chose deputies to agree on some mode of government, and finally determined to return to their ancient union with Massachusetts.

In 1692, Samuel Allen obtained a commission for the government of New-Hampshire. Having purchased of Mason's heirs the lands of the colony, they were embroiled with new controversies for several years.

Previous to this, in 1688, an Indian war broke out in New England; various were the provocations plead by the natives in their justification. The first blood was shed at North Yarmouth, in September. In the spring, the Penicook Indians joining those of Saco, made a dreadful slaughter at Cocheco. Mesandouit, being hospitably lodged at major Waldron's, in the night opened the gate, and a hundred, some say 500 Indians rushed into the garrison, murdered the major, and 22 others, took 29 prisoners, burned 4 or 5 houses, and fled, loaded with plunder. The captives were sold to the French in Canada. Four young men of Saco, being abroad were killed; 24 men armed went forth to bury them, and were assaulted by such a number, that they retreated, leaving 5 or 6 of their number dead. In August, the enemy took the fort at Pemaquid; and so frequent were their assaults, and so great the public alarm, that the country round retired to Falmouth for safety. The same month, major Swayn, with 7 or 8 companies from Massachusetts, relieved the garrison at Blue Point, which was beset with Indians. Major Church, with another party of English and christian Indians from Plymouth colony, marched to the eastward. Swayn, making his head-quarters at Berwick, sent Capt. Wiswell, and Lieut. Flag on a scout. Near Winnipisioke pond, Flag left a number of his friendly Indians, who continued there a number of days. It was afterwards discovered, that they had an interview with the hostile natives, and gave them all the information in their power. So strong is the attachment, which binds us to our native country, that often the bonds of gratitude, oaths, and religion, like Sampson's cords, burst asunder, when they interfere with this passion. Feeble then, is that government, which depends on *foreigners* for defence or counsel. It is hazardous to any government to trust foreigners with a share in its administration. It is enough that they have protection and a participation in its blessings.

This month, Casco was assaulted, and Capt. Bracket was killed; but Captain Hall arriving, a serious engagement followed, which was supported several hours. Of the English 10 or 12 were killed; the enemy fled; and in November our troops were dismissed, excepting a few in the garrisons at Wells, York, Berwick and Cocheco. The next spring, 1690, the French and Indians fell upon Salmon

Falls, burned the greatest part of the town, killed about 30 persons, and took 50 prisoners. *Artel* was the French commander of this party. On their way to Canada, one of their captives, Robert Rogers, endeavouring to escape, was overtaken, stripped, beaten, tied to a tree, and burned alive; the savages dancing and singing round him, cutting off pieces of his flesh and throwing them in his face.

As the French were the malignant instigators of the Indians in their bloody assaults, it was thought essential to the peace of New-England, that these enemies should be attacked in their own dominions. Hence, vigorous exertions were made for an expedition against Canada. The command was given to sir William Phips. His first object was to subdue Nova-Scotia. Accordingly, he sailed from New-England, April, 28, with a force of 700 men, and in a fortnight arrived at Port Royal. The fort surrendered, and he took possession of the province for the crown of England. Returning, he sailed again from Hull, August 9th, 1690, with a fleet of 32 sail, and arrived before Quebec, Oct. 5th; but the season being far spent; the army from Connecticut and New-York, which was to have entered the province, having returned after visiting the lake; and the troops with sir William being sickly and discouraged, the expedition failed, and in November the troops arrived at Boston. This expedition involved the government in a heavy debt; a thousand men perished, and a general gloom spread through the country.

The latter part of May, the Indians fell upon Casco, and assaulted all the garrisons; the soldiers defended themselves while their ammunition lasted; they then, concealed by the night, fled to the fort; when the whole force of the enemy was directed to this spot, first having burned the whole town. The fort was badly situated, having near it a deep gully, into which the enemy rushing, the guns could not reach them. They immediately began their mine, and nearly reached the fort, when the English, having fought 5 days and 4 nights, and the greater part of them having been killed or wounded, began a parley. Articles were agreed upon; the English were to have the liberty of going to the next town; they were to have a guard for their protection. The French commander, lifting his hand, swore by the eternal God punctually to perform the articles. It was French faith; he immediately suffered a part of his prisoners to be killed, and a part to be carried to Canada.

The garrisons at Papoodack, Spurwink, Black Point, and Blue Point, were so alarmed, that without orders, they retreated to Saco, 20 miles within Casco; and from Saco, 20 miles further to Wells, and some of them came on further; but recruits arriving, they were inspired with new courage. Soon after, Hopehood, a chief warrior, who had lived in Boston, had a skirmish with Capt. Sherburn, and the next sabbath his party killed a man, and burned several houses at Berwick. Three days after, at Fox Point, on Piscataqua, he burned a number of houses, took 6 prisoners, and killed 12 persons. Captains Greenleaf and Floyd came up with him soon after, killed part of his company, retook some of the captives, and a great part of their plunder.

At Spruce Creek, they killed an old man, and took a woman captive. July 4, 9 persons being at work in a field by Lampereel river, all were killed. The same day, captains Wiswel and Floyd marched from Portsmouth to search the woods. The next day, the garrison at Exeter was assaulted, but relieved by Lieut Bancroft, with the loss of several men. One of them, Simon Stone, being shot in 9 places, lay as if dead among the slain; the Indians coming to strip him, attempted by two blows of a hatchet to sever his head from his body: though they did not effect it, the wounds were dreadful; our people coming upon them suddenly; they did not scalp him; while burying the dead, Stone was observed to gasp; an Irishman present, advised them to give him another blow of the hatchet, and bury him with the rest; but his kind neighbours poured a little water into his mouth, then a little spirits, when he opened his eyes; the Irishman was ordered to haul a canoe on shore, in which the wounded man might be carried to a surgeon; carelessly pulling it along with his gun, it went off, broke his arm, and rendered him a cripple while he lived. Stone, in a short time, perfectly recovered. In 2 days, Floyd and Wiswel came upon the enemy at Wheelwright's pond. Fifteen of our people were slain, among whom were Capt. Wiswel, Lieut. Flag, and sergeant Walker; a great number were wounded. Capt. Convers was sent to bury our dead, and bring off the wounded.

The same week, Amesbury was assaulted, 3 persons killed, and 3 houses burned; Capt. Foot was tortured to death. In September, major Church, with 300 men, landed in Casco bay, at Macquoit, and marched to Androscoggin fort, took and killed 20 Indians, set 5 captives at liberty, and burned the fort. On their return they sent a party from Winter Harbour up the river, who fell on the enemy, killed some, took considerable plunder, and relieved an Englishman from captivity. At Casco Harbour the enemy, in the night, fell on them and killed 5, but were soon driven to the woods. The army, excepting 100 men, were then dismissed.

The country was now in a distressed situation; the disappointment and losses in the Canada expedition, and a murderous Indian war, which lasted for several years, had exhausted the resources and sunk the spirits of the country. In this period of discouragement, the people were joyfully surprised with overtures of peace from the Indians; a conference was held at Sagadahoc, 10 prisoners were restored, and a truce established, till the 1st of May, 1692. Instead of appearing in May at the garrison in Wells, with all their captives, to sign articles of a lasting peace, according to agreement, on the 9th of June, the place was assaulted by 200 Indians, but, being courageously repulsed, they retired. About the same time, they killed 2 men at Exeter, 2 at Berwick, and 5 or 6 at Cape Neddock. In the latter part of July, a number of troops having explored the Pejepscot region, to no purpose, while going on board their vessels, at Macquoit, they were violently assailed all night; but their vessels secured them, in a great measure, against harm.

In mercy to New-England, the force of the Indians was this year exceedingly restrained. Yet, September 28th, 7 persons were killed and taken captive at Berwick, and the next day, 21 were taken from Sandy Beach. Oct. 23d, in Rowley, Byfield parish, Mr. Goodridge, his wife, and 2 of his daughters, were killed. He was shot while praying in his family; it was sabbath evening. As he fell, he exclaimed, "I am a dead man; fly to the garrison." As they fled from the house, the wife and daughters were killed. A son and daughter were taken captive, the daughter was redeemed the next spring, at the expense of the province. She lived 82 years after, and died in Beverly, 1774, aged 89. Her name was Deborah Duty.

On the 25th of January, 1692, several hundred Indians assaulted York, took a hundred captives, and killed fifty, among whom was their faithful minister, the Rev. Shubael Dummer. The remaining people were so discouraged, that they were about leaving the town, when the government sent Capt. Greenleaf and Convers to protect them.

About this time, our people fell on a party in Cocheco woods, took and killed all but one; but the most valorous exploit happened at Wells. Capt. Convers displayed the courage of Leonidas, with more success. He had 15 men in the garrison; little more than a gunshot off, in 2 sloops, were 15 more, who had just brought ammunition and stores for the garrison. In this situation, he was assaulted by an army of 500 French and Indians. Monsieur Burn ff was general, and Labocree a principal commander. They were supported by the most distinguished chieftains of different tribes. Warumbo, Egremet, Moxus, and Modocawando, names of terror in those times, were present, with their chosen warriors. After a speech from one of their orators, with shouts and yells, they poured a volley upon the garrison, which returned the fire with so much spirit and success, that the besiegers retired to attack the sloops. The vessels lay in a creek, rather than a river, which at low water was barely wide enough to prevent the enemy from leaping on board. From a turn of the creek, they could approach so near, as to throw handfuls of mud on board, without being exposed themselves. A stack of hay and a pile of plank, were also places of security, whence they could pour showers of balls upon the sloops; while their great numbers allowed them to place parties of men to prevent any assistance from the garrison. Several times they set the sloops on fire, by shooting burning arrows; but by the vigilance of the crews, under Capt. Storer and Capt. Gouge, they were extinguished. Resistance was so formidable, that they again returned to the garrison, and then again they assaulted the sloops. Various and bold were their stratagems. On a pair of wheels they built a platform, with a raised front that was bullet proof. This, loaded with French and Indians, was pushed toward the sloops; the terrific machine of death slowly advanced; it proceeded by the side of the channel, bursting with smoke and fire, till within 15 yards of the sloop; one wheel sunk in the mire; a Frenchman stepped to lift the wheel; Storer levelled his gun, and he fell; another took his place; and again Storer took aim, and he fell by his fellow. Soon the tide rose and overturned their rolling battery; the men were exposed to the deadly fire of the sloops, and fell or fled in every direction.

Their next project was to build a kind of fireship, 18 or 20 feet square, loaded with combustible substance; this raft of fire they guided as near the vessels as they dared, and the tide wafted the blazing pile directly toward the trembling sloops. Never were men in a more awful situation. In this moment of distress, they cried unto God and he heard them. To the amazement of all, the wind suddenly changed, and with a fresh gale drove the floating destruction on shore, so shattered, that the water broke in, and extinguished the fire. Thus, after alternately attacking the garrison and vessels for 48 hours, exhausting their strength, expending their ammunition, losing one of their French commanders, and a number of their men; they sullenly retreated, having killed 1 man, and a number of cattle, and taken 1 prisoner; him they tortured, and killed in a most terrible manner.

This summer, a formidable stone fort was built at Pemaquid, called William Henry. Early in the summer of 1693, major Church received the command of the troops in the eastern country, with orders to raise 350 more. He surprised and took a party of the enemy not far from Wells; then marched to Pemaquid, Taconet, and Saco, but found no enemies. At Saco, he ordered a fort to be built.

About this time, the Indians alarmed Quabaog, or Brookfield, and killed a number of persons; but they were pursued, most of them killed, and their captives and plunder retaken. The Indians had now become tired of the war; they had some serious fears respecting the Maquas, and sued for peace, which was willingly granted them. A treaty was signed, May, 11, 1693.

In 1691, the general court employed two of their members, with Sir Henry Ashhurst, and the Rev. Dr. Mather, to solicit the restoration of their charter. In this they were disappointed; but a new charter was given, including the colony of Plymouth, Province of Maine, and Nova-Scotia, with all the country between Nova-Scotia and Maine, to the river St. Lawrence; also Elizabeth Islands, Nantucket, and Martha's Vineyard, in the government of Massachusetts. But the people were greatly disappointed in their new charter. Many of their invaluable privileges were taken from them. They no longer chose their governor, secretary, or officers of admiralty. The militia was under the controul of the governor. A house of representatives was not mentioned. To levy taxes, grant administrations, prove wills, and try capital offenders, was the office of the governor and council. But in the true spirit of their native independence, the first act of the legislature, in Massachusetts, after receiving the charter, contained the following clause: "No aid, tax, tollage, assessment, custom, loan, benevolence, or imposition whatsoever shall be laid, assessed, imposed, or levied on his majesty's subjects, or their estates, on any pretence whatever, but by the act and consent of the governor, council and *representatives* of the people, assembled in general court."

CHAP. XXII.

Witchcraft.

It was now 72 years since the first settlement of Plymouth. During this period, making their own laws, and choosing their own rulers, New-England had established regulations for promoting learning and religion, not equalled perhaps in any nation. In 1643, there were 36 churches in New-England; in 1650, there were 40, which contained 7750 communicants;* and though the philosophist points the finger of derision at the pious founders of these republics, the history of man does not present any people adopting wiser measures, productive of more permanent blessings. No where was knowledge more generally diffused, morals more correct, religion more pure, or the inhabitants more independent and happy.

But the fairest day has its cloud. Sir William Phips, the first governor under the new charter, found the province in a deplorable situation. An Indian war was wasting the frontiers. An agitation, a terror of the public mind, in the greater part of Essex county, like a tornado, was driving the people to the most desperate conduct. In the tempest of passion, a government of laws, trial by jury, all the guards against oppression, were too feeble to protect the person or property of the most worthy and loyal subject. The pillars of civil government were shaken to their foundation, by the amazing power of supposed *witchcraft*. In the beginning of 1692, the Rev. Samuel Paris, of Salem village, now Danvers, had a daughter aged 9, and a niece aged 11, "who were distressed with singular distempers." The means used by the physician being ineffectual, he gave it as his opinion, that *"they were under an evil hand."* The neighbours immediately believed that they were bewitched. An Indian servant and his wife privately made some experiments "to find out the witch." The children being informed of this, immediately complained of Tituba, the Indian woman, that she pinched, pricked and tormented them. They said she was visible to them, here and there, where others could not see her. Sometimes they would be dumb,

* Dr. Stiles' M.S.

and choked, and have pins thrust into their flesh. Mr. Paris, being deeply affected with the distress of his family, invited a number of his brethren in the ministry to visit him, and give their advice. They advised him "to wait on the providence of God, and to be much in prayer." Accordingly, 2 or 3 private fasts were kept at his house, at one of which several ministers came and joined with him. After this, there was a public fast in the village, and afterward, in several congregations in the neighbourhood; and finally, the general court appointed a fast throughout the colony, "to seek the Lord, that he would rebuke Satan." Still the distresses increased, more persons complained of their sufferings, and more were accused. At the sight of these, the sufferers would swoon and fall into fits; at the touch of the same persons they would revive. The public mind was shocked and alarmed; the most decisive proceedings followed. For a time, all, or most of, the people were of one mind. March 2d, there was a public examination at the village, and several were committed to prison. March 21, the magistrates met in Salem, and Mr. Noyes opened with prayer. On the 24th of March, they met at the village, and Mr. Hale prayed. On the 26th, they met again in Salem, and kept the day in fasting and prayer. There was another examination at Salem, April 22d, and a number more imprisoned. June 2d, an old woman was tried and condemned at Salem, and executed on the 10th, making no confession. Five more were tried June 30th, and executed July 19th; six more were tried August 6th, and all executed the 19th, except one woman, who pleaded pregnancy. One of these was Mr. George Burroughs, sometime minister at Wells; he had also preached at the village, but met with great opposition. A great number of witnesses appeared at his trial; specimens of their testimonies, still extant, excite compassion for the errors of those days.

Nine persons received sentence of death, Sept. 17th, 8 of whom were executed Sept. 22d, one woman being reprieved, pleading pregnancy. Giles Cory had been pressed to death, Sept. 16th, because he would not (seeing all were convicted) put himself on trial by the jury. Previous to this, numbers had confessed themselves guilty of witchcraft, it being the only way of saving their lives, none, who confessed, being executed. Terrible was the day. Every man was suspicious of his neighbour, and alarmed for himself. Business was interrupted; many people fled from their dwellings; terror was in every countenance, and distress in every heart. Every place was the subject of a direful tale, and the most common incidents received some fanciful construction to cover them with mystery, or load them with infamy.

The agency of invisible beings, whether true or false, constitutes a part of every religion under the sun. The first page of the Jewish scriptures introduces the subject; the New-Testament constantly supposes the powerful influence of spiritual beings. Mahometans, and pagans, civilized and savage nations have for substance but one creed on the subject.

The people of Essex county had lived among the Indians; they had heard their narratives of Hobbamocko, or the devil, of his frequent appearance to them, of their conversations with him, and of his sometimes carrying them off. These were the familiar tales of their winter evenings, which confirmed their opinions, roused their admiration, laid the basis of much superstition, and furnished materials for approaching terrours. The circumstances attending the first strange appearances, were most unfortunate, and tended powerfully to give them currency. They first appeared in the family of their minister; he was credulous; this excited belief in others. An Indian and his wife were in the family; they were supposed adepts in the science of witchcraft; their opinions were important. To complete the misery, the physician united his suffrage. The evidence now in the public mind was conclusive. No wonder the alarm was sudden and terrible. Children not 12 years of age were allowed to give in their testimony. Indians related their own personal knowledge of invisible beings, and women told their frights. The testimonies then received, would now be considered a burlesque on judicial proceedings. One circumstance, however, ought to be noticed. The persons accused had generally, if not universally, been in some obnoxious situation, or done some singular or forbidding action. Giles Cory had confessed himself a scandalous person, and been accepted by the church, at 80 years of age. Mr. Burroughs had been greatly disliked as a preacher; he was a stout man, and performed athletic exploits, which were thought preternatural. Another person was an object of envy, on account of superiour wealth; but most of those accused were in the lower walks of life, whose misfortunes or accidents, of 20 or 30 years standing, were now brought as fatal charges against them. Some evil of private life was the ground of suspicion. These circumstances perplexed the judges, and increased the public fury. The frenzy lasted from March to October. The supposed sufferers now becoming more daring, accused some of the best people in the country. Suspicion roused from its lethargy; condemnation ceased; the accusers were silent; those under sentence were reprived, and afterwards pardoned.

If we can be convinced by the uniform protestations of those executed, or the confessions of numbers, who had been accusers, or the deliberate recantations of others, who had confessed themselves witches, or the universal conviction of error in the minds of those, who had been leading actors in these awful scenes, or the entire change of public opinion, we shall be satisfied, that the whole originated in folly and delusion. All these are facts. All those executed, the first excepted, protested their innocence with their dying breath, when a confession would have saved their lives. Several years after, persons, who had been accusers, when admitted to the church, confessed their delusion in such conduct, and asked "pardon for having brought the guilt of innocent blood on the land." The following is an extract from the confession of 6 persons belonging to Andover, who had owned themselves witches; "We were all seized as prisoners; knowing ourselves altogether innocent, we were all exceedingly astonished, and amazed, and affrighted out of our reason; and our dearest relations, seeing us in this dreadful condition, and knowing our great danger, apprehending there was no other way to save our lives, persuaded us to confess; we said any thing and every thing which they desired."

On the day of a public fast, in the south meeting-house of Boston, one of the judges, who had been concerned in the condemnation of these unhappy victims at Salem, delivered in a paper, and while it was reading stood up: it was to desire prayers, &c. "being apprehensive he might have fallen into some errors at Salem."

The following is from the declaration of 12 men, who had been jurymen at some of these trials; "We do therefore signify our deep sense of, and sorrow for, our errors in acting on such evidence; we pray that we may be considered candidly and aright, by the living sufferers, as being then under the power of a strong and general delusion." Mr. Paris, who was active in the prosecution, and evidently a serious and conscientious man, in his public confession, Nov. 26, 1694, says, "I do acknowledge, upon after consideration, that were the same troubles again to happen, which the Lord of his mercy forever prevent, I should not agree with my former apprehensions in all points; as for instance," &c.

Martha Cory, a member of the church in Salem village admitted April 27th, 1690, was, after examination upon suspicion of witchcraft, March 21st, 1692, committed to prison, and condemned to the gallows yesterday. This day in public, by general consent, she was voted to be excommunicated out of the church. The following will show, in a most affecting manner, the light in which the church viewed this vote, 10 years after. In "Dec. 1702, the pastor spoke to the church on the sabbath, as followeth. Brethren, I find in your church book a record of Martha Cory's being excommunicated for witchcraft; and the generality of the land being sensible of the errors, that prevailed in that day, some of her friends have moved me several times to propose to this church, whether it be not our duty to recal that sentence, that so it may not stand against her to all generations. And I myself, being a stranger to her, and being ignorant of what was alledged against her, I shall now only leave it to your consideration, and shall determine the matter by a vote, the next convenient opportunity. Feb. 14th, the pastor moved the church to revoke Martha Cory's excommunication: a majority voted for revoking it."* So deep was the people's sense of the errors of those transactions, that a great part of Mr. Paris's congregation could not persuade themselves to sit under his ministry. Accordingly, after great difficulty, after a respectable council had laboured in vain for their reconciliation, after an arbitration respecting the business, Mr. Paris was dismissed July 24th, 1697, as the agrieved state to the arbitrators, "for being an instrument to their miseries."

If any reader point the finger of scorn at the people of Essex, or the judiciary of Massachusetts, for their credulity

---

* Church Records of Danvers.

and errors, he is informed, that they acted in conformity to the public opinion of the world at that time; that they were guided in their judicial proceedings by the writings of Keeble on the common law, Sir Matthew Hale, Glanvil, Bernard, Baxter, &c. He is informed, that while the people of this once devoted neighbourhood soon saw and retracted their errors, and would now be the last people to fall into such a delusion, other parts of the world have been more slowly convinced. At Tring, in Hertfordshire, 20 miles from London, in 1751, 2 aged persons were drowned, supposed to be guilty of witchcraft. At Huntingdon, the anniversary of the execution of a family for witchcraft is celebrated to this day. A preacher from Cambridge, delivers a discourse against witchcraft. At Embo, in Scotland, a person was executed for witchcraft, in 1727. At Rome, the Rev. Father Altizza was lately seized for the crime of sorcery.

CHAP. XXIII.

French war; Complaint against governor Phips; his character; Indian and French ravages; Yale college; Indian war; Peace; Death of Queen Ann; George I. crowned; Small Pox; Earthquake; Burnet governor; his death.

In 1694, the sword was drawn again, after being sheathed about a year. The Sieur Villion, commander of the French at Penobscot, with 250 Indians from the tribes of St. John, Penobscot, and Norridgewock, assaulted the people on Oyster river, in New Hampshire; killed and captured about 100 persons, and burned 20 houses, 5 of which were garrisons.

During these distresses, the people became uneasy, ascribing their sufferings to the government, and a number made complaint to the king against governor Phips. He and his accusers were summoned to Whitehall. In November he embarked for England. A majority of the general court being in his favour, he carried a recommendation from the legislature. But before his trial he was seized with a malignant fever, of which he died in the 54th year of his age. Sir William Phips was born of poor parents, on the bank of the Kennebec. He was first a shepherd, then a ship carpenter, then a seaman. By discovering a Spanish wreck, near Port de la Plata, he became rich, and was brought into notice. He was a man of enterprise, diligence, and perseverance, religious himself, and disposed to promote piety in others.

The Indians continued to ravage the frontiers, and in Oct. 1695, a party penetrated to Newbury, and made captives of John Brown and his family, excepting 1 girl, who escaped, and ran 5 miles to the water side, near Newburyport, and alarmed the people. Capt. Greenleaf instantly pursued, and, before it was light the next day, overtook and rescued the captives, 9 in number. The Indians, when they found it impossible to carry them off, determined to kill them; but such was their hurry, the wounds they gave them were not mortal; all recovered. Capt. Greenleaf received a musket ball in his arm, when he made this attack, which is now preserved in the family.

The French and Indians, in 1696, took and demolished the fort at Pemaquid.

In 1697, the French projected an invasion of the country. A fleet arrived at Newfoundland, expecting an army from Canada, to assault Boston, and ravage the coast to Piscataqua; but the season was advanced, provisions failed, and the design was relinquished. After the peace of Ryswick, 1698, the French could no longer assist the savages; they therefore buried the hatchet, restored their captives, ratified their former engagements, and, in 1699, submitted to the British crown.

At the close of the war in Europe, the king appointed the earl of Bellamont governor of New-York, Massachusetts, and New-Hampshire. He resided at New-York; Mr. Stoughton conducted the affairs of New-England. In May, lord Bellamont visited Boston. He was a nobleman of polite, conciliating manners, and professed great esteem for the congregational ministers, and with the general court, as was customary at that time, attended the stated Thursday lectures at Boston. In his time, the pirates, who had been connived at for 30 or 40 years, were arrested and punished. Numbers were executed at Boston. Bradish, Kidd and others were carried to England, tried, and executed.

Soon after the session of the general court, in May, 1700, lord Bellamont returned to New-York, where he died the 5th of March following.

Yale College was founded by a number of clergymen, in 1701, and had its charter in 1702. It was named after ELIHU YALE, Esq. of London, governor of the East-India company, who was its principal early benefactor. It was originally fixed at Killingworth, afterward removed to Saybrook; and thence in 1717, to New-Haven. Its legislature is a corporation, consisting of the president of the college, who is also president of the corporation; the governor of the state, the lieutenant-governor, and 6 senior assistants, *ex officio*, and 10 fellows, who are all clergymen; who, with the president fill their own vacancies. Other powers are possessed by all the members of the board in common. The corporation meet annually. A committee of 3 or 4 members, of whom the president ex officio is one, is appointed by them, every year, to superintend the concerns of the institution. This committee meets 4 times a year. The immediate government and instruction of the students is committed to a president, to professors of divinity, of mathematics and natural philosophy, of chemistry and mineralogy, and of languages and ecclesiastical history, and to 6 tutors. The number of students (1812) was 305, in 1818, 283. They are divided into 4 classes. The senior class recites only to the president, and, with the junior, attends the lectures of the professors. The 3 lower classes are divided each into 2 divisions, and each of the divisions is committed to its own tutor, who has the sole instruction of it. The library contains 7 or 8000 volumes, and has a fund yielding about $200. The students have libraries amounting to 2500 more. The philosophical and chemical apparatus are very handsome, and are complete. The chemical laboratory is considered one of the best in the U. States. The college possesses a very handsome mineralogical cabinet, containing about 2500 specimens; and, in 1811, 2 cabinets, one consisting of more than 6000 choice specimens, and the other of about 18,000; the two noblest collections ever opened in the United States, were deposited in this seminary by Col. Gibbs of Boston. This respectable stranger has been invited by the corporation to deliver lectures on his favourite science. The academical buildings consist of 3 colleges, each 4 stories high, and 104 feet by 40, all standing in a line, fronting S. E. and containing 96 convenient chambers: a chapel, having in the third story, a philosophical chamber and rooms for the philosophical apparatus, a lyceum, resembling the chapel in form, and containing a chemical laboratory, and its appendages; 7 large recitation rooms, 2 chambers, and a library; and a large dining hall and kitchen in the rear of the other buildings. The chapel and lyceum are between the colleges, and project beyond them. A medical institution was established in the seminary in 1813. It consists of 4 professorships, of the materia medica, of anatomy and surgery, of the theory and practice of physic, and of chemistry. It has about 60 students. The funds of the college are small.

In 1702, Queen Ann appointed Joseph Dudley, Esq to succeed Bellamont as governor of Massachusetts and New-Hampshire. According to his instructions, he required a permanent salary, and maintained a long and obstinate struggle with the general court of Massachusetts, but was finally obliged to relinquish the object.

In 1703, the Indians, aided as usual by the French, attacked all the settlements from Canso to Wells; killed and took about 130 people, and burned many houses. Women and children fled to garrisons; the men carried their arms into the field of labour, and posted sentinels round them; small parties of the enemy were frequently making assaults; and the whole country, from Deerfield to Canso, for some time was in constant alarm. Towards the close of the year, 300 French and Indians fell upon Deerfield, murdered 40 of the inhabitants, took 100 captives, and left the village in flames. To repel such bloody foes, the famous Col. Church, so distinguished in the wars of Philip, in 1704, was ordered to the eastward. At Piscataqua, he was joined by major Hilton; they destroyed Minas and Chignecto, and did some damage to the French at Penobscot and Passamaquoddy.

The following year, a number of captives taken at Deerfield were redeemed. In April, 1706, the Indians killed 8 people at Oyster river. The garrison was near, but not a man in it. The women put on hats, loosened their hair, and fired so briskly, that the enemy fled, without burning or plundering the house they had assaulted. The year following, the Indians came to Reading, within 10 miles of Boston, killed a woman and 2 children, and carried off 5 captives.

Persons were also killed and prisoners taken this year, at Chelmsford, Sudbury, Groton, and Exeter.

On the 27th of November, 1707, died John Winthrop, Esq. governor of Connecticut, and was buried in Boston. The bones of John Winthrop, the first governor of Massachusetts, his son and grandson, governors of Connecticut, rest in the same tomb, in the oldest burying ground in Boston. There was this year an unsuccessful expedition against Port Royal.

On the 29th of August, 1708, Haverhill was assaulted by the Indians; thirty or forty persons were killed, among whom was their minister, Mr. Rolf; 20 or 30 houses were burned, and the rest plundered. Such had been the loss of men in Massachusetts, by their dreadful wars with the French and Indians, that in 1713, the province had not doubled in half a century. The same observations may be made respecting the period from 1722 to 1762. Had the French in Canada been subdued 100 years sooner, it is supposed there would have been more than 300,000 souls in New-England, more than the present number.

In 1710, the territory of Acadia was subdued by the surrender of Port Royal. The name of the place was changed to Anapolis, in honour of the queen. Samuel Vetch, a colonel in the victorious army, was appointed governor.

This success encouraged New England to attempt, the next year, the conquest of Canada. General Nicholson was successful in soliciting aid from the British court. The combined army of Old and New-England troops, being 6500 men, with a fleet of 5 ships of war, engaged in the enterprize; but in the way, 8 transports were wrecked on Egg Island, and a thousand people perished, among whom was but one man from New-England. The expedition was relinquished; the consequence was, new assaults from the savages. But news of the peace of Utrecht arriving, a suspension of arms was proclaimed at Portsmouth, Oct. 29, 1712. The Indians came in, and agreed upon articles of peace.

Never was an event more welcome to the provinces. They had been bleeding for almost 40 years; 5 or 6000 men had fallen in battle, or by disease in the army. Massachusetts and New-Hampshire were the principal sufferers.* The inhabitants of Connecticut had increased to about 17,000. The people were religious; their righteousness exalted their character. In 1696, there were 130 churches in these colonies, 35 of which were in Connecticut. At this period, Connecticut had 45 towns. The number of ordained ministers was 43. There was an ordained minister to every 400 persons, or to every 80 families. There was not one vacant church in the colony. A number of candidates were preaching in the new towns, where no churches were formed. The year before this, a valuable part of Boston was laid in ashes by an accidental fire, but was soon rebuilt in a more elegant style.

The death of queen Ann, and the accession of George I. was announced in New-England, Sept. 15, 1714. Col. Shute being appointed governor of Massachusetts, and New-Hampshire, Mr. Dudley retired to a private station. Gov. Shute was a man of ambition, possessing too high ideas of royal authority to accord with the republican feelings of New-England. Their controversies with him, and with other governors, proved that they never could be enslaved, till their character should be totally changed. He arrived in Boston, Oct. 5th, 1716, and was received with great parade. The summer following, he with a number of the council from both provinces, met the Indians at Arrowsic Island, to confirm their friendship, to persuade them to relinquish popery, and embrace the Protestant religion. He

* Trumbull.

offered them an Indian bible, and a Protestant missionary; they rejected both.

Some time elapsed before the opposition, usually displayed against royal governors, shewed itself; but, in 1720, the storm rose higher than it had for a number of years. The governor negatived the speaker, chosen by the house; they refused to choose another; he dissolved them. The flame of popular resentment blazed through the province. He revived the old controversy of a fixed salary, and met with the fate of his predecessors. But the people of New-Hampshire were satisfied with Gov. Shute's administration, and contributed more than their proportion toward his support. So strong was the tide of opposition at Boston, that the governor, in 1720, returned to England, and presented a variety of complaints against the house of representatives. Among other things, he complained that they had usurped his right of appointing days of fasting and thanksgiving. The British ministry justified the governor, and the province was obliged to accept an explanatory charter, dated August 12th, 1724. This confirmed the right of the governor to negative the speaker, and forbid the house to adjourn for more than two days, without his consent.

In 1721, the small pox was very mortal in Boston, and several adjacent towns. In Boston 5889 caught it, and 844 died. The Rev. Dr. Cotton Mather had read of innoculation among the Turks. He recommended it to the physicians. Dr. Boylston alone complied. He was first successful in his own family, and afterward gave it to many others in the same way; but the business was, in general, very unpopular, and finally forbidden by the general court.

In the winter, an unsuccessful attempt was made to seize Ralle, the French missionary at Norridgewock. This provoked the Indians to vengeance; and, after various hostilitics, they destroyed Brunswick. By these things, the government was induced, in 1722, to make another attempt upon Norridgewock. Captains Moulton and Harman of York, surprised the village, killed the Jesuit and about 80 Indians; rescued 3 prisoners, burned the wigwams and chapel, and brought away the plate and furniture. The military spirit was roused: government offered £100 for every scalp. Capt. Lovell, of Dunstable, became a daring adventurer. At one time he brought in 10 scalps; but soon after fell in battle, with more than a 4th part of his companions, near Winnipisioke pond.*

After governor Shute's departure, lieutenant governor Dummer managed the affairs of Massachusetts, and Mr. Wentworth those of New-Hampshire. Fort Dummer was built in Hinsdale, 1724, and the first settlement made in Vermont. At his decease, Gov. Dummer bequeathed a valuable estate in Byfield to that parish, toward supporting a grammar school. This is now Dummer Academy.

The year 1727 was remarkable for the greatest earthquake, which had ever been known in New-England. It happened Oct. 29, at 10 o'clock, P. M. The heavens were clear, the atmosphere perfectly calm, the moon shining in her glory. The shock extended several hundred miles; its greatest force was displayed at Newbury, in Essex county; the earth burst open in several places; more than a hundred cartloads of earth were thrown out, which, in a few days, emitted a loathsome smell. But the most remarkable and important effect was the panic, which seized the public mind, and the general seriousness, which followed. In many towns, numbers were awakened, a reformation of morals was visible, family prayer was more generally attended, and great additions were made to many churches.†

*Hutchinson. †Foxcroft.

Upon the accession of George II. this year, Mr. William Burnet, son to the good bishop of Sarum, was appointed governor of Massachusetts and New-Hampshire. He had been popular as a governor of New-York and New-Jersey, and was received in Boston with great pomp, being met there by the lieutenant governor of New-Hampshire, and a committee of the council and assembly. The government of New-Hampshire gave him a fixed salary, on certain conditions; but in Massachusetts there was soon a warm altercation between him and the general court on this subject. His nerves should have been "made of sterner stuff," to contend with Massachusetts. He was disappointed; he was depressed; and died in a few months. When the news of this reached England, the resentment there was so great, that a proposal was made to reduce the colony to absolute dependence on the crown; but milder measures prevailed, and Mr. Jonathan Belcher, a native of the province, son of a wealthy farmer, then a merchant in London, was appointed governor of Massachusetts and New-Hampshire.

CHAP. XXIV.

Public ferment in Massachusetts; Dreadful mortality; line established between Massachusetts and New-Hampshire; Shirley governor; Louisbourg taken; French invasion; Congress at Albany; Nova-Scotia taken; Braddock's defeat.

WHILE these provinces were in a constant ferment by their contentions with their governors, Connecticut and Rhode-Island, under their ancient charters, enjoyed tranquillity, chose their own rulers, and enacted their own laws. The altercations of Massachusetts fanned the coals of independence, and finally produced the explosion, which has forever separated the two countries.

In August, 1730, Gov. Belcher was received with great joy; like his predecessors, he proposed a fixed salary; like them, he saw his proposal repelled with violence. He saw the cause was desperate, and obtained leave from the British court to receive such sums as should be granted him. So terminated the long, the tedious contest respecting the governor's salary.

In 1735 was the most extensive and fatal epidemic, which has been known in New-England since its settlement by the English. It was called the *throat distemper*. The throat swelled with white or ash-coloured specks, an efflorescence appeared on the skin; with great debility of the whole system, and a strong tendency to putridity. Its first appearance was in May, 1735, at Kingston, in New-Hampshire. The first person seized was a child, who died in 3 days. In about a week, it appeared 4 miles distant, 3 children died on the third day. During the summer, it spread through the town; of the first 40 who had it, not one recovered. In August it appeared in Exeter, an adjacent town, where 127 died; In September, at Boston, 50 miles south, where 114 died; at Byfield, 15 miles south of Kingston. Oct. 23d; nor was it known in Chester, an adjoining town, till this month. At Byfield, only 1 died in October,* in November 2 died, in December 10, in January 7, in February 3, in March 6, in April 5, in May 7, in June 4, in July 9, in August 25, in September 13, in October 8, in November 4; the last of which died on the 23d, so that in just thirteen months 104 persons died, which was about the 7th part of the population of the parish. Eight children were buried from one family, 4 of them in the same grave; another family lost 5 children.

* Church Records of Byfield.

In other places, from 3 to 6 children were lost out of a family. In some towns 1 in 3, and others 1 in 4, who were sick, died. In Hampton Falls, 20 families buried all their children; 27 persons were lost out of 5 families, and more than a sixth part of the inhabitants died. In the province of New-Hampshire alone, which then had only 15 towns, not less than 1000 persons, of whom 900 were under 20 years of age, fell victims to this terrible malady.*

It was not an enemy of any particular season or situation. It continued through the whole year. It appeared afterwards, in 1754 and 1755, spreading mortality through New-England. In some places in Connecticut, it was quite as fatal as in Massachusetts. It again alarmed New-Hampshire and Massachusetts in 1784, 5, 6 and 7, and 1802. It has of late been much more under the controul of medicine; but still it is a formidable enemy, walking in darkness; appearing here to-day, and perhaps to-morrow in the remotest place in the neighbourhood, without any intercourse or similarity of situation; the distress and anguish it brings is often indescribable; the writhings and contortions of the patient seem as great, as if he were on a bed of burning coals.

The divisional line, in 1740, was finally determined by the lords of the council, between New-Hampshire and Massachusetts. New-Hampshire obtained 14 miles in breadth, and about 50 in length more than they had claimed. A party, the following year, opposed Gov. Belcher, and by incessant applications to the ministry, by falsehood and forgery, they finally prevailed. He was succeeded in New-Hampshire, by Benning Wentworth; in Massachusetts, by William Shirley. Gov. Belcher repaired to court; demonstrated his own integrity and the baseness of his enemies, was

* Belknap.

appointed governor of New-Jersey, passed a quiet life, and his memory has been treated with merited respect.

In 1744, news of war with France and Spain being received, forces were raised to attack Nova-Scotia. Gov. Shirley projected an invasion of Louisbourgh, the *Dunkirk of America*. Its fortifications had employed French troops 25 years, and cost 30,000,000 livres. A majority of one in the general court voted for the expedition. The land forces were commanded by Col. William Peperell, of Kittery; the English squadron, by commodore Warren. The last of April, the following year, the troops, 3800 in number, landed at Chapeaurogue bay. The transports had been discovered early in the morning from the town, which was the first notice they had of the design. In the night of May 2, 400 men burned the warehouses containing the naval stores. The French were alarmed, spiked their guns, flung their powder into a well, and, abandoning the fort, fled to the city. The New-England troops cheerfully submitted to extreme hardships; for 14 nights successively, they were yoked together like oxen, dragging cannon and mortars through a morass of 2 miles. The commanding artillery of the enemy forbade this toil in the day. No people on earth, perhaps are more capable of such laborious and daring exploits, than the independent farmers of New-England. On the 17th of June, the garrison capitulated, but the flag of France was kept flying, which decoyed into the harbour, ships of the enemy, to the value of £600,000 sterling. The weather, during the siege, was fine, but the day following rains began, which continued 10 days, and must have proved fatal to the provincial troops, had not the capitulation prevented. The good people of New-England were deeply affected by this evident interposition of divine providence.

The next year, 1746, a French fleet sailed to pour destruction on New-England. Twenty men of war, 100 transports, 8000 veteran troops, made the country tremble. In their consternation, they were disappointed of a squadron of defence, from the mother country. God interposed. A mortal sickness spread through the fleet; a tempest scattered them; the commander, disappointed, and mortified, poisoned himself; his successor fell on his sword. Never was the hand of divine providence more visible; never was a disappointment more severe to the enemy; never a deliverance more complete without human aid, than this in favour of New-England.

As the distresses of war ceased, the people were alarmed, in 1749, with the report of an American episcopacy; but the design was not executed. Dr. Mayhew, of Boston, distinguished himself in this controversy. This year Benning Wentworth made a grant of Bennington, Vermont.

In 1754, a congress met in Albany, consisting of delegates from New-Hampshire, Massachusetts, Rhode-Island, Connecticut, New-York, Pennsylvania, and Maryland; but the plan of government they proposed was rejected, both in England and America. Had this instrument been accepted, the mind is lost in conjecturing what might have been the consequences. Perhaps the revolution of 1776 had been postponed a long period; perhaps the millions and millions of the human race, lately destroyed in Europe and Asia by the demon of revolutionary madness, might have long survived, to swell the tide of human felicity.

Preparations were made in 1755, to dislodge the French from Nova-Scotia. Col. Winslow raised 2000 men, but the command of the expedition was given to Col. Monkton. The French were subdued. The inhabitants had taken the oath of allegiance to the British crown, but were accused of furnishing support and intelligence to Indians and French, in annoying the colonies; some of them were in arms. It was determined to remove them; about 2000 souls were accordingly transported to New-England. The cloud of their sorrows was never dispelled; in a land of strangers, most of them pined away and died. They were remarkable for the simplicity of their manners, the ardour of their piety, and the purity of their morals.

Gen. Braddock, with 2200 regular and provincial troops, marched this year for Fort Du Quesne, but fell into an ambuscade, and was fatally wounded; a panic seized his regular troops, but Col. Washington, his aid-de camp, with his militia, covered their retreat, and saved the shattered army.

The 18th of November, this year, was a memorable day on account of the earthquake. The wooden spindle of the vane on Fanueil Hall was broken; and an iron one, which supported the vane on Springfield steeple, was bent to a right angle: stone walls were thrown down, and the tops of chimnies shaken off.

In 1758, Louisbourgh, Frontenac, and Fort Du Quesne, submitted to the English; a small compensation for more than 2000 men killed and wounded in the rash and unsuccessful attack upon Ticonderoga. Splendid were the victories of the year 1759. Niagara, Ticonderoga, Crown Point, and Quebec submitted to the English. At the taking of Quebec, Wolf, the British commander, after being wounded in the wrist, received a fatal ball in his breast. Leaning on the shoulder of a lieutenant, sinking in the agonies of death, he heard a cry, "they run." For a moment reviving, he asked, who ran? It was answered, "the French." He replied, "I thank God, I die happy," and expired. Montcalm, the French commander, and also the second in command, were killed. Quebec surrendered, and the whole province, was soon annexed to the British empire.

In 1762, Martinico, Grenada, St. Vincents, and Havanna submitted: English valour was triumphant in every quarter of the globe: peace followed.

CHAP. XXV.

Stamp Act; Dartmouth college founded; Lexington and Bunker Hill battles; Expedition to Canada; Boston evacuated; Ticonderoga taken; descent on Rhode-Island; Tryon's expedition to Connecticut; American academy incorporated; New-London burnt; Insurrection in Massachusetts; Federal Constitution; Colleges in Vermont and Maine.

It was now thought a proper time to tax America. The stamp act, which passed in 1765, roused New England. Every mean was used to inform the minds and kindle the patriotism of the people. Massachusetts made the proposal, and a congress assembled. In Connecticut the people met; the stamp master resigned. The 1st of November, when the stamp act was to operate in Boston, the bells tolled, shops were shut, effigies of the royalists were carried about in derision, and torn in pieces. At Portsmouth, the bells tolled; a coffin was prepared; on the lid was inscribed, "Liberty, aged 145;" a procession moved with unbraced drums; minute guns were fired; an oration was delivered at the grave. At the close, the coffin was taken up, signs of life appeared in the corpse; "Liberty revived," was substituted; the bells struck a cheerful key; joy sparkled in every countenance. All was decency and order. At Rhode-Island the day passed in a similar manner. In March, 1766, the obnoxious act was repealed; ships in the Thames displayed their colours; houses were illuminated through the city of London; the colonies rejoiced in their deliverance.

In 1769, Dartmouth College was established by a royal charter; the pious and laborious Dr. Eleazer Wheelock, the founder, was appointed the first president, with power of appointing his successor. He removed Moor's Indian charity school from Lebanon, in Connecticut, to Hanover in New-Hampshire, where the college was established. A principal object with this good man was, to civilize and spread the gospel among the Indians of the country. Persevering were his exertions, and indefatigable his labours for the accomplishment of this benevolent and noble design. Considerable numbers were taught in the grammar school, and made some advance in collegiate studies; only one or two, however, obtained the honours of college. A number of schoolmasters and missionaries were sent to different tribes with some success; but the revolutionary war cut off supplies from England, and, for a time, interrupted the good work.

The college stands on a beautiful and elevated plain, half a mile east from Connecticut river. The place is very healthy, and the prospect commanding. About 80,000 acres of land constitute the permanent funds of the college. Their value is constantly increasing; their annual income is about 1600 dollars. This, with the tuition, amounts to about 8700 dollars. The number of undergraduates is generally about 150, and from 50 to 80 medical students. The students are under the immediate government and instruction of a president, a professor of divinity and moral philosophy, a professor of mathematics, and natural philosophy, of Hebrew and other languages, of chemistry and medicine, and 2 tutors. The college building is 150 feet by 50; 5 stories high. It has a good library and philosophical apparatus.

The same year that Dartmouth college was founded, 1769, the first commencement of Rhode-Island college was attended. It was incorporated in 1764, and was organized at Warren, where it continued till 1770. It was then removed to Providence, where a handsome brick building had been erected for its accommodation. It stands on the hill east of the town, has a healthy air, and beautiful prospect. The edifice is 4 stories high, 150 feet long, 46 wide, with a projection of 10 feet on each side in the centre. From Dec. 1776, to June, 1782, it was used as a hospital and barrack by the French and American troops. The president and a majority of the trustees must always be of the Baptist denomination. They have a valuable library and philosophical apparatus.

The limits of this little volume prevent a detail of the various events, which produced the revolutionary war, and the independence of the United States. Numerous other works contain these details. We only observe that new duties on various articles; the sending of troops to Boston; the firing of the guard, after they had been highly provoked, which was *called* a massacre; the shutting up of the port of Boston, &c. again roused the indignation of the country. Votes of legislatures, committees of correspondence, liberty poles in towns and villages, displayed the zeal and resolute determination of the people to defend their rights.

In the night of April 18th, 1775, Gen. Gage sent 800 troops to destroy the stores at Concord. At 11 o'clock they embarked at Boston common, and landed at Phips' farm with all possible stillness. But so watchful were the people, so alive to every motion of the British troops, that nothing could be obtained by stratagem. News was instantly carried to Concord, and the country was alarmed. By 2 in the morning, 130 of the Lexington militia had assembled to oppose them. Between 4 and 5 o'clock the enemy appeared. Major Pitcairn rode up, ordered the militia to disperse, fired his pistol, and ordered his men to fire. Some were killed; several returned the fire; but the British proceeded to Concord, and executed their commission. Here a skirmish took place between the British and the militia under major Buttrick. The British having accomplished their object in destroying the stores at Concord, began their retreat to Boston. The Americans closely followed, firing from fences and walls. At Lexington, lord Percy met them with 900 men. These, having two pieces of cannon, kept their pursuers at a great distance. Before dark, they reached Bunker Hill, having travelled that day about 40 miles. The next day they returned to Boston. Sixty-five of their number had been killed, 180 wounded, 28 taken prisoners. The Americans had 50 killed, 38 wounded and missing.

The provincial congress of Massachusetts, then sitting, voted an army of 30,000 men; 13,600 to be from their own province. They sent to the other New-England colonies; an army of 20,000 men shortly invested Boston, under the command of Gen. Ward. Soon after, these were joined by a large body from Connecticut, under Gen. Putnam, whose name was then a host. The continental congress resolved to organize an army, and recommended a general fast. The clergy, in their sermons and prayers, consecrated the cause, and kept alive the ardour of the people. Col. Arnold, sent from Connecticut, being joined by Col. Allen, May 10th, took Ticonderoga and Crown Point, with all their military stores.

On the night of June 16th, 1775, Gen Putnam*, with 1000 men, took possession of Breed's, erroneously called

---

* It has been questioned, who was commander in this action: but if any credit can be given to respectable human testimony, this matter is settled. Col. Grosvenor, who was an officer in the action, writes to me that Gen Putnam did command in the battle of Breed's Hill. Another officer, who was there wounded, and saw Warren fall, has assured me that Putnam commanded in the action A son of the general has given me the same assurance, having heard it from his father. The Rev. Dr Whitney, in a note of his sermon, occasioned by the death of the general, says, "The detachment at first was put

Bunker's Hill. They laboured with such diligence and ardour, that by the dawn of light, they had thrown up a redoubt of 8 rods square. As soon as the British ships discovered them in the morning, they began a heavy fire, which was supported by a fort on Copp's hill, in Boston. An incessant storm of balls and bombs was poured on this handful of farmers, the greater part of whom had probably never heard the roar of artillery before. They diligently continued their work, and had almost completed a breastwork to the water, eastward. They had been laborious through the night; and had not been relieved, nor supplied with refreshment. In this exhausted situation, they were destined to meet the fury of British valour.

A little after noon, boats and barges, filled with 3000 veterans, the flower of the royal army, landed in Charlestown. Generals Howe and Pigot commanded. Burgoyne and Clinton stood watchful on Copp's hill. British troops and citizens of Boston crowded the roofs, houses and steeples, to witness the dubious conflict. The American army and the country people thronged the surrounding hills. The fleet, as well as the camps, gazed at the opening scene. The king's troops deliberately advanced, that their artillery might demolish the new raised works. Charlestown was now set on fire, by order of the British commander, and immediately about 400 houses were in a blaze. The lofty steeple of the meeting-house formed a pyramid of flame, magnificent and awful, in view of many thousand

under the command of Gen. Putnam; with it he took possession of the hill, and ordered the battle from beginning to the end. These facts Gen. Putnam himself gave me soon after the battle, and repeated them after his life was printed." The honesty and veracity of Putnam were never suspected. The hero ought not to be robbed of his glory.   E. P.

This subject has been put at rest, in favour of Gen. Putnam, by the late controversy with Gen. Dearborn.

anxious spectators. The slow approach of the enemy gave time to assume greater presence of mind. In this crisis, Gen. Putnam made an harangue; he reminded the troops, "that they were all marksmen, and could bring a squirrel from the highest tree." He charged them "to be cool, and reserve their fire till the enemy were near; till they could see the white of their eyes." They obeyed. At the distance of 10 rods, they began a furious discharge of small arms. The British, whose ranks were thinned, retreated with precipitation. Again the general addressed his men. He told them "they had done well, and would do much better, and directed them to aim at the officers. The British returned. The fire was terrible. Their officers exclaimed, "it is downright butchery to lead the men against the lines."

In telling the story, Gen. Putnam exclaimed, "I never saw such a carnage of the human race." At the next assault, the enemy receiving new strength by the arrival of Gen. Clinton; the cannonade from the ships, and the batteries of Boston, and the field artillery, increasing their fury, and the powder of the Americans failing, a retreat was ordered. Fifteen hundred Americans were engaged; 77 were killed, among whom was the brave Gen. Warren, a volunteer, who refused any command, though it was offered him by Putnam; 278 were wounded and missing. The British lost 1054 killed; of whom 19 were commissioned officers. A greater number than they lost at the battle of Quebec, which gave them the province of Canada.

The people of Falmouth, now Portland, violently opposing the loading of a mast ship, Capt. Mowat received orders, which he executed, to burn the town. Privateers at this time were successful. Capt. Manly brought in a vessel, loaded with military stores, valued at £50,000. This was a most providential and seasonable supply; and inspired the army with courage. This summer, a detachment was sent from Cambridge to Quebec, under the command of Col. Arnold; they ascended the Kennebec, and had a dismal march thence into Canada. Many of the men became sickly; one third were discouraged and returned; those who bravely persevered were compelled to eat their dogs, their shoes, and even their cartridge boxes. In 31 days they found inhabitants. They joined Gen. Montgomery, and with him scaled the walls of Quebec. American valour was unsuccessful. The brave Montgomery fell; Arnold was wounded; 100 men were killed or wounded, 300 taken prisoners. These Gen. Carlton treated with his accustomed delicacy and humanity, highly honourable to his character.

On the night of March 4th, 1776, works were raised on the hills of Dorchester; 1200 men were employed, and 200 teams. So prodigious were their labours, that in the morning the whole seemed to the British "like enchantment and invisible agency." Gen. Howe was seized with consternation, and in confusion and hurry evacuated Boston.

In 1777, astonishment and terror spread through New-England, by the flight of Gen. St. Clair from Ticonderoga. The rear of his army was attacked at Hubbardston, a few miles from lake Champlain. The brave Col. Francis, of Beverly, fell, with a number of his men. Gen. St. Clair was at Castleton, within hearing of the musketry, but though his officers entreated with tears, that they might return to succour their brethren, he forbade them. Gen. Stark afterward turned the alarming tide of affairs, by his gallant action at Bennington. He routed Col. Baum, and killed or wounded a great part of his detachment. This kindled new courage through the eastern states. It was the first step to the capture of Burgoyne, which procured us succour in Europe, and insured the independence of the country. This year Vermont declared itself a sovereign state.

Five hundred British and Hessian troops burned the meeting house in Warren (R. I.) the church in Bristol, and a number of houses in each town, in 1778. Newport was soon threatened by land and sea. Gen. Sullivan passed to the island with 10,000 troops in high spirits, and nothing forbade the conquest of the British, who took possession of this island in 1776, but a failure of aid from the French fleet. This brought on them many execrations in New-England. Gen. Pigot, the British commander, had so placed himself, that a fleet was necessary to attack them with hope of success.

Gen. Sullivan, therefore, retired to the north end of the island, intending to fortify his camp, and wait till it should be ascertained whether the French fleet would return. But in a few hours he was attacked in his new situation; the action became general; it was a bloody day; 2 or 300 fell on each side. The fleet of lord Howe appeared off the coast, and Gen. Sullivan determined to leave the island. The day of the battle had been windy, so that a retreat would have been dangerous, if not impracticable; but the evening was calm, and in a few hours the army, with the sick and wounded, all the artillery and baggage, with a great number of sheep and cattle, passed in safety to the main.

In the summer of 1779, Gov. Tryon landed at New-Haven, and plundered the town; proceeding by water, he burned Fairfield; continuing the work of destruction, he burned part of Green's Farms, and the pleasant town of Norwalk.

On the 4th of May, 1780, the American Academy of Arts and Sciences was incorporated by the general court of Massachusetts.

Early in the morning of Sept. 6th, 1781, Gen. Arnold landed a detachment of troops on Groton Point, and proceeded up to New London with his fleet. He set fire to the town, and immediately 60 houses and 84 stores were destroyed, without opposition. But the party at Groton found more bloody work. The men in fort Griswold, who had hastened there in the morning, from the neighbourhood, defended themselves to the last extremity. The British finally entered the fort, sword in hand, and killed every man they found. Col. Ledyard, resigning his sword, the officer who received it plunged it into his heart. One man escaped by concealing himself in the magazine, another by climbing up a chimney in the barrack; 1 or 2 who fell wounded among the slain, recovered. Awful was this day to Groton. The compact part of the town was in ashes; 70 of her valuable citizens, who in the morning rushed to arms, lay dead in the fort; they were conveyed to their families for interment. Peace between the belligerent powers, put an end to these bloody scenes, in 1783.

In 1784, New Hampshire established a constitution of civil government, as Massachusetts had done in 1780. Connecticut and Rhode-Island continued their ancient constitutions, and experienced no sensible change by the revolution.

Owing to their embarrassed circumstances, from the decay of trade, the loss of public credit, the weight of public and private debts, in the fall of 1786, the 3 western counties of Massachusetts obstructed the judicial courts; but were soon brought to submission, and are now very generally among the zealous friends of good government.

The next year the federal constitution was formed, and in 1788, adopted by all the states of New-England; and went into operation April 30, 1789, when Gen. Washington was installed first president of the U. States, at New-York. New-England, with the other parts of the union, have liberally shared the blessings of that event, in the revival of commerce, and public credit, the increase of wealth, the promotion of the liberal arts, and all that exalts or adorns civil society. Long may these enterprizing states remain solid pillars in the federal edifice! and long maintain the pure morals, the serious and sound religion, and wise institutions of their pious forefathers.

The emigrants to Vermont, carrying a good portion of the virtue and intelligence of their native states into their new settlements, founded institutions of science, as soon as they were able to support them. In 1791, the legislature established a college at Burlington, on lake Champlain, pleasantly situated on the south side of Onion river. Large sums of money were subscribed for erecting buildings, and the establishment of a fund. Ten trustees were appointed, who have since elected a president, and the other officers usual in our literary institutions, under whom a course of collegiate studies has since been pursued by a number of youth. The state has granted about 33.000 acres of new land for the support of a college. In 1800, another college was incorporated in Middlebury, which is now flourishing under a president and other officers. The college edifice is the largest building in the state. In 1793, Williamstown College was incorporated. By a generous legacy from Col. Ephraim Williams, and various donations, a fund has been established and the necessary buildings erected. The number of students is about 100, under the care and instruction of a president, professor of law, of mathematics, and natural philosophy, and 5 tutors.

In 1795, Bowdoin College, at Brunswick, in Maine, was incorporated. Ten thousand dollars, by the Hon. James Bowdoin, Esq. and 5 townships by the legislature, have been given for the benefit of this institution, beside other smaller donations. It is under the government of two boards, one of 13 trustees, one of 45 overseers. Two college edifices of brick are erected, with a chapel. This institution is remote from any other college, and bids fair to be useful, under a president, a professor of languages, of philosophy, chemistry, and four tutors. It has about 60 students, and the number is increasing.

CHAP. XXVI.

Population; Character; Amusements; Learning; Religion.

NEW-ENGLAND is the most populous part of the United States. It contained, in 1790, 1,009,522 souls, in 1800, 1,233,011; and in 1810, 1,471,973. The great body of these are landholders and cultivators of the soil. As they possess, in fee simple, the farms which they cultivate, they are all attached to their country; the cultivation of the soil makes them robust and healthy, and enables them to defend it.

New-England may with propriety be called a nursery of men, whence are annually transplanted, into other parts of the United States, thousands of its natives. Vast numbers of them, since the war, have emigrated into the northern parts of New-York, into Canada, and indeed into every state, and town of note in the union; particularly the new states northwest of the Ohio river.

The inhabitants of New-England are almost universally of English descent: and it is owing to this circumstance, and to the great and general attention that has been paid to education, that the English language has been preserved among them so free from corruption.

The New-Englanders are generally tall, stout and well built. Their education, laws and situation serve to inspire them with high notions of liberty. Their jealousy is awakened at the first motion toward an invasion of their rights.

A chief foundation of freedom in the New England States, is a law by which intestate estates descend to all the children, or other heirs in equal proportions. In consequence of these laws, the people of New-England enjoy an equality of condition unknown in any other part of the world; and it is in this way that the people have preserved that happy mediocrity among themselves, which, by inducing economy and industry, removes from them temptations to luxury, and forms them to habits of sobriety and temperance. At the same time their industry and frugality exempt them from want, and from the necessity of submitting to any encroachments on their liberties.

In New-England, learning is more generally diffused among all ranks of people, than in any other part of the United States; a fact arising from the excellent establishment of schools in every town.

In these schools, which are generally supported by a public tax, and under the direction of a school committee, are taught the elements of reading, writing and arithmetic; and of late very commonly the higher branches of grammar, geography, history, &c.

A very valuable source of information to the people is the newspapers, of which more than 30,000 are printed every week in New-England, and circulated in every town.*

A person of mature age, who cannot both read and write, is rarely to be found. By means of this general establishment of schools, the extensive circulation of newspapers,

* In 1798, there were 120 different newspapers printed in the United States, many of them daily papers, and more printed twice a week. In 1788, it was estimated, that no less than 4,000,000 of newspapers were circulated through the country every year. They have probably more than trebled since.

and the consequent diffusion of learning, every township throughout the country is furnished with men capable of conducting the affairs of their town with judgment and discretion: these men are the channels of political information to the lower class of people, if such a class may be said to exist in New-England, where every man thinks himself at least as good as his neighbour.

The people from their childhood, form habits of canvassing public affairs, and commence politicians. This naturally leads them to be very inquisitive. It is with knowledge as with riches, the more a man has, the more he desires to obtain. This desire after knowledge, in a greater or less degree, prevails throughout all classes of people in New-England; and from their various modes of expressing it, some of which are blunt and familiar, bordering on impertinence, strangers have been induced to mention *impertinent inquisitiveness*, as a distinguishing characteristic of New-England people. But this inquisitiveness is rarely troublesome, and generally pleasing. The common people in New-England are excelled by no common people in the world, in civility to strangers.

Before the late war, which introduced into New-England a flood of corruptions and errors, together with many improvements, there was a general uniformity in the faith of the churches; the sabbath was observed with great strictness; no unnecessary travelling, no secular business, no visiting, no diversions, were permitted on that sacred day. The people considered it as consecrated to divine worship, and were generally punctual and serious in their attendance upon it. Their laws were strict in guarding the sabbath against every innovation. The supposed severity with which these laws were composed and executed, together with some other traits in their religious character, have acquired for the New-Englanders the name of a superstitious, bigotted people. But all persons are called superstitious by those less conscientious, and less disposed to regard religion with reverence, than themselves. Since the war, a catholic, tolerant, spirit, occasioned by a more enlarged intercourse with mankind, has become general; and as mankind are wont to vibrate from one extreme to the other, New-England is now experiencing all the effects of a variety of discordant opinions concerning the faith of the gospel, of its ordinances, and discipline.

There is one distinguishing characteristic in the religious character of this people, which me must not omit to mention; and that is, the custom of annually celebrating fasts and thanksgivings. In the spring, the governors of the several New-England states issue their proclamations, appointing a day to be religiously observed in fasting, humiliation, and prayer, throughout their respective states; in which the predominating vices, that particularly call for humiliation, are enumerated. In autumn, after harvest, that gladsome era in the husbandman's life, the governors again issue their proclamations, appointing a day of public thanksgiving, enumerating the public blessings received in the course of the foregoing year.

This pious custom originated with their venerable ancestors, the first settlers of New-England; and has been handed down as sacred, through the successive generations of their posterity. A custom so rational, and so happily calculated to cherish, in the minds of the people, a sense of their dependence on the Great Benefactor of the world, for all their blessings, it is hoped will ever be sacredly preserved. Other states in the union are adopting this wise practice.

The people of New England generally obtain their estates by hard and persevering labour: of course they know their value, and are frugal. Yet in no country do the indigent and unfortunate fare better. Their laws oblige every town to provide a competent maintenance for their poor, and the necessitous stranger is protected and relieved by their humane institutions. It may in truth be said, that in no part of the world are the people happier, better furnished with the necessaries and conveniences of life, or more independent, than the farmers in New-England. As the great body of the people are hardy, independent, freeholders, their manners are, as they ought to be, congenial to their employment, plain, simple, and manly. Strangers are received and entertained among them with a great deal of artless sincerity, and friendly, plain, hospitality. Their children, those imitative creatures, to whose education particular attention is paid, early imbibe the manners and habits of those around them; and the stranger, with pleasure, notices the honest and decent respect that is paid him by them as he passes through the country.

As the people, by representation, make their own laws, and appoint their own officers, they cannot be oppressed; and, living under governments, which have few lucrative places, they have few motives to bribery, corrupt canvassings, or intrigue. Real abilities, and a moral character unblemished, have hitherto been the qualifications requisite, in the view of most people, for officers of public trust. The expression of a wish to be promoted, was, and is still, in some parts of New-England, the direct way to be disappointed.

The inhabitants are generally fond of the arts and sciences, and have cultivated them with great success. Their colleges have flourished. The illustrious characters they have produced, who have distinguished themselves in politics, law, divinity, the mathematics, and philosophy, natural and civil history, and in the fine arts, particularly in poetry and painting, evince the truth of these observations.

Many of the women in New-England are handsome. They generally have fair, fresh, and healthful countenances, mingled with much female softness and delicacy. Those who have had the advantages of a good education, and they are numerous, are genteel, easy, and agreeable in their manners, are sprightly and sensible in conversation. They are early taught to manage domestic concerns with neatness and economy. Ladies of the first distinction and fortune, make it a part of their daily business to superintend the affairs of the family. Employment at the needle, in cookery, and at the spinning-wheel, with them is honourable. Idleness, even in those of independent fortunes, is universally disreputable. The women in country towns, manufacture the greater part of the clothing of their families. The linen and woollen cloths are strong and decent. Their butter and cheese is not inferior to any in the world.

Gaming is practised by none but those who cannot, or rather will not, find a *reputable* employment. The gamester, the horse-jockey, and the knave, are equally despised, and their company is avoided by all who would sustain fair and irreproachable characters.

The athletic and healthy diversions of cricket, football, quoits, wrestling, jumping, hopping, foot races, and prison bass, are universally practised in the country, and some of them in the most populous places, and by people of almost all ranks.

The people of New-England are Protestant christians, excepting a few Jews, who have a synagogue in Newport, and a few Roman Catholics, principally in Boston. The Protestants are divided into Congregationalists, which is the prevailing denomination, Episcopalians, Baptists, Friends or Quakers, Methodists, and Universalists. As in other parts of the United States, so in the part we are describing, there are numbers, who have their religion yet to choose. They have *liberty of conscience*, but no *religion*.

The clergy of New-England are a numerous body of men, and, in general, are respectable for their piety, morals, and learning. The cause of general literature is much indebted to their labours. Probably nineteen twentieths of the publications in New England, from its first settlement, have been from the pens of the clergy.

The number and pious exertions of missionary societies, some of them patronized by the government, do honour to the religious character of New-England. At the expense, and under the direction of these societies, a large number of missionaries are annually sent among the Indians and frontier settlers, who are destitute of religious instruction, and some to foreign countries. The business of our domestic mission, particularly, is to instruct from house to house, the inhabitants of waste places, to preach publicly, to administer ordinances, and distribute bibles and various other religious books. The good effects which have followed these exertions, in preserving and cherishing the early religious habits of the people, and guarding them against the poison of infidelity and vice, are great beyond calculation.

HISTORY OF NEW-YORK.

CHAP. XXVII.

Discovery by the Dutch; Patent; Submission to the English; Government resumed by the Dutch, who erect a fort on Connecticut river; Their extravagant claims; Surrender of the country to the English; Its seizure by the Dutch, who soon surrendered it permanently to the English; Indians.

As early as 1607, and 1608, Henry Hudson, an Englishman, an experienced, intrepid, and enterprizing seaman, under a commission from king James, in the employ of certain merchants, made several voyages for the discovery of a northwest passage to the East-Indies. In 1609, in consequence of some misunderstanding between him and his employers, he engaged in the Dutch service. Their East-India company fitted out a ship for discovery, of which they gave Hudson the command. He sailed from Amsterdam, March 1609, and during his voyage he ranged the American coast, touching at different parts, from lat. 71° 46, to lat. 39° 5, N.; and, in September, of the same year, entered the fine river, which bears his name. He penetrated this river, according to his own account, 53 leagues; which must be as far as where the city of Albany now stands. This discovery gave the Dutch at once an entrance into the heart of the American continent, where the best furs could be procured, without interruption from the French or English, both which nations claimed this territory.

Within four years after this discovery, a company of merchants, who had procured from the States General a patent for an exclusive trade to Hudson's river; built a fort and trading house, where Albany now stands.

In 1614, Capt. Argal, under sir Thomas Dale, governor of Virginia, visited the Dutch, on Hudson's river, who, being unable to resist him, prudently submitted for the present to the king of England, and, under him, to the governor of Virginia. Determined upon the settlement of a colony, the States General, in 1621, granted the country to the West-India company; and in the year 1664. Wouter Van Twiller arrived at fort Amsterdam, now New-York, and took upon himself the government.

In 1615, a fort was built on the southwest point of Manhattan's, now York, island; but the first settlers planted themselves about 2 miles from this fort, and built a church there, the ruins of which, not many years since, were visible, near the two mile stone, on the public road. In this situation, finding themselves insecure, during the wars between the English and Dutch, they left this place, and planted their habitations under the guns of the fort, which laid the foundation of the present city of New-York.

In 1621, the Dutch made a grant of this country to the West-India company. In 1623, a company of Dutch traders came to Connecticut river, to the place where Hartford is now built, and erected a small fort, in which they planted 2 cannon, and built a trading house, which they called the *Hirse of Good Hope*. In 1635, the English, from Massachusetts, planted a colony near fort Good Hope, at Hartford, Weathersfield, and Windsor; and 4 years after, seized the Dutch garrison, and drove them from the banks of the river, having first, in 1632, settled New-Haven.

In consequence of their discoveries and settlements, the Dutch claimed all the country, extending from Cape Cod to Cape Henlopen, along the seacoast, and as far back into the country as any of the rivers, within those limits, extend, and named it *New* NETHERLANDS. But these extravagant and unfounded claims were never allowed to the Dutch. This nation, and after them the province of New-York, for a long time, claimed as far east as the western banks of Connecticut river, and this claim was the ground of much altercation, till 1664, when the partition line between New-York, and Connecticut was run from the mouth of Memoroncock river (a little west of Byram river) N. N. W. and was, according to Dr. Douglass* "the ancient easterly limits of New-York, until November 23, 1683, when the line was run nearly the same as it is now settled."

In 1664, Aug. 27, Gov. Stuyvesant surrendered the colony to Col. Nicolls, who had arrived in the bay a few days

* Summary, vol. ii. p. 161.

before, with 3 or 4 ships, and about 300 soldiers, having a commission from king Charles II. to reduce the place, which was then called New-Amsterdam, afterwards New-York. Very few of the inhabitants removed out of the country; and their respectable descendants are still numerous in many parts of this state, and of New-Jersey. A league of friendship was at this time entered into with the Five Indian nations, which has never since been broken.

In 1667, at the peace of Breda, New-York was confirmed to the English, who in exchange ceded Surrinam to the Dutch.

The English kept peaceable possession of the country, until the year 1673, when the Dutch, with whom the English were then at war, sent a small squadron, which arrived at Staten island on the 30th of July. John Manning, a captain of an independent company, who had at that time the command of the fort, sent a messenger down to the commodore, and like Benedict Arnold in later times, turned traitor to his country, and made his terms with him. On the same day, the ships came up, moored under the fort, landed their men, and entered the garrison, without giving or receiving a shot. All the magistrates and constables from East Jersey, Long Island, Æsopus, and Albany, were summoned to New-York; and the major part of them swore allegiance to the States General, and the prince of Orange. The conquerors, however, did not long enjoy the fruits of their success; for on the 19th of February, the year following, a treaty of peace between England and Holland, was signed at Westminster; by the sixth article of which, this province was restored to the English, in whose hands it remained until the late revolution, when it became one of the United States.

The confederated tribes of Indians, before the incorporation of the Tuscaroras, a people driven by the Carolinians from the frontiers of Virginia, consisted of *Five Nations,* viz. the Mohawks, Oneidas, Senecas, Onondagas, and Cayugas. The Tuscaroras made the sixth, and ever since their arrival, they have been called *"the Six Nations."* The alliance and trade of these six nations, inhabiting the territory west of Albany, to the distance of more than 200 miles, though much courted by the French of Canada, with few interruptions, have been enjoyed by the English.

In 1684, the French attempted the destruction of these Indians, because they interrupted their trade with the more distant tribes, called the *Far Nations*. The Seneca Indians interrupted this trade, because the French supplied the Miamies, with whom they were at war, with arms and ammunition.

To effect the destruction of the Indians, great preparations were made by the French. But famine and sickness prevailing among them, the expedition proved fruitless. Four years after this, 1200 Indians attacked Montreal, burnt many houses, and put to death 1000 of the inhabitants.

Each of these Six Nations was divided into 3 families, or clans, of different ranks, bearing for their arms, the *tortoise*, the *bear*, and the *wolf*; by which names they were distinguished. Their instruments of conveyance, &c. were subscribed by representations of these animals. They had high notions of military glory, and were among the most formidable body of Indians in all the country around them. Many of the neighbouring tribes were their tributaries. They were contented, without riches, merely with a freedom from want. An Indian once asked what the white people meant by *covetousness*. The reply was, "a desire of more than a man had need of." The Indian replied, "Ah, that is strange."

After their acquaintance with Europeans, their war implements were a musket, long knife, and a *hatchet;* hence a declaration of war, on their part, was called, "taking up the hatchet;" and burying it, denoted a determination to be at peace. When the Indians were inclined to make peace, a messenger was despatched to their enemies with a pipe ornamented with the plumage of birds, who made his proposals; which, if accepted, the preliminaries of peace, were ratified by smoking this pipe; and this was a signal for a cessation of hostilities. This pipe the French call a *calumet;* hence the phrase, "smoking the calumet of peace." It is used generally, as far as we know, among all the Indian tribes on this continent.*

The language of the Six Nations, except the Tuscaroras, is radically the same.† It is masculine and sonorous. Their chiefs study the art of speaking, and in all their speeches strictly observe method. Their speeches are highly figurative, short, and impressive. In conversation they are sprightly, but solemn in the transaction of their public affairs. Their speakers deliver themselves with surprising force and propriety of gesture. Their manly and fierce countenances, erect attitude, elevated tone of voice, and distinct and deliberate enunciation, the flowing blanket, the naked arm, and easy and graceful gesture, their auditors seated in the open air, in a semicircle before them, all together forcibly remind the spectator of the orators of Greece and Rome, in their best days. These once formidable tribes are much reduced in numbers, and character, and are but the feeble remnant of what they once were. Their numbers in 1818, inhabiting within the limits of this state, were 4,871, whose several reservations together amounted to 275,323 acres. These reservations are among the best lands in the state.

* Smith's Hist. New-York. † Rev. Mr. Spencer, a missionary among them.

CHAP. XXVIII.

Governor Dongan recalled; Jacob Leister traitorously assumes the government; The French instigate the Indians to make war on the colonies; Dreadful massacre of the inhabitants of Schenectady; Leister and his son condemned to die, as guilty of treason; Commencement of dissentions between Episcopalians and Presbyterians; Indians cede a large tract of land to the English; Abortive plans for attacking Canada; Five sachems visit England, and are introduced to Queen Anne; 3000 Palatines from Germany, brought over by Gov. Hunter; Troubles with the merchants respecting the Indian trade; Project for a settlement of Highlanders, fails; Cession of lands to New-York, by Massachusetts.

In 1689, Col. Dongan, the governor, being called home by king James, and a general disaffection to government prevailing at New-York, one Jacob Leister took possession of the garrison for king William and queen Mary, and assumed the supreme power over the province. His reduction of Albany, held by others for William, and the confiscation of the estates of his opponents, were impolitic measures, which sowed the seeds of mutual animosity, the ill effects of which were felt for a long time after, in the embarrassments of the public affairs.

The French, in 1689, in order to detach the Six Nations from the British interest, sent out several parties against the English colonies; one of which, consisting of about 200 French, and some of the Cagnawaghga Indians, commanded by D'Ailldebout, de Mantel, and le Moyne, was intended for New-York. But by the advice of the Indians, they determined first to attack Schenectady.

For this place they accordingly directed their course, and after 20 days' march, in the depth of winter, through the snow, carrying their provisions on their backs, they arrived in the neighbourhood of Schenectady, on the 8th of February, 1690. Such was the extreme distress to which they were reduced, that they had thoughts of surrendering themselves prisoners of war. But their scouts, who were a day or two in the village, entirely unsuspected, returned with such encouraging accounts of the absolute security of the people, that the enemy determined on the attack. They entered the town on Saturday night, about 11 o'clock, at the gates, which were found open; and, that every house might be invested at the same time, they divided into small parties of 6 or 7 men. The inhabitants were in a profound sleep, and unalarmed, until their doors were broken open. Never were people in a more wretched consternation. Before they had time to rise from their beds, the enemy entered their houses, and began the perpetration of the most inhuman barbarities. No tongue can express the cruelties that were committed. The whole village was instantly in a blaze. Women with child ripped open, and their infants cast into the flames, or dashed against the posts of the door. Sixty persons perished in the massacre, and 27 were carried into captivity. The rest fled naked towards Albany, through a deep snow, which fell that very night in a terrible storm; and 25 of the fugitives lost their limbs in the flight, through the severity of the frost. The news of this dreadful tragedy reached Albany, about break of day, and universal dread and dismay seized the inhabitants of that city, the enemy being reported to be 1400 strong. A party of horse was immediately despatched to Schenectady, and a few Mowhawks, then in town, fearful of being intercepted, were with difficulty sent to carry intelligence to their own castles, and to put them on their guard Owing to the great depth of the snow, and the extreme difficulty of travelling, the Mohawks, though near, remained unacquainted with this bloody scene for two days after it happened. The enemy pillaged the town of Schenectady until noon the next day; and then went off with their plunder, and with about 40 of the best horses. The rest, with all the cattle they could find, were left slaughtered in the streets.

Upon the arrival of a governor at New-York, commissioned by the king, Leister refused to surrender the garrison, for the seizure of which, he and his son were tried and condemned to die, as guilty of high treason.

The whole province of New-York was originally settled by non-episcopalians, chiefly by Presbyterians, except a few episcopal families in the city of New-York. In 1693, Col. Fletcher, then governor of the province, projected the scheme of a general tax for building churches, and supporting episcopal ministers, and by artifice effected his design in part. This overture laid the foundation for a controversy between the Presbyterians and Episcopalians, which, until the revolution, was maintained on both sides with great warmth and animosity, and which has never since been suffered uninterruptedly to sleep. Several of the governors, particularly lord Cornbury, showed great partiality to the Episcopalians, and oppressed and persecuted the Presbyterians.

In 1701, (July 19,) the confederated tribes of Indians, at Albany, surrendered to the English their beaver hunting country, lying between lakes Ontario and Erie, to be by them defended for the said confederated Indians, their heirs and successors forever. This transaction was confirmed, Sept. 14, 1726, when the Senecas, Cayugas, and

Onondagas, surrendered to the English, for the same use, their habitations, from Cayahoga to Oswego, and 60 miles inland.

In 1709, a vigorous expedition was meditated against Canada; in making preparations for which, this province expended above £20,000; but the expected assistance from Britain failing, it was never prosecuted. Soon after Col. Schuyler, who had been very influential with the Indians, visited England with five sachems, who were introduced into the presence of queen Anne. The object of this visit was to stimulate the ministry to the reduction of Canada. Afterward, in 1711, a considerable fleet was sent over for that purpose; but 8 transports being cast away on the coast, the rest of the fleet and troops returned without making any attempt to reduce Canada.

In 1710, Gov. Hunter brought over with him about 3000 Palatines, who, the year before, had fled to England from the rage of persecution in Germany. Many of these people settled in the city of New-York; others settled on a tract of several thousand acres, in the manor of Livingston, and some went to Pennsylvania, and were instrumental in inducing thousands of their countrymen afterwards to migrate and settle in that province.

The prohibition of the sale of Indian goods in France, in 1720, excited the clamour of the merchants at New-York, whose interest was affected by it. The measure was undoubtedly a futile one; and the reasons for it were these: the French, by this trade, were supplied with articles which were wanted by the Indians. This prevented the Indians from coming to Albany, and drew them to Montreal; and they, being employed by the French as carriers, became attached to them from interest. About the same time, a trading house was erected by the English at Oswego, on lake Ontario; and another by the French at Niagara.

In 1729, the act prohibiting the trade between Albany and Montreal, was imprudently repealed by the king. This naturally tended to undermine the trade at Oswego, and to advance the French commerce of Niagara; and at the same time to alienate the affections of the Indians from the English. Not long after this, the French were suffered to erect a fort on lake Champlain. To prevent the ill consequences of this, a scheme was projected to settle the lands near lake George, with loyal Protestant Highlanders, from Scotland. Accordingly, a tract of 30,000 acres was promised to Capt. Campbell, who, at his own expense, transported 83 Protestant families to New-York. But through the sordid views of some persons in power, who aimed at a share in the intended grant, the settlement was never made.

In 1787, the legislature of this state, ceded to the commonwealth of Massachusetts, all the lands, within their jurisdiction, west of a meridian to be drawn from a point in the north boundary line of Pennsylvania, 82 miles west from Delaware; (excepting one mile along the east side of Niagara river) and also 10 townships between the Chenango and Oswego rivers, reserving the jurisdiction to the state of New-York. This cession was made to satisfy a claim of Massachusetts, founded upon their original charter.*

* The authors are not in possession of the necessary materials for bringing the history of this respectable and increasing state down to the present time. It is their intention to do it hereafter.

HISTORY OF NEW-JERSEY.

CHAP. XXIX.

The Dutch settled E. Jersey, and the Swedes and Finns W. Jersey; grant of this territory by Charles II. to the duke of York, and by him to others; Lands purchased of the Indians; The Dutch and Swedes inhabit the country together; Indian murders, causes and effects of them; character and customs of the Indians; The Dutch conquered the country, but soon relinquished it; new Patent division into East and West Jersey; sold to Fenwick, who makes the first English settlement in Jersey; New partition of the country; New grant of West Jersey, and sale of East Jersey; Difficulties in managing the government; Surrendered to the crown 1702; Remained a royal government, till it became in 1776, an independent state. The patriotism and sufferings of its inhabitants during the war; College and Theological Seminary at Princeton.

The first settlers of New-Jersey were a number of Dutch emigrants, who came over between the years 1614, and 1620, and settled in the county of Bergen, on the west side of Hudson's river, opposite New-York. Next after these, in 1627, came over a colony of Swedes and Finns, and settled on the river Delaware, below Philadelphia. They afterwards purchased of the Indians, the land on both sides of New Swedeland stream, (now called Delaware river) from cape Henlopen to the falls at Trenton; and by presents to the Indian chiefs, obtained peaceable possession of it. The settlers of New-Jersey appear to have been scrupulous on the subject of purchasing their lands of the Indians, which is the more creditable to them as there were but few Indians within their territories. The Dutch and Swedes though not in harmony with each other, kept possession, each of their respective territories many years.

In 1668, the Mantas Indians murdered 7 persons. On hearing this news, the Indians in the vicinity desired that there should be an absolute prohibition upon the whole river, of selling strong liquor to the Indians generally; the late murders having been probably the consequence of a drunken frolic; this is the more likely, as the whole body of the Indians in the first settled part of the lands on Delaware, afterwards, through a long course of years manifested an open, hospitable disposition toward the English, and generally manifested no hostile designs.

The year following, Gov. Carteret made a purchase of the lands of the Indians, for "funds inconsiderable," for the security of the settlements. For though the Indians in their vicinity were not numerous, they were "strong in their alliances, and besides of themselves could easily annoy the frontier settlers; and there having been before several considerable skirmishes between the Dutch and them, in which some blood had been spilt, their friendship, on this consideration, it was thought, stood but ticklish: upon the whole, the governor so ordered it that the comers were either to purchase of the Indians themselves, or if the lands were before purchased, they were to pay their proportions. The event answered his expectation; for as the Indians parted with the lands to their own satisfaction, they became, of a jealous, shy people, serviceable, good neighbours; and though the circulation of reports of their coming to kill the white people, sometimes disturbed their repose, no instance occurs of their hurting them in those early settlements."*

* Smith's Hist. New-Jersey.

New-Jersey was originally inhabited by many small Indian tribes, distinguished by the names of the creeks on which they resided. Among them were the Assunpink, i.e. *Stoney Creek* Indians; the Rankokas, the Mingos,* the Andastakas, the Neshamines, and the Mantas, or *Frogs*, who lived about Burlington. These and other tribes were distinguished from the *back Indians*, who bore the general name of *Delawares*, and who were more warlike. On the banks of the Delaware, below the falls, are monuments of forts erected against their incursions. Mr. Smith, in his history of New Jersey, gives the following account of the tribes within this province. We quote this account more fully, because, from it, the reader may form some pretty correct ideas of the Indians generally throughout our country.

"When they buried their dead, it was customary to put family utensils, bows and arrows, and sometimes money, (wampum) into the grave with them, as tokens of their affection. When a person of note died far from the place of his own residence, they would carry his bones to be buried there; they washed and perfumed the dead, painted the face, and followed singly; left the dead in a sitting posture, and covered the grave pyramidically. They were very careful in preserving and repairing the graves of their dead, and pensively visited them; did not love to be asked their judgment twice about the same thing. They generally delighted in mirth; were very studious in observing the virtues of roots and herbs, by which they usually cured themselves of many bodily distempers, both by outward and inward applications. They besides frequently used sweating,

* A sachem of this tribe was observed to look intently at the great comet which appeared Oct. 1680. When asked what he thought of it; he answered gravely, "It signifies that we Indians shall melt away, and this country be inhabited by another people."

and the cold bath. They had an aversion to beards, and would not suffer them to grow; but plucked the hair out by the roots. The hair of their heads was black, and generally shone with bear's fat, particularly that of the women, who tied it up behind in a large knot; sometimes in a bag.

"They were very loving to one another; if several of them came to a christian's house, and the master of it gave one of them victuals, and none to the rest, he would divide it into equal shares amongst his companions; if the christians visited them, they would give them the first cut of their victuals; they would not eat the hollow of the thigh of any thing they killed.

"Their chief employment was hunting, fishing, and fowling; making canoes, bowls, and other wooden and earthen ware; in all which they were, considering their means, ingenious; In their earthen bowls they boiled their water. Their women's business chiefly consisted in planting Indian corn, parching or roasting it, pounding it to meal in mortars, or breaking it between stones, making bread, and dressing victuals; in which they were sometimes observed to be very neat and cleanly, and sometimes otherwise. They also made mats, ropes, hats and baskets, (some very curious) of wild hemp and roots, or splits of trees; their young women were originally very modest and shame-faced, and at marriageable ages distinguished themselves with a kind of worked mats, of red or blue bays, interspersed with small rows of white and black wampum, or half rows of each in one, fastened to it, and then put round the head, down to near the middle of the forehead. Both young and old women would be highly offended at indecent expressions, unless corrupted with drink.

"The Indians would not allow of mentioning the name of a friend after death. They sometimes streaked their faces with black, when in mourning; but when their affairs went well, they painted red. They were great observers of the weather by the moon; delighted in fine clothes; were punctual in their bargains, and observed this so much in others, that it was very difficult for a person who had once failed herein, to get any dealings with them afterwards. In their councils they seldom or never interrupted or contradicted one another, till two of them had made an end of their discourse; for if ever so many were in company, only two must speak to each other, and the rest be silent till their turn. Their language was high, lofty, and sententious. Their way of counting was by tens, that is to say, two tens, three tens, four tens, &c when the number got out of their reach, they pointed to the stars, or the hair of their heads.

"They lived chiefly on maize, or Indian corn roasted in the ashes, sometimes beaten and boiled with water, called hominy; they also made an agreeable cake of their pounded corn; and raised beans and pease; but the woods and rivers afforded them the chief of their provisions. They pointed their arrows with a sharpened flinty stone, and of a larger sort, with withs for handles, cut their wood; both of these sharpened stones are often found in the fields. Their times of eating were commonly morning and evening; their seats and tables the ground. They were naturally reserved, apt to resent, to conceal their resentments, and retain them long; they were liberal and generous, kind and affable to the English. They were observed to be uneasy and impatient in sickness for a present remedy, to which they commonly drank a decoction of roots in spring water, forbearing flesh, which if they then eat at all, it was of the female. They took remarkable care of one another in sickness, while hopes of life remained; but when that was gone, some of them were apt to neglect the patient.

"Their government was monarchical and successive, and mostly of the mother's side; to prevent a spurious issue.* They commonly washed their children in cold water as soon as born; and to make their limbs straight, tied them to a board, and hung it to their backs when they travelled; they usually walked at 9 months old. Their young men married at 16 or 17 years of age, if by that time they had given sufficient proof of their manhood, by a large return of skins. The girls married about 13 or 14, but stayed at home with their mothers to hoe the ground, and to bear burdens, &c. for some years after marriage. The women, in travelling, generally carried the luggage. The marriage ceremony was sometimes thus; the relations and friends being present, the bridegroom delivered a bone to the bride, she an ear of Indian corn to him, meaning that he was to provide meat, she bread. It was not unusual, notwithstanding, to change their mates upon disagreement; the children went with the party that loved them best, the expense being of no moment to either; in case of difference on this head, the man was allowed the first choice, if the children were divided, or there was but one.

"Very little can be said as to their religion; much pains were taken by the early christian settlers, and frequently since, to inform their judgments respecting the use and benefit of the christian revelation, and to fix restraints; but generally with unpromising success, though instances have now and then happened to the contrary. They are thought to have believed in a God and immortality, and seemed to aim at public worship; when they did this, they sometimes sat in several circles one within another; the action consisted of singing, jumping, shouting and dancing; but mostly performed rather as something handed down from their ancestors, than from any knowledge or inquiry into

* That is, the children of him now king, will not succeed, but his brother by the mother, or children of his sister, whose sons (and after them the male children of her daughters) were to reign; for no woman inherited.

the serious parts of its origin. They said the great king that made them, dwelt in a glorious country to the southward, and that the spirits of the best should go there and live again. Their most solemn worship was the sacrifice of the first fruits, in which they burnt the first and fattest buck, and feasted together upon what else they had collected; but in this sacrifice broke no bones of any creature they ate; when done, they gathered and buried them, very carefully; these have since been frequently plowed up. They distinguished between a good and evil man-etta, or spirit; worshipped the first for the good they hoped: and some of them are said to have been slavishly dark in praying to the last for deprecation of evils they feared; but if this be generally true, some of the tribes much concealed it from our settlers.

"They did justice upon one another for crimes among themselves, in a way of their own; even murder might be atoned for by feasts, and presents of wampum; the price of a woman killed was double, and the reason, because *she bred children, which men could not do*. If sober they rarely quarrelled among themselves. They lived to 60, 70, 80 years, and more, before rum was introduced, but rarely since. Some tribes were commendably careful of their aged and decrepid, endeavouring to make the remains of life as comfortable as they could, except in desperate decays, then they were apt to neglect them.

"Strict observers of property, yet to the last degree, thoughtless and inactive in acquiring or keeping it. None could excel them in liberality of the little they had, for nothing was thought too good for a friend; a knife, gun, or any such thing given to one, frequently passed through many hands. Their houses or wigwams were sometimes together in towns, but mostly moveable, and occasionally fixed near a spring, or other water, according to the conveniencies for hunting, fishing, basket-making, or other business of that sort, and built with poles laid on forked sticks in the ground, with bark, flags or bushes on the top and sides, with an opening to the south, their fire in the middle. At night they slept on the ground with their feet towards it. Their clothing was a coarse blanket or skin thrown over the shoulder, which covered to the knee, and a piece of the same tied round their legs, with part of a deer skin sewed round their feet for shoes. As they had learned to live upon little, they seldom expected or wanted to lay up much. They were also moderate in asking a price for any thing they had for sale. When a company travelled together, they generally followed each other in silence, scarcely ever two were seen by the side of one another. In roads, the man went before with his bow and arrow, the woman after, not uncommonly with a child at her back, and other burdens besides: but when these were too heavy, the man assisted. To know their walks again, in unfrequented woods, they heaped stones or marked trees.

"In person they were upright, and straight in their limbs, beyond the usual proportion in most nations. Their bodies were strong, but of a strength rather fitted to endure hardships, than to sustain much bodily labour, very seldom crooked or deformed: their features regular: their countenances sometimes fierce, in common rather resembling a Jew than Christian: the colour of their skin a tawney reddish brown. The whole fashion of their lives of a piece; hardy, poor and squalid. When they began to drink, they commonly continued it as long as the means of procuring it lasted. While intoxicated, they often lay exposed to all the inclemencies of weather, which introduced a train of new disorders among them. They were grave, even to sadness, upon any common, and more so upon serious, occasions; observant of those in company, and respectful to the old; of a temper cool and deliberate; never in haste to speak, but waited for a certainty, that the person who spoke before them had finished all he had to say. They seemed to hold European vivacity in contempt, because they found such as came among them, apt to interrupt each other, and frequently speak all together.

"Their behaviour in public councils, was strictly decent and instructive, every one in his turn was heard, according to rank of years or wisdom, or services to his country. Not a word, a whisper, or a murmur, while any one spoke; no interruption to commend or condemn; the younger sort were totally silent. They got fire by rubbing wood of particular sorts, (as the ancients did out of the ivy and bays) by turning the end of a hard piece upon the side of one that was soft and dry. To forward the heat they put dry rotten wood and leaves; with the help of fire and their stone axes, they would fall large trees, and afterwards scoop them into bowls, &c. From their infancy they were formed with care to endure hardships, to bear derision, and even blows patiently; at least with a composed countenance. Though they were not easily provoked, and hard to be appeased.

"Liberty in its fullest extent, was their ruling passion; to this every other consideration was subservient. Their children were trained up so as to cherish this disposition to the utmost; they were indulged to a great degree, seldom chastised with blows, and rarely chided; their faults were left for their reason and habits of the family to correct; they said these could not be great before their reason commenced; and they seemed to abhor a slavish motive to action, as inconsistent with their notions of freedom and independence. Even strong persuasion was industriously avoided, as bordering too much on dependence, and a kind of violence offered to the will. They dreaded slavery more than death. They laid no fines for crimes; for they had no way of exacting them. The atonement was voluntary. Every tribe had particular persons in whom they reposed a confidence, and unless they did something unworthy of it they were held in respect. Their kings were distinguished sachems; the respect paid them was voluntary, and not exacted or looked for, nor the omission of it regarded. The sachems directed in their councils, and had the chief disposition of lands. To help their memories in treaties, they had belts of black and white wampum; with these closed their periods in speeches, delivering more or less according to the importance of the matter treated of; this ceremony omitted, all they said passed for nothing. They treasured these belts when delivered to them in treaties, kept them as the records of the nation, to have recourse to upon future contests. Governed by customs and not by laws, they greatly revered those of their ancestors, and followed them implicitly. They long remembered kindnesses, families or individuals that had laid themselves out to deal with, entertain and treat them hospitably, or even fairly in dealings, if no great kindness was received, were sure of their trade. This also must undoubtedly be allowed, that the original and more uncorrupt, very seldom forgot to be grateful, where real benefits had been received.

"Notwithstanding their government was successive, it was, for extraordinary reasons, sometimes ordered otherwise; of this there is an instance in the old king Ockanickon, who, before his death, at Burlington, declared himself to this effect:

" 'It was my desire, that my brother's son Iahkursoe, should come to me, and hear my last words; for him have I appointed king after me.

" '*My brother's son*, This day I deliver my heart into your bosom; mind me. I would have you love what is good, and keep good company; refuse what is evil, and avoid bad company.

" 'Now having delivered my heart into your bosom, I also deliver my bosom to keep my heart in; be sure always to walk in a good path; and if any Indians should speak evil of Indians or christians, do not join in it, but look at the sun from the rising of it to the setting of the same: In speeches that shall be made between the *Indians* and the christians, if any wrong or evil thing be spoken, do not join with that; but join with the good: When speeches are made, do not you speak first; be silent and let all speak before you, and take good notice what each man speaks; and when you have heard all, join to that which is good.

" '*Brother's son*, I would have you cleanse your ears, and take all foulness out, that you may hear both good and evil, and then join with the good and refuse the evil; and also cleanse your eyes, that you may see good and evil, and where you see evil, do not join with it, but join to that which is good.

" '*Brother's son*, I advise you to be plain and fair with all, both *Indians* and christians, as I have been; I am very weak, otherwise I would have spoken more.' "

In 1683, the Dutch had a house devoted to religious worship at Newcastle, within the territories claimed by the Swedes; who, at the same time, had three, viz. one on the island of Tenecum, one at Christiana, and one at Wicoco. The descendants of these first settlers now live in Gloucester county, in this state, and in Philadelphia.

In March, 1634, Charles II. granted all the territory, called by the Dutch New-Netherlands, to his brother the duke of York; and in June, 1664, the duke granted that part now called New-Jersey, to lord Berkley, of Stratton, and Sir George Carteret, jointly; who, in 1665, agreed upon certain concessions, with the people for the government of the province, and appointed Philip Carteret, Esq. their governor. He purchased considerable tracts of land of the Indians, for small considerations, and the settlements increased.

The Dutch took possession of the country in 1672, or 1673, but it was restored by the peace of Westminster, Feb. 9, 1674.

In consequence of the conquest made by the Dutch, and to obviate any objections that might be made against the former grant; a new patent was issued in 1674, to the duke of York, for the same country. He appointed Andros his lieutenant, who entered on his charge the November following. In July, 1674, New-Jersey was divided, and West Jersey was granted by the duke of York to the assigns of lord Berkley; and East Jersey to Sir G. Carteret. The division line was to run from the southeast point of Little Egg-Harbour, on Barnegate creek, being about the middle between cape May and Sandy Hook, to a creek, a little below Ancocus creek, on Delaware river, thence about 35 miles, a strait course, along Delaware river, up to lat. 41° 40′ N. This line has never been settled, but has ever since continued to be a subject of contention. Carteret, who had been expelled, with outrage, in 1672, returned again to East Jersey, early in 1675, and was now kindly received by the inhabitants, having felt the rigours of conquest, which had not been softened, but much increased by Andros.

In 1675, West Jersey, which had been granted to lord Berkley, was sold to John Fenwick, in trust for Edward Bylinge. Fenwick came over with a colony, principally Quakers, or Friends and Baptists, and settled at Salem. These were the first English settlers in West Jersey. In 1676, the interest of Bylinge in West Jersey was assigned to William Penn, Gavin Laurie, and Nicholas Lucas, as trustees, for the use of his creditors. Mutual quit-claims were executed between Sir George Carteret and the trustees of Bylinge. This partition was confirmed in 1719, by an act of the general assembly of the Jerseys.

In 1678, the duke of York made a new grant of West Jersey to the assigns of lord Berkley.

Agreeably to Sir George Carteret's will, dated Dec. 5, 1678, East Jersey was sold, in 1682, to 12 proprietors, who by 12 separate deeds, conveyed one half of their interest to 12 other persons, separately, in fee simple. This grant was confirmed to these 24 proprietors, by the duke of York, the same year. These 24 shares, by sales of small parts of them, and by these small parts being again divided among children of successive families, became at last subdivided in such a manner, as that some of the proprietors had only one 40th part of a 48th part of a 24th share. West Jersey was in the same condition. This created much confusion in the management of the general proprietors, particularly in regard to appointing governors. These inconveniences aided by other causes of complaint, which had been increasing for several years, and were fast advancing to a dangerous crisis, disposed the proprietors to surrender the government to the crown; which was accordingly done, and accepted by Queen Ann, on the 17th of April, 1702, who immediately appointed lord Cornbury governor. Till this time, the government of New-Jersey was proprietory; and for 26 years preceding, had remained two distinct provinces; it now became royal, and so continued till the memorable 4th of July, 1776. This state was the seat of war for several years, during the bloody contest between Britain and America. Her losses, both of men, and property, in proportion to her population and wealth, were greater than those of any other of the thirteen states. When Gen. Washington was retreating through the Jerseys, almost forsaken by all others, her militia were at all times obedient to his orders; and, for a considerable length of time composed the strength of his army. There is hardly a town in the state, that lay in the progress of the British army, which was not rendered signal by some enterprize or exploit. At Trenton the enemy received a check, which may be said, with justice, to have turned the tide of war. At Princeton, the seat of the muses, they received another, which, united, obliged them to retire with precipitation, and to take refuge in disgraceful winter quarters. The many military achievements performed by the Jersey soldiers, give this state one of the first ranks among her sisters in a military view, and entitle her to a share of praise that bears no proportion to her size, in the accomplishment of the revolution which gave independence to our country.

The principal ornament of this state, has been, since its establishment in 1738, its college at Princeton; to which was annexed, in 1812, a Theological seminary. This has been under the government and instruction of a succession of some of the most distinguished men, for learning and piety, which our country has produced, and its fruits have been of incalculable benefit to the civil and religious interests of our country. The Theological seminary is fast rising in reputation and usefulness, and multiplying the blessings of the more ancient institution with which it is associated.

INDEX.

A.

ANAWON, an Indian Warrior, interesting account of, 226, 228 he is beheaded, 230
Andros, Sir Edmund, appointed captain general of N. England 244, his oppression 245, made a prisoner and sent to England — — — 246
Arabella, lady — — — — 92
Arnold's expedition against Quebec — 282
Awashonks, a squaw sachem, anecdotes of 216, 222

B

Baptism, disputes about 234 decision of Synod 236
Belcher appointed governor of Massachusetts 270
Boston settled, 95 description of, 96 fires 97
Bowdoin college some account of — 285
Bradford Wm. chosen governor — 73
Brownists — — — — 36
Bunker-hill battle — — — 279
Burnet appointed governor of Massachusetts 270

C.

Canada, expedition against, in 1690 — 248
Canonicus threatens war — — 75
Cape Cod, landing of our forefathers — 53
Carver, John, chosen governor 55, death — 72
Charlestown settled — — — 89

Church, Capt. Benj. makes several successful attacks upon the Indians 214, account of his life 216, 232, remarkable preservation - - 218, 219
Churchmembership, disputes about 234, decision of Synod - - - - - 236
Coddington, Mr. some account of - - 151
Comet of 1664 - - - - 205
Conant, Roger settles on Naumkeag river 88
Concord, stores destroyed by British - 278
Connecticut, how divided among the Indians 123, charter granted 127, 144, reserve of lands 145, character of the inhabitants 146, school fund 145, charter demanded by Andros 244, ancient government dissolved - - - - - 245
Consociation, decision of the synod respecting 237
Cranmer, archbishop burnt - - 26
Crimes capital, of Massachusetts colony - 113

D

Dartmouth college founded - - 276
Davenport, Rev. Mr. account of 131, 132, 133, 134
Deerfield burnt by the Indians 208, a second time 265
Dissenters, their origin - - - 33
Dorchester heights fortified - - 282
Dress of clergy, disputes about 30, 31, 32
Drought, distressing - - - 79
Dudley appointed governor of Massachusetts 244
Duel between two servants - - 76
Dutch establishment at Hartford - - 125

E.

Earthquake throughout New-England 166, another 269
Eastham settled - - - - 179

Edward VI. - - - - 20, 21
Eliot Rev. John, apostle to the Indians, account of 193,
   194, 195, translates the Bible into Indian   194
Elizabeth, Queen, her reign - - 29
Extempore prayers 22

F.

Fasts customary in New-England - 289
Five Nations of Indians - - - 295
Forefathers' rock - - - - 66
French war of 1694 - - - 261
French fleet for invasion of New-England scattered 274

G.

Gorges, his patent confirmed by Charles I. 120

H.

Hampton, in N. Hampshire settled 167
Hartford settled - - - - 127
Harvard college established 167, account of 168
Hatfield, victory there, over the Indians 208
Henry VIIIth. - - 15, 16, 17, 18, 19, 20
Higginson Rev. Francis, account of 107, 108, 109
History, advantages of the study . . 13
Hobbamac resides at Plymouth . . 74
Hobbamoc; the devil of the Indians, account of 185
Hooker, Rev. Thomas, account of 136
Hooper, Dr. some account of . . 22
Hudson, Henry, discovers New-York . 293

I.

Indians of New-England, nature of their title to lands 618,

Their religion 184, their customs and character 188, 189, 190, 191, instructed by Eliot and others 193, 194, 195, 196, 197, anecdotes of 211, 212, 213, 214
Indian wars . . 246, 247, 248, 265
Indians of New-Jersey, their customs 306, 307, 308, religion 308
Ipswich settled . . 99, 110

J.

James King . . . 37
James II. ascends the throne, and is proclaimed at Boston 243

K.

Kennebec Indians, their conspiracy detected 170

L.

Lateran council - - - - 14
Lathrop Capt. and 70 men slaughtered by the Indians 208
Latimer, bishop, burnt - - - 26
Laud, archbishop, his persecution of the Puritans 85
Louisburg invaded - - - 273
Luther - - - - - 14

M.

Maguas Indians attack Philip . . 213
Marlborough burnt 211
Marriage customs among New Jersey Indians 308
Mary Queen 25
Mason and Gorges obtain grants of the Plymouth council 119, attempt to divide New-England into lordships 120

Massachusetts charter lost . . 242
Massasoit, first visit to Plymouth 71, is sick 77, informs of conspiracy among the Indians . 77
Mendon burnt 211
Mohegans, extent of their country . . 123
Morton tried for stealing . . . 94

N.

Narragansets, war with Massasoit 72, their religion 186
Newbury settled 99, description of . . 100
New-Hampshire purchased from the Indians 119, ceases to be a separate province . . . 123
New-Haven settled 130, character of colonists 134
New-England, boundaries &c. 56, name 59, patent 69, character of first settlers 115, confederation of the colonies 135, 178, population 286, character 286, 287, 2 0, learning, schools, newspapers 287, fasts and thanksgivings 289
New-Jersey, history of 303, customs of N. Jersey Indians 305
Newport settled 152
New-York, history of 292, confirmed to the English 295, taken by the Dutch . . . 295
Nipmuck Indians assist Philip . . 207
Norridgewog Indians, tradition of . . 58
Noyes Rev. James, account of . . 103

O.

Oceanus born 55

P.

Panieses, account of . 186
Papists, their creed 42

Parker, Rev. Thomas, account of . 102
Peperell's expedition against Louisbourg . 273
Pequots, extent of their country 123, Pequot war 158,
   terrible slaughter of Indians . . 163
Philip's war 205, 226, his death . . 225
Phips, Sir Wm. expedition against Canada 248, his
   character 262
Pierce John, obtains a patent . . 78
Plymouth discovered . . . 65
Podunk Indians 124
Prayers extempore, and written . . 22
Printing office established at Cambridge . 170
Providence settled . . . 150
Puritans, origin of the name 27, 28, testimony of Burnet and Hume respecting them . . 39

Q.

Quaboag attacked by Philip . . . 207
Quakers, laws against 143, persecuted . 198
Quebec taken by the British under Wolf 275, unsuccessful expedition against, under Arnold . 282

R.

Representative form of government established 112
Revolutionary war; history of . . 278
Rhode Island settled 148, patent 154, universal toleration Roman Catholics excepted 156, charter surrendered 157, charter resumed . . 158
Ridley, bishop, burnt . . . 26
Robinson, Rev. John, death and character . 81
Rogers, Rev. Ezekiel, account of . . 170
Rogers, John, burnt 26

Rowley settled . . . 170
Roxbury settled 95

S.

Salem witches 255
Salem settled 88
Samoset visits Plymouth . . . 71
Sassacus, a mighty Indian warrior 162, killed by the
   Mohawks 165
Sausaman reveals Philips's plot . . 206
Saybrook fort built, 125, Saybrook platform 242
Schenectady attacked by French and Indians and inhab-
   itants massacred . . . 299
Six nations, anecdotes of 296, customs, language, num-
   bers 297
Small Pox in Boston in 1721 . . 268
Society for propagating the gospel . 193
Springfield, houses burnt by the Indians . 208
Squanto's first visit to Plymouth 71, his character 76
Stamp act rouses New-England . . 276
Standish, Capt. Miles makes discoveries on Cape Cod,
   64, chosen captain 67, his character 199, interesting
   anecdotes of 200, 201, 202, 203, 204
Sudbury suffers from Indians . . 212
Sufferings of our forefathers . . 52, 68
Swansey suffers from Indians . . 217
Synod at Cambridge 150, at Boston 236, 238, 240, at
   Saybrook 241

T.

Thanksgiving common in New-England . 289
Throat distemper prevails in New-England 271
Tispaquin beheaded . . . 230

Tobacco, the use of it prohibited in Connecticut 142
Treat, Rev. Samuel, account of . . 180

U.

Uncas visits Boston . . . 166

V.

Virginia colony massacred by Indians 75

W.

Watertown settled . . . 95
Weathersfield settled . . . 127
Wells attacked by French and Indians . 252
White, Peregrine, first child in New-England born 64
Wickliffe 14
Williams, Roger, his sentiments 149, banished 149, settles in Providence . . 150
Williams College, some account of . . 285
William and Mary proclaimed in Boston . 246
Wilson, Rev. Mr. ordained at Charlestown . 94
Winslow, General, attacks an Indian fort in a swamp and gains a bloody victory . . 209
Winthrop, governor, his speech 182, his character 183, 184
Witches at Salem, account of . . . 255
Woburn settled 175
Wolf, General takes Quebec . . 275
Woodbridge, Rev. John, account of . . 104

Y.

Yale College, account of . . . 263
Yellow fever, dreadful ravages of . . 59

THE END.

Milton Keynes UK
Ingram Content Group UK Ltd.
UKHW040046180324
439604UK00006B/1019